EDUCATION IN CRISIS

Selected Titles in ABC-CLIO's
**CONTEMPORARY
WORLD ISSUES**
Series

For a complete list of titles in this series, please visit
www.abc-clio.com.

Books in the Contemporary World Issues series address vital issues in today's society such as genetic engineering, pollution, and biodiversity. Written by professional writers, scholars, and nonacademic experts, these books are authoritative, clearly written, up-to-date, and objective. They provide a good starting point for research by high school and college students, scholars, and general readers as well as by legislators, businesspeople, activists, and others.

Each book, carefully organized and easy to use, contains an overview of the subject, a detailed chronology, biographical sketches, facts and data and/or documents and other primary-source material, a directory of organizations and agencies, annotated lists of print and nonprint resources, and an index.

Readers of books in the Contemporary World Issues series will find the information they need in order to have a better understanding of the social, political, environmental, and economic issues facing the world today.

(Overview). The state of Minnesota enacted the first charter law in 1991, and soon after, 39 states, Puerto Rico, and the District of Columbia have enacted laws to establish and regulate charter schools. In general, charter schools are granted their charters, or contracts, typically by states, local school boards, or other state-authorized chartering agencies or sponsors; they include, in most states, universities. Typically, state laws allow only a certain number of charter schools to be operated within the school district, and often for a period of three to five years, and they may be renewed. While charter schools are exempt from many policies of the school districts in which they are located, charter schools are accountable to their chartering agencies, whether those are state, local school district, or other entities, for student achievement and for fiscal responsibility.

Charter schools are generallyประoted by those in that an independent part can school districts or states. The governance boards or sponsors they represent allow for-profit or nonprofit groups, where charter schools are organizationally structured in ways that are different from the typically represented by public schools. Both private themes within an annual schedule, sponsors, structure, pedagogy, service language, dimensions, lengthof and expectations, and learning. Most often charter schools are located within urban school districts, and they may be comprised of lower enrollment. Low-proportion enrollments, or low enrollment, or, per capita, or according to U.S. charter school data, there were around 3,000,000 for schools across the United States and Puerto Rico with more than 2 million children enrolled in over 6,000 charter schools.

Analyses of the demographics of the US charter reveals that participated in the 2009 National Assessment of Educational Progress (NAEP) showed that, in comparison to other public schools, higher percentages of charter schools enroll poorer students, or black (National Center for Education Statistics 2009), suggesting that minority families are more likely to take advantage of the opportunity to attend charter schools. This same study showed that the performance in both reading and mathematics for fourth-graders attending charter schools "was not measurably different" from the performance of fourth-grade students "with similar racial/ethnic backgrounds." In other words, while there have been many other studies of charter school performance (Center, Loveless, and Hassel 2006; Henig 2008; Hoxby 2004; Ravitch 2010, with interpretations about whether charter schools differ markedly in terms of improved student learning.

EDUCATION IN CRISIS

A Reference Handbook

Judith A. Gouwens

**CONTEMPORARY
WORLD ISSUES**

A B C CLIO

Santa Barbara, California
Denver, Colorado
Oxford, England

Library of Congress Cataloging-in-Publication Data

Gouwens, Judith A.
   Education in crisis : a reference handbook / Judith A. Gouwens.
      p. cm. — (Contemporary world issues)
   Includes bibliographical references and index.
   ISBN 978–1–59884–170–1 (hardcover : alk. paper) — ISBN
   978–1–59884–171–8 (e-book)
   1. Education—Handbooks, manuals, etc.   2. Education—United
States—Handbooks, manuals, etc.   I. Title.   II. Series.
   LB17.G6   2009
   370.973—dc22   2009003075

13 12 11 10 09   1 2 3 4 5

This book is also available on the World Wide Web as an eBook.
Visit www.abc-clio.com for details.

ABC-CLIO, LLC
130 Cremona Drive, P.O. Box 1911
Santa Barbara, California 93116-1911

This book is printed on acid-free paper. ∞™
Manufactured in the United States of America.

This book is dedicated to all of the teachers on the front line of education reform, teachers who believe that the children whose lives they touch can learn well, who go to work every day committed to helping the children in their classrooms learn well, and who make a difference in those children's learning and lives.

Comprehensive School Reform

Contents

Preface

Public education in the United States is in crisis. Nearly every day there is a media report that keeps the failures of public education at the forefront of our national consciousness. Our government and media fuel that fire with reports that describe schools that are failing and that place the blame for our economic woes on our system of public education. Nearly everyone knows that there is a crisis in education. But not everyone agrees on what the nature of that crisis is.

Some say that the crisis is one of *quality*, predicting a dismal future for the economic viability of the United States in the global marketplace based on what they perceive is the inadequacy of our system of public education. They point to international rankings that purport to show that the scores of children in the United States fall short of those of our international competitors. The most recent Trends in Mathematics and Science Study (TIMSS) and Progress in International Reading Literacy Study (PIRLS) show average student scores from the United States on these tests rank below the scores of students from several other developed or industrialized countries in reading, mathematics, and science. More information about these tests and test scores can be found in Chapters 3 and 6 of this book.

Interestingly, many of the countries whose students score higher on the tests than U.S. students look past the rankings of test scores in their determination that what makes the United States strong in the global marketplace is the creativity and innovation that U.S. students learn. Those countries, including China and Japan, understand that standardized test scores do not measure creativity and innovation. China, Japan, and several other countries are seeking to implement curriculum and teaching practices that foster creativity and problem solving, curriculum and teaching practices that have all but been abandoned in the United States in the pursuit of knowledge- and skills-based teaching and learning in efforts to improve standardized test scores.

Other analysts have reviewed and reanalyzed both national and international test scores and used them to show that the majority of students in the United States *are* learning well, and that the crisis is one of *equity*. They point to the achievement gap as evidence that our schools are failing minority children and children whose families live below the poverty line. According to UNESCO figures, the rate of poverty among school-aged children, nearly 22 percent, is higher in the United States than in any other industrialized nation except Mexico. Gerald Bracey's reanalysis of the test data that links students' achievement to the level of poverty in their schools should be a wake-up call for policy makers in the United States. (See Chapter 3 for more information about Bracey's analysis.) It is not enough to improve schools; the issue of childhood poverty must be addressed if we really want all children to learn to high levels.

Linda Darling-Hammond, George Wood, and a number of other education reformers who make up the Forum for Education and Democracy published a report, "Democracy at Risk: The Need for a New Federal Policy in Education." These reformers assert that all children in the United States have the right to a high-quality education, and they point to inequity as a critical impediment to improved public education. Based on the premise that it is the federal government that has the most leverage for equity in education, they argue that "underlying all federal efforts should be a commitment to paying off the long-standing educational debt our nation has accrued by allowing an unequal system to self-perpetuate for hundreds of years" (2008, 19).

No Child Left Behind (Elementary and Secondary Education Act, 2002; PL107–110) is intended to provide additional teaching and support services for children who live in poverty or who attend schools with high levels of poverty to help fill the gap between their learning and that of their more affluent peers. Unfortunately, many educators believe, some of the provisions of No Child Left Behind have actually resulted in more inequity for the children most in need. The accountability requirements of No Child Left Behind have narrowed the curriculum to include, in many schools, only reading, mathematics, and science—the subjects that are tested to determine the quality of schools. Social studies, the arts, physical education, recess, and even lunchtimes have been cut so that there is more time for teaching the subjects that are tested.

Although one of the provisions of No Child Left Behind is the requirement that school districts employ only highly qualified teachers, children in the poorest schools continue to have teachers with the least experience and who are the least qualified. They attend schools whose facilities are in need of renovation, with larger class sizes, and with fewer libraries, less technology, fewer high-quality instructional materials, and more outdated textbooks.

Between the *Brown v. Board of Education* decision in the 1950s and about 1990, schools in the United States made progress toward equity; the gap in achievement between African American and Hispanic children on the one hand and white children on the other narrowed considerably. In the last decade and a half, however, not only has no progress been made in paying off the educational debt but the debt has actually grown as the courts have either refused to hear cases about civil rights and segregation of schools or even reversed earlier decisions that impact equity in schools. According to a wide variety of sources, schools are as racially segregated as, and in some cases even more so than, they were before *Brown*. Jonathan Kozol's latest book, *The Shame of the Nation: The Restoration of Apartheid Schooling in America* (2005), documents the deplorable conditions in many of these resegregated schools.

Still other observers of education believe that the real crisis in education in the United States is the *impending demise of our entire system of public education*. They point to the neoliberal agenda of right-wing think tanks and business groups that view education as an opportunity for financial profit and that work toward privatizing education and dismantling the system of public education that has been a pillar of our democratic society. Kenneth Saltman (2007), DePaul University professor, speaks for critical educators in asserting that "a number of privatization initiatives are being enacted through a process involving the dismantling of public schools followed by the opening of for-profit, charter, and deregulated public schools" (p. 5).

Critics of the neoliberal agenda argue that the use of public resources for such private schools is part of a redistribution of economic wealth that goes against the democratic principles upon which our country was founded. In effect, these critics warn that school privatization is part of the neoliberal "class warfare waged by the rich on the rest" (Saltman 2007, 8), and that inequity in the education system serves the purpose of the neoliberal agenda for privatization.

I believe that the crisis in education involves quality, equity, and the threat of privatization. All of these issues must be addressed to close the achievement gap and to ensure that public education in the United States continues as one of the pillars of our democratic way of life.

So What Are We to Do?

Nel Noddings, professor emerita from Stanford University, argues that before beginning any reform, we need to identify the problem. According to Noddings, solutions are often sought and enacted without identifying the problem—and then they solve nothing. Noddings argues also that the problem might not be the same for all schools or all school districts (2007). But agreeing on what the problem is, is the first step to finding solutions.

Once there is consensus about what the problem is, we should look to past education reform efforts to understand what has worked, what has not worked, and what the effects of those efforts have been. According to Noddings, there is much to be learned from our history with education reform. Finding *a* solution might not be the answer because "one size fits all" really fits no school or school districts; reforming U.S. education may require a whole array of solutions. Chapters 1 and 2 describe the history of education reform in the United States and a variety of reform efforts that could serve as possible solutions. We can also look to what other countries are doing and have done to reform education, and Chapter 3 provides accounts of some other countries' education systems and reform efforts.

Teachers must be at the forefront of the process of identifying problems and proposing solutions. In the United States, teachers have often been left out of the process of education reform. Very few teachers, for example, were involved in the development of the national goals, and similarly, few teachers were involved in the development of No Child Left Behind. But the responsibility for implementing reforms falls to teachers, and their commitment to any reform effort is critical to success.

I have spent nearly 40 years in education—as an elementary teacher; as a school and school district administrator; as a senior research associate consulting and working with schools, school districts, and state departments of education in the process of education reform; as an evaluator of educational programs; and as a university professor and researcher. During my career, I have met countless numbers of teachers who are committed to the learning of their students and truly making a difference, not only in their students' learning, but also in their students' lives. These teachers work hard, not because of mandates or legislated accountability, but because of their commitment to the learning of their students.

Real education reform doesn't happen in legislative bodies or through mandates. It doesn't happen because members of the media or government officials describe teachers as not doing their jobs or not qualified. It doesn't happen because teachers are offered bonuses to improve their students' test scores or because their jobs are threatened if they don't. Real education reform happens in the hearts and minds of teachers who come to know and understand the children they teach, their lives outside school, and the myriad strengths the children bring into their classrooms. These committed teachers design learning opportunities for the children in their classrooms that connect the curriculum to the children's real lives outside school so that the children see value in learning. It is then and only then that children will learn well. It is the work of good teachers to mentor and coach that learning.

Noddings tells us that it will take creativity and innovation (what we Americans are known for internationally) to identify the problems in our public education system and to find solutions that will truly address the problems. "We need to engage in fresh thinking," she says.

> We should draw back from standardization and outmoded structures of schooling, but remain willing to analyze, adapt, and revise promising old ideas. In the process, we should avoid dehumanizing teachers and students and explore new ways to educate for genuine intellectual growth, moral commitment, and democratic citizenship. (2007, 83)

We can view the crises in our education system as occasions to wring our hands and place blame. Or we can view the crises as opportunities for real reform of our schools. In 1978, Ronald Edmonds, one of the first researchers to investigate the characteristics of effective schools, challenged educators to look forward to new solutions. In a speech titled "Some Schools Work and More Can," he said,

> We can whenever, and wherever we choose, successfully teach all children whose schooling is of interest to us. We already know more than we need in order to do this. Whether we do it must finally depend on how we feel about the fact that we haven't so far. (1979, 32)

References

Baer, J., S. Baldo, K. Ayotte, and P. J. Green. 2007. *The Reading Literacy of U.S. Fourth-Grade Students in an International Context: Results from the 2001 and 2006 Progress in International Reading Literacy Study (PIRLS)* (NCES 2008–017). Washington, DC: National Center for Education Statistics, Institute of Education Sciences, U.S. Department of Education.

Darling-Hammond, L., and G. Wood. 2008. "Democracy at Risk: The Need for a New Federal Policy in Education." Athens, OH: Forum for Democracy and Education.

Edmonds, R. R. 1979. "Some Schools Work and More Can." *Social Policy* 9, 28–32.

Gonzales, P., J. C. Guzman, L. Partelow, E. Pahlke, L. Jocelyn, D. Kastberg, and T. Williams. 2004. *Highlights from the Trends in International Mathematics and Science Study (TIMSS) 2003* (NCES 2005–005). U.S. Department of Education, National Center for Education Statistics. Washington, DC: U.S. Government Printing Office.

Kozol, J. 2005. *The Shame of the Nation: The Restoration of Apartheid Schooling in America*. New York: Crown.

Noddings, N. 2007. *When School Reform Goes Wrong*. New York: Teachers College Press.

Saltman, K. J. 2007. *Capitalizing on Disaster: Taking and Breaking Public Schools*. Boulder, CO: Paradigm.

Acknowledgments

There are a number of people whom I would like to thank for their help and encouragement throughout the process of writing this book. Holly Heinzer, Mim Vasan, Kim Kennedy-White, and Lauren Thomas from ABC-CLIO worked so patiently and encouragingly with me as I developed the manuscript for this book. The advice and feedback that they provided helped immeasurably.

I would also like to thank Janice Mulqueeny, a wonderful friend who is a school administrator, for her support and expert advice throughout the development of this book. Jan's intuition about when I needed encouragement is uncanny—she called or e-mailed often when I had run into a snag and helped me to get past it! Many thanks also to Karen McElvogue, one of my former students at Roosevelt University, for reading and providing feedback and suggestions on a draft of the manuscript.

Special thanks go to my life partner and best friend, Thomas Gouwens. His love, support, and encouragement always help me to persevere.

1

Background and History

Reform of public education has become a key element of public discussion and political platform in the United States. The report "39th Annual Phi Delta Kappa/Gallup Poll of the Public's Attitudes Towards the Public Schools" affirms that "K-12 schooling is near the top of the agenda in state and national policy discussions, and the efforts to improve student achievement dominate those discussions" (Rose and Gallup 2007, 34). One cannot open a newspaper or news magazine in the United States without a headline, article, or editorial that addresses the quality of public education in the United States. Googling "education reform" results in more than 14 million hits, which include papers and articles that critique the state of education, organizations that offer support and technical assistance for reforming or improving education, and a wide variety of strategies for doing so. Bookstores are full of books describing what is wrong with public education or explaining how to "fix" the problems of public education. Education reform is a hot topic.

Policy makers and business people often link student achievement with the ability of the United States to compete in the global marketplace, and they believe that student achievement must be improved so that the United States can continue to be competitive in the global market. This discourse has been based on comparisons of student achievement in the United States with that of other countries. Since the International Association for the Evaluation of Educational Achievement conducted its first pilot study (between 1959 and 1962) comparing the achievement of 13-year-olds from 12 countries in mathematics, reading comprehension, geography, science, and nonverbal ability, such comparison studies have been conducted periodically. Recent comparisons have shown that student achievement in reading, mathematics, and science, for example, in the Trends in International Mathematics and Science Study (TIMSS) administered in 2003, showed the average score of fourth-graders in the United States to rank 15th out of the 25 countries that participated in the study. Similarly, at the eighth grade level, students from the United States ranked 15th of the 44 countries in the study. These data, as well as more comparisons of U.S. student achievement in mathematics, science, and reading, can be found in Chapter 6.

Many educators, on the other hand, believe that the purpose of schooling is not related to the economy or improving the standing of the United States in the global marketplace. Instead, they believe that the purpose of schooling is to develop productive citizens who are prepared to participate actively in the democratic process in the United States. They believe that schools should be reformed to provide opportunities for children to learn more and to learn better for the benefit of our democratic society, and they believe that schools can and should reform or reorganize to ensure those opportunities.

In general, there is a consensus in the United States that schools should reform and that children could learn more and better. The debate about school reform has focused not on whether reform is necessary but on the purpose of reform and on how to accomplish this monumental task. Perspectives on school reform and how schools should be reformed are directly related to their proponents' view of society in general and what their proponents believe is the purpose and function of public education.

One can see how such differing perspectives have been at play from the beginnings of public education in the United States. Benjamin Franklin and Thomas Jefferson, signers of the Declaration of Independence and early statesmen of the United States, both independently set forth propositions for public education because they believed that the democratic form of government outlined in the new Constitution would require an educated citizenry. Franklin's and Jefferson's ideas for education were different in many ways, representing their very divergent views of human nature and society. Franklin (1749) proposed that education be available to all boys, and that it be publicly funded, while Jefferson's proposal would have created a system to educate an elite class to serve as leaders of the new nation and the state of Virginia. Even though their visions for public education differed, founders of our country like Franklin and Jefferson laid the foundation for the system of free, public education that has developed in the United States.

Franklin's and Jefferson's ideas demonstrate how education can be and has been viewed as reflecting society and as shaping it. As our society has changed, there have been calls for schools to change or reform. One example of societal change was the great influx of immigrants into the United States in the 19th century. Horace Mann, who was appointed secretary of the first Massachusetts board of education in 1837, is often called the father of public education in the United States. As secretary of the board of education, Mann worked to raise public support for education, to improve the education and working conditions of teachers, and to establish libraries in public schools. Mann called for universal public education to help new immigrant children to assimilate into American culture, as well as to have some measure of social control over a population that was both booming and becoming more diverse. Interestingly, Mann also visited schools in other countries and promoted educational ideas that he learned in his travels in a publication that he edited, the *Common School Journal,* and in a series of reports that he wrote about the state of schools in Massachusetts. Educational historians agree that schools in Massachusetts improved greatly as a result of Mann's work to reform them.

Another example of early school reform was a response to the progression in the United States from a predominantly agrarian society to a more industrial society that began in the 19th century and continued into the 20th century. Frederick W. Taylor, an industrial engineer, developed his principles of "scientific management" to promote efficiency and productivity in industry by observing people doing their jobs in their workplaces and finding ways to make them more productive by increasing their efficiency. Taylor is often called the first efficiency expert. In the early 20th century, those principles were also applied to the management and organization of schools (Callahan 1962). As schools and school populations became larger, reformers called for regulation and efficiency, drawing on the ideas of Taylor. Raymond Callahan describes how schools used Taylor's ideas to organize schools and classrooms and to view students as workers and their learning as the product of schooling. Taylor is often cited as influencing the organization of the modern high school, where teachers are specialized and students move from teacher to teacher to learn the subjects they specialize in.

The ideas of Franklin and Jefferson foreshadowed a discourse in the United States on the purpose of schooling and on two major goals of educational reform—quality and equity—that often seem to be in conflict with one another. While Franklin believed that all boys should have the opportunity to be educated through a comprehensive and practical curriculum—equity, Jefferson believed that public education should be available in three levels, with only the lowest level of basic education available to all free children and the other levels whose curriculum included sciences and philosophy available based on merit—excellence or quality. The tension between equity and quality is evident in the debate and discourse in the United States to this day.

Until the middle of the 20th century, school reform efforts in the United States generally reflected societal changes in the United States; reforms were instituted slowly and generally by way of local initiatives in response to societal changes, identification of specific needs, or the setting of new priorities. For example, as families left farms and rural areas and moved into towns and cities and as bus transportation became available and practical for children who lived in rural areas, the one-room schoolhouse gradually became a thing of the past. Such a reform was usually the result of a community deciding that it could save money or offer more educational opportunities for children in a larger school. Such reforms, initiated as responses to locally identified needs, according to Merilee Grindle (2004), "rarely . . . get on national political agendas" (p. 28).

In the 1950s, however, two things happened that thrust education into the political, and thus national, spotlight. They generated the political action that Grindle (2004) argues is necessary to put education reform on the public agenda. These two events brought about reform on a scale and at a pace not previously imagined; they set the stage for school reform efforts through the last half of the 20th century and into the 21st. The reform efforts precipitated by these events were not intended to reflect societal changes as had school reform efforts prior to the 1950s. Instead, the purpose of these new reforms was to *bring about* societal change. Those two events were the *Brown v. Board* Supreme Court decision and the successful launch of Sputnik I, the first artificial satellite sent into orbit by the Soviet Union and the impetus for the U.S.–U.S.S.R. space race. The effects of these two events on education represent what often seem to be the competing goals of equity in and quality of schooling in general, and in school reform in particular. They also represent the first significant federal involvement in education in the United States, since education was a responsibility traditionally reserved for the states by the framers of the U.S. Constitution.

The first of those events, the U.S. Supreme Court decision in *Oliver L. Brown et al. v. the Board of Education of Topeka (KS) et al.* (347 U.S. 483), announced in 1954, laid the foundation for massive educational reform efforts centered on equity. Although there had been many lawsuits arguing against racial segregation at the state level before this, no case had been argued before the Supreme Court since its 1896 decision in *Plessy v. Ferguson* (163 U.S. 537). The *Plessy v. Ferguson* decision had upheld the doctrine of "separate but equal" that had been used to justify segregation not just in schools, but also in all areas of American life. The separate schools and dual school districts affirmed by the *Plessy* decision were rarely equal, with schools for black children having fewer resources, older textbooks, and poorer facilities.

In the 1950s, there were many schools in the United States that were segregated, and a large number of states had laws that prohibited African American and white children from going to schools together. Linda Brown, a third-grader in Topeka, Kansas, was one of those children. She was not allowed to attend the elementary school only seven blocks from her home because it was a school for white children. Instead, she had to walk a mile, through a railroad switching station, to a bus stop where she caught a bus that took her to an elementary school for black children. In the summer of 1950, the National Association for the Advancement of Colored People (NAACP) asked Linda Brown's father, Oliver Brown, and 12 other black families to attempt to enroll their children in "white" schools in Topeka. The children were all denied enrollment, and the NAACP filed suit against the Topeka school district on behalf of the 13 families. The *Brown* case (so named because Brown was the first in alphabetic order of the last names of all the plaintiffs) brought together the Topeka case with four other cases on appeal to the U.S. Supreme Court. Together the appeal represented about 200 plaintiffs who sought the dismantling of racial segregation in schools. Into the 1950s (and even beyond in a few states, including Alabama which *still* has a segregation law on its books), there were laws in several states in the United States that required school districts to provide dual school systems, one to educate white children and another to educate black children. In those states, it was illegal to educate white and black children in the same classrooms in the same school buildings.

The five individual cases that formed the *Brown* case before the U.S. Supreme Court were all initially filed in 1950 and 1951; they had originated in Delaware, Kansas, South Carolina, Virginia, and the District of Columbia. Charles Hamilton Houston, NAACP attorney, was instrumental in bringing the cases together on appeal, and Thurgood Marshall, also of the NAACP (who would go on to serve as the first black associate justice of the U.S. Supreme Court), headed a team of attorneys who argued the case before the Supreme Court. The Supreme Court ruled that racial segregation in schools "violates the Fourteenth Amendment to the U.S. Constitution, which guarantees all citizens equal protection of the laws" (*Brown v. Board of Education*), and ordered the dismantling of separate school systems for black children. This ruling overturned the "separate but equal" doctrine that had been in place since *Plessy v. Ferguson*.

In a subsequent ruling, sought in 1955 because some of the states involved in the original *Brown* case had not yet begun to implement the remedies required by the 1954 ruling, the U.S. Supreme Court affirmed its *Brown* decision and ordered that children be admitted to schools "on a racially nondiscriminatory basis with all deliberate speed" (*Brown v. Board of Education*, 349 U.S. 294). The NAACP initiated these cases to begin to dismantle segregation wherever it existed in U.S. society, but the *Brown* decisions have had far-reaching effects in terms of equity in U.S. public schools as well as in society in general. The transcripts of the *Brown* decisions are found in Chapter 6.

The second of those events focused the attention of the country on improving the quality of students' learning in schools, colleges, and universities in the United States. Shortly after the second *Brown* decision, in 1957, the Soviet Union launched Sputnik I, the first artificial satellite to orbit the earth. In the context of the distrust, tension, and competition between the United States and the Soviet Union during the Cold War, the successful launch of Sputnik I generated a furor in the United States. While there had been many calls for improving the content and the teaching of mathematics and science before the successful launch, Sputnik I thrust those calls into the public eye as the space race had the public looking to place blame for the Soviet Union having taken first place in that race. Interestingly, there had been few comparisons of education quality between the United States and other countries before Sputnik I, but the space race seems to have been the beginning of global comparisons of educational outcomes.

The U.S. Congress began hearings to determine why the Soviet Union was ahead of the United States in the space race and what could be done to be competitive in the future. The hearings identified the quality of science and mathematics education in the United States as one of the issues that kept the United States from being competitive. In 1958, Congress enacted the National Defense Education Act (NDEA), the first comprehensive federal education legislation that linked education to national defense. According to the U.S. Department of Education,

> To help ensure that highly trained individuals would be available to help America compete with the Soviet Union in scientific and technical fields, the NDEA included support for loans to college students, the improvement of science, mathematics, and foreign language instruction in elementary and secondary schools, graduate fellowships, foreign language and area studies, and vocational-technical training. (U.S. Department of Education 2007)

In other words, the enactment of the NDEA linked school outcomes with the ability of the United States to compete internationally, a theme that echoes throughout educational reforms into the 21st century. The NDEA also initiated an agenda of U.S. federal involvement in and funding of educational reform, a responsibility previously left entirely to individual states.

These two events, the *Brown* decisions and the beginning of the space race, began two threads that wind throughout educational reform in the United States. Those two threads, equity and quality, have run their courses from the 1950s into the 21st century, sometimes far apart, sometimes intertwining, but always evident in calls for and responses to educational reform.

Education Reform for Equity

The two landmark Supreme Court decisions, *Brown* and *Brown II*, mark the beginning of the march to equity in the United States, not only in education, and not only for racial minorities, but also in nearly every aspect of our society. In terms of equity in the education specifically of African American children and of racial and ethnic minorities in general, court decisions have often paved the way to reform, even though that reform happened very slowly.

After the *Brown* decisions, there were several other U.S. Supreme Court cases that led to significant educational reforms in terms of equity. Among them are *Green v. County School Board of New Kent County* (391 US 430; 1968); *Swann v. Charlotte-Mecklenberg Board of Education* (402 US 1; 1971); and *Keyes v. Denver School District No. 1* (413 US 187; 1973). The decision in the *Green* case ordered school districts to dismantle dual school systems, and required districts to desegregate facilities, staff, faculties, extracurricular activities, and transportation—factors that came to be called the "Green factors" and that were subsequently used to guide the development of desegregation plans for many school districts. The *Swann* decision allowed for busing to achieve integration, and the *Keyes* decision awarded to Hispanic children the same rights earlier decisions had awarded to African American children.

In his analysis of the history of school desegregation, Robert Lowe, professor of educational policy and leadership at Marquette University in Milwaukee, Wisconsin, argues that although the courts were slow to enforce the integration of schools,

> the [Supreme Court] decisions provided federal legitimacy to the fight against discrimination and helped inspire a variegated movement for civil rights of which the demand for school desegregation would be a part—in fact perhaps the most recalcitrant part, as the pace of school desegregation was glacial after *Brown*. (Lowe 2004)

Instead of waiting for the courts to enforce integration, and fortified by the Supreme Court's decision, the NAACP worked with black families to force the issue in school districts throughout the South. In 1957, in Little Rock, Arkansas, for example, the school board was set to implement its integration plan with the enrollment by the NAACP of nine students in the formerly all-white Central High School. When Governor Orval Faubus called out the Arkansas National Guard to keep the nine black students from entering the school, and white parents protested to keep the black students out of the school, the NAACP persisted, and eventually federal marshals escorted the nine students into the school.

The Civil Rights Movement of the 1960s, and particularly the March on Washington in 1963, where Dr. Martin Luther King delivered his famous "I Have a Dream" speech, led to the passage in

1964 of the Civil Rights Act (PL 88–352). The 1964 Civil Rights Act outlawed segregation in U.S. schools and other public places, as well as discrimination in government, housing, and employment. The *Brown* decisions and the Civil Rights Act provided the impetus for a great expansion of educational opportunity for children in poverty, children with special needs and disabilities, children who spoke languages other than English as their first languages, and the children of migrant agricultural workers.

President Lyndon Johnson announced the "War on Poverty" in his inaugural address. Johnson's "war" saw education as one of the ways to combat poverty, and along with a number of other social and economic programs also aimed at reducing poverty. Johnson proposed several compensatory education initiatives. The first among them was the Head Start program. Head Start began in 1965 as a preschool program for children from low-income families. Based on the view of education as the great equalizer, the Head Start program was designed to address the social, emotional, educational, health, nutrition, and psychological effects of poverty that stood in the way of the children's educational success, in other words, to make up for the disparity in school readiness between these children and those of middle- and upper-income families. Over the years since its inception, Head Start has served many, many children, and it is one of only a handful of educational programs that has been studied longitudinally. According to W. Steven Barnett (2002), director of the National Institute for Early Education Research (NIEER), "Nearly four decades of research establish that Head Start . . . improves the lives and development of the children and families it serves" (p. 1).

In a study of the effects of Head Start, UCLA researchers Eliana Garces, Duncan Thomas, and Janet Currie (2000) found that Head Start did indeed have long-term effects. Interestingly, the effects seemed to differ by the race of the participants. For white Head Start participants, the researchers found a "significantly increased probability of completing high school and attending college, as well as elevated earnings in one's early twenties" (p. 1). Head Start participants who were African Americans were found to be "less likely to have been charged or convicted of a crime" (p. 1). The study also found that African American males were more likely to have completed high school, when compared to their siblings. In other words, Head Start has affected its participants not only during preschool but also long after they had left the Head Start program.

The federal government also enacted the Elementary and Secondary Education Act (ESEA) in 1965. While the ESEA included provisions for funding school libraries, supplemental services, and state departments of education, the most significant part of ESEA was, and continues to be, Title I. Title I, subtitled "Education of Children of Low Income Families," was intended to provide federal funds to supplement the education of elementary and secondary school children in poverty—to provide services that would make up for the detrimental effects of poverty on their learning, particularly in the areas of reading, language arts, and mathematics. The successful authorization of ESEA led to the addition of provisions for education of children whose parents are migrant agricultural workers in 1966, and Title VII, which supports bilingual education for children who are "limited English proficient" (LEP), in 1968. In the 1988 reauthorization of ESEA, the addition of the Jacob Javits Gifted and Talented Students Education Act recognized the special needs of children identified as gifted and talented. Subsequent reauthorizations of the ESEA changed the specifics of the law, but the basic intent of providing supplemental educational services to children in poverty remained the same until No Child Left Behind (NCLB; PL 107–110, 2002). NCLB, the latest reauthorization of the ESEA, greatly expanded the scope of the legislation to include the achievement of state-developed educational standards by all public school children, not just those living in poverty.

Shortly after the ESEA was first enacted, Congress commissioned a study to determine the level of educational inequity in the United States. James Coleman, then a sociologist at Johns Hopkins University, conducted a large-scale study of U.S. children and schools. His report, issued in 1966, concluded that there were inequities both in the quality of schools and in the quality of children's learning. Coleman's report was controversial, however, because one of his findings was "that a child's early years at home had a significant impact on later performance in school and that an achievement gap existed between blacks and whites despite similarities in their teachers' training, salaries, and curriculum" (Hanna 2005, 4). The identification of an achievement gap supported the notion of compensatory education for poor and minority children; at the same time, Coleman argued that differing levels of financial support for schools had little effect on how well children learned. While many people saw Coleman's report as a call for high-quality preschool education to help minority children and children in poverty begin to address the achievement gap before they began elementary school, others viewed the Coleman findings as a rationale for not addressing the achievement gap more rigorously.

The Civil Rights Act also gave rise to a more critical look at education as gendered practice. Title IX of the Education Amendments of 1972 states succinctly, "No person in the U.S. shall, on the basis of sex be excluded from participation in, or denied the benefits of, or be subjected to discrimination under any educational program or activity receiving federal aid." Originally intended to address inequities for women in higher education, Title IX has been enforced by the U.S. Office of Civil Rights, ensuring both academic and athletic opportunities for girls and women. Initially, Title IX was used almost exclusively to support the provision of athletics and sports opportunities for girls and women that were equitable to those provided for boys and men. But the gender equity proposed in Title IX soon was applied to all areas of education. To provide support for the implementation of gender equity, the Women's Educational Equity Act (WEEA) was passed in 1974. WEEA provides "funding at all levels of education for programs of national, statewide, or general significance to overcome sex stereotyping and achieve educational equity for girls and women" (Valentin 1997, 4). The American Association of University Women has worked to support the implementation of both Title IX and WEEA, funding research that identifies gender inequities in schools (see Orenstein 1994; Sadker and Sadker 1995), providing professional development to teachers focused on how to ensure gender equity in their classrooms, and advocating for gender equity through continued enforcement of and funding for both Title IX and WEEA.

Parent groups had organized as early as the 1930s to advocate for public education for their children with disabilities. Spurred on by the *Brown* decisions and the Civil Rights Act, they continued to struggle for educational rights for their own children. In 1975, Public Law 94–142, the Education of All Handicapped Children Act, was enacted. This law requires states to develop programs that provide "a free appropriate public education" to all children with disabilities. Prior to 1975, many children with disabilities were excluded from public schools. PL 94–142, according to Priscilla Pardini (2002), proved to be landmark legislation, requiring public schools to provide students with a broad range of disabilities—including physical handicaps, mental retardation, speech, vision and language problems, emotional and behavioral problems, and other learning disorders—with a "free appropriate public education." Moreover, it called for school districts to provide such schooling in the "least restrictive environment" possible.

This law, renamed the Individuals with Disabilities Education Act (IDEA), has been reauthorized twice, in 1990 and 1997. Each of these reauthorizations has strengthened the law, ensuring that more and more children with disabilities are served in schools in ways that allow them to reach their full potential. Schools are required to develop an individual education plan (IEP) for each child who has a disability; an IEP specifies the educational services, the setting, the curriculum, and the types of instruction that will most appropriately address that child's learning needs. Today, children who have disabilities are "included" as much as possible in regular education classrooms; they are served by special education teachers and other support staff who work in tandem with regular education teachers so that the children who have disabilities become part of the social interaction of the regular classroom. Currently, according to the National Center for Education Statistics, more than 13 percent of U.S. public school children qualify for and receive special education services.

All of these reforms, whether the result of legislation or of court decree, have greatly expanded access to the educational system in the United States. Many more children have opportunities for a free, appropriate, and public education as a result. But educational equity is only one part of educational reform.

Education Reform for Quality

Parallel to educational equity is the theme of educational quality. The launch of Sputnik focused the United States on the quality of mathematics and science programs across the nation in the 1950s, and the National Defense Education Act provided more than a billion dollars of federal funds to address what were viewed at the time as shortcomings in the educational system. In addition to funds for improving the content and the teaching of mathematics and science, the NDEA supported the development and expansion of school libraries, the improvement of teacher education, the teaching of foreign languages in elementary and secondary schools, vocational and technical education, graduate fellowships, and loans for college students.

According to Larry Abramson (2008), as a result of NDEA's focus on improving science instruction in schools and classrooms, "Educational tools began to change. Lab kits and overhead projectors were added, and educational films became part of the curriculum." There were changes, also, in mathematics education. Reform in mathematics curriculum, begun with little notice before the launch of Sputnik, came from many different directions and organizations, among them the University of Illinois Committee on School Mathematics and the Commission on School Mathematics of the College Entrance Examination Board. The calls for reform, strengthened by NDEA, resulted in the introduction of calculus courses in high school, as well as what came to be known as "new math," an approach to the teaching and learning of mathematics that focused on theoretical and abstract concepts rather than basic arithmetic computation.

Before the 1980s, the rhetoric about the quality of education in the United States was just rhetoric; there had been no large-scale study of the quality of education that paralleled the Coleman study of educational equity. In 1981, the U.S. secretary of education, Terrell Bell, established a National Commission on Excellence in Education and charged that commission with conducting a comprehensive review of education in the United States. Bell asked the commission to place particular emphasis on programs and practices that produced high levels of learning and prepared children for college and university entrance. That commission held hearings and gathered and analyzed data on the quality of education in the United States. In 1983, it issued a report, "A Nation at Risk: The Imperative for Educational Reform," that has shaped the discourse about educational reform since its publication. The report, like the calls for school improvement that led to the NDEA, linked the quality of education in the United States and the educational achievement of U.S. children to our national defense and our standing as a global power.

The report began with a letter to President Ronald Reagan and the nation, opening with these words:

> Our nation is at risk. Our once unchallenged preeminence in commerce, industry, science, and technological

innovation is being overtaken by competitors throughout the world. This report is concerned with only one of
the many causes and dimensions of the problem, but it
is the one that undergirds American prosperity, security,
and civility.

The language of the report is strong and direct; it characterized education in the United States as being "eroded by a rising
tide of mediocrity that threatens our very future as a Nation and a
people." The commission chided the American public and educational community for allowing this to happen. According to the report, "If an unfriendly foreign power had attempted to impose on
America the mediocre educational performance that exists today,
we might well have viewed it as an act of war. . . . We have, in effect, been committing an act of unthinking, unilateral educational
disarmament." The commission concluded its analysis of the
quality of education with recommendations for the improvement
of education, public, private, and parochial, at all levels, that "the
American people can begin to act on now, that can be implemented
over the next several years, and that promise lasting reform."

The Nation at Risk report challenged parents and students to
become involved in school reform and in improving learning. For
parents, the commission described a dual role in school reform—
that of setting expectations for their children and that of advocating for real reforms in their children's schools. The commission
exhorted children to take advantage of the educational opportunities afforded them.

The Nation at Risk report is important because it was the
first real blueprint for comprehensive school reform centered
on the quality of student learning. It addressed nearly every
aspect and every level of schooling, and at least a decade before
reformers were calling for educators to view schools as systems,
the report recognized that comprehensive reform must involve
all of the parts of the system at once, rather than the "tinker-
ing around the edges" approaches often taken by schools. The
authors of the report made recommendations for curriculum
and expectations for learning that foreshadowed the standards-
based education reform that did not begin until nearly a decade
later. They also recognized the critical role that parents and students themselves play in improving schools and learning. The
report, which was forward-looking in its comprehensiveness,
lacked strategies for implementing recommended reforms.

Unfortunately, the commission had no authority to do anything other than make recommendations, and the federal government provided no resources for any organized implementation of the reforms the report recommended. The introduction of "A Nation at Risk" can be found in Chapter 6.

The Nation at Risk report generated a public focus on school quality, a focus that led to a proliferation of school reform research, as well as consultants, organizations, and programs, all promising to improve the quality of schools and the outcomes for children. Schools and school districts also began to look to successful business models, such as management by objective, the Deming management method, and others, for help in reorganizing their school operations.

At the same time, during the 1980s, many of the nation's governors were working both within and across their states on education reform. At the National Governors Association (NGA) meeting in Idaho in the summer of 1985, school reform was high on the agenda. Governor Lamar Alexander, chair of the NGA, shared his concern about the link between education and the economy in general, and in particular, the availability of an able workforce and global competitiveness. As a result of their discussion at that meeting, the governors set seven school reform tasks for themselves. The reform tasks included improving school leadership and teaching, raising standards for learning and helping at-risk children to meet them, promoting parent involvement and school choice, and using technology more effectively in education (Vinovskis 1999).

The governors continued to work on their education reform agenda, and when George Herbert Walker Bush was elected president with education as a key part of his campaign platform, the governors held him to his promise as the "education president" to meet with them to discuss education reform. That meeting took place in Charlottesville, Virginia, in September 1989. At the meeting, the governors and President Bush agreed that there should be a set of national education goals that could provide a direction for school reform in the United States, and they set six goals to be met by the nation and by the schools by 2000. A list of the goals is found in Chapter 6. They also agreed that states and local communities should determine how the goals would be met. The goals were announced by President Bush in 1990.

The National Education Goals Panel (NEGP) was established by Congress in July 1990 to monitor, assess, and report on the progress of the nation's schools in reaching the national education goals. The bipartisan NEGP was made up of federal and state officials; they were charged with issuing annual reports on the progress toward the goals in the nation and in the states. The first report of the NEGP was released in 1991; the NEGP continued to publish annual reports about the progress of education reform each year until 2000. The NEGP published numerous other reports on a wide variety of educational reform topics related to the goals, including indicators and strategies for reaching the national educational goals and "tool kits" for various stakeholders in school reform. One of the most significant of the reports, in terms of future education reform, was "Promises to Keep: Creating High Standards for American Students" (1993), which was a call for the development of national curriculum standards. In 2000, the NEGP was disbanded by Congressional mandate.

At the same time that Congress established the NEGP, several states and urban school districts joined forces in 1990 to begin the New Standards Project to support the National Educational Goals and the development of the new national standards. According to Elizabeth Spalding (2000), the New Standards Project was made up of

> a national coalition of approximately 17 states and seven urban school districts, co-directed by Lauren Resnick of the Learning, Research, and Development Center of the University of Pittsburgh and Marc Tucker of the National Center on Education and the Economy in Washington, D.C. (p. 758)

This project brought hundreds of educators together to develop assessments that were aligned with both the National Education Goals and curriculum standards that were being developed by a number of professional education associations such as the National Council of Teachers of Mathematics, the National Council of Teachers of English, the National Council for Social Studies, and so on. (The U.S. Department of Education funded the development of standards for the arts, civics and government, English language arts, foreign languages, geography, history, and science.) One of the goals of the New Standards Project was to create performance assessments and portfolios that allowed children "to demonstrate their ability to meet performance standards that were being developed simultaneously"

(Spalding 2000, 759). In other words, the performance assessments and portfolios informed the development of the standards as the development of the standards informed the assessments.

In 1991, at the request of Secretary of Education Lamar Alexander, Congress also established the National Council on Education Standards and Testing (NCEST) and charged that council with examining the feasibility of national curriculum standards and a method of assessing them. Although no national curriculum standards have been adopted and declared mandatory by the federal government, the standards developed by the professional education organizations have been debated nationally, and many states have either adopted them or modeled state standards after them.

In 1994, President Bill Clinton signed the Goals 2000: Educate America Act (PL 103–227) into law. The purpose of the Goals 2000 legislation was to provide funding to states and school districts to support their own standards-based education reform processes and projects. According to the text of the legislation, the law was based on the following principles of effective change:

1. All students can learn;
2. Lasting improvements depend on school-based leadership;
3. Simultaneous top-down and bottom-up reform is necessary;
4. Strategies must be locally developed, comprehensive, and coordinated; and
5. The whole community must be involved in developing strategies for system-wide improvement. (Title III. Sec. 301. Findings)

The Goals 2000: Educate America Act required states to develop or adopt rigorous content, performance, and opportunity to learn standards and to measure children's achievement relative to those standards, and for school districts to align their curricula with the standards. (Content standards specify what children should learn, performance standards specify how well they should learn, and opportunity to learn standards describe the resources that should be available to children to support the learning.) The law also required states to publish report cards of their progress toward standards-based reform.

For the first time, this legislation allocated federal funds for states and school districts to support their school reform efforts. And for the first time, federal legislation demonstrated the understanding that *teachers* are on the front lines of education reform by including provisions and substantial funding for professional development, as well as for the development of professional development standards and models. At the same time, the legislation maintained state autonomy in terms of the standards and assessments to measure achievement of the standards, as well as the processes states might use to reform education to meet the national goals. In 1996, the Goals 2000: Educate America Act was amended to eliminate the requirement for opportunity to learn standards.

According to the U.S. Constitution, the administration of education is not a federal responsibility; it is left to the states. The Goals 2000 legislation was the first federal legislation that intervened in general education. In states whose constitutions or laws supported control of education by local communities, adopting state standards and assessments interfered with local control. Most of the states participated in the Goals 2000 initiative; a few, however, chose not to. Among them was Iowa, where the state constitution explicitly reserved control of public education for local communities. To address the issue of local control, the Goals 2000: Educate America Act included provisions for local school districts or consortia of local districts to apply for funding for standards-based school reform in states that had opted not to participate.

Bringing Equity and Quality Reforms Together

Throughout the recent history of education reform in the United States, the balance has shifted back and forth between equity and quality. But until the current authorization of the Elementary and Secondary Education Act, No Child Left Behind (PL 107–110), no initiative has brought them together so explicitly. No Child Left Behind (NCLB) brings together the equity historically intended by the ESEA and the quality represented by the standards-based reforms of America 2000 and Goals 2000. Its provisions, however, go far beyond those of earlier authorizations of the ESEA and Goals 2000, especially in terms of accountability for meeting the goals set by the law. NCLB revised the national goals enacted by

Congress in America 2000 and Goals 2000, replacing them with the following performance goals:

> By 2013–2014, all students will reach high standards, at a minimum attaining proficiency or better in reading/language arts and mathematics.

> All limited English proficient students will become proficient in English and reach high academic standards, at a minimum attaining proficiency or better in reading/language arts and mathematics.

> By 2005–2006, all students will be taught by highly qualified teachers.

> All students will be educated in learning environments that are safe, drug-free, and conducive to learning.

> All students will graduate from high school.

The law includes performance indicators for each of the five goals, as well as penalties and sanctions for schools and school districts that do not achieve what the law calls "adequate yearly progress" (AYP) toward all students meeting the state standards.

NCLB not only requires that schools meet the standards overall or that only the average students meet the standards. It also requires that schools consider and be evaluated by the performance of the many subgroups that make up the schools' populations. For the first time, schools are being held accountable for the academic progress of every child, and schools are required to report separately on the progress of minority groups, children in poverty, homeless children, children whose first languages are other than English, and children with disabilities. One of the great strengths of NCLB is that schools must make plans to improve the achievement of *all* children.

But NCLB has also been criticized by states, school districts, parent groups, and many special interest groups for a number of reasons. Among the many criticisms of NCLB are that the law requires annual testing of all children in school districts that receive funding under the law, that it is unrealistic to think that all children will demonstrate proficiency on such tests, that the law has not been fully funded, and that the law far oversteps the Constitutional right of the federal government to regulate education in the states. The analysis of some critics of NCLB is that the standards have been set so high that by 2014, nearly all schools in the United States will be considered failing, and some studies are beginning to support that analysis. (See Cavanaugh and Hoff 2008.)

Since the *Brown* decisions, which set precedent for and resulted in equity of access to education for so many children previously not served by U.S. public education, and the launch of Sputnik I, which spurred the first federal foray into improving the quality of learning in the United States, great strides have been made, particularly in the expectations of the public and the federal government about the outcomes of public education. But we have far to go to realize those expectations. There are still many children in the United States whose access to a high-quality education is challenged by a number of factors that have yet to be adequately addressed.

The State of Public Education in the United States and the Continued Need for Reform

Although the system of public education in the United States has been involved in some level of reform for more than half a century, the visions of many reformers for equity and quality have not been realized. There are many challenges to education reform in the United States. Among them are the increasing diversity of the school population, including the number of children living in poverty and the number of children whose home language is not English; inequity in school funding and other resources, including the quality of teaching, for education both among and within the states; and a political climate that seems not to support the equity envisioned by the *Brown* decisions.

Diversity of the U.S. School Population

One of the biggest challenges to education reform in the United States is the increasing diversity of the U.S. population in general, and in particular, the diversity of the children enrolled in public schools. According to the Center for Public Education (2007), in 1970, 79 percent of the children enrolled in public schools were white, 14 percent were black, 6 percent were Hispanic, and 1 percent were Asian or Pacific Islander. In 2006, of the 49,676,964 children enrolled in kindergarten through grade 12 in public schools in the United States, 55.9 percent were white, 16.9 percent black, 20.5 percent Hispanic, 4.5 percent Asian and Pacific Islander, and 1.2 percent American Indian or Alaska Native. Of those students, 8.5 percent were English language learners, and 13.6 percent were identified as having disabilities. The demographics of most urban school districts in the United States are very different from these, however, with fewer than 10 percent of the school population consisting of white students, and many individual urban schools consisting of nearly 100 percent minority students.

The number of children who are English language learners (whose first language is not English) is growing as well. According to Jeanne Batalova (2007), the number of LEP (limited English proficient) children enrolled in U.S. public schools increased 65 percent between 1994 and 2004, with about 5 million LEP children enrolled in kindergarten through grade 12 in the 2003–2004 school year. Some large urban school districts serve as many as several hundred different language groups; a typical urban school in an area where new immigrants settle may serve children who speak 40 or more languages. Batalova (2007) also cites statistics from the U.S. Census Bureau that show that LEP children are twice as likely to live in poor families as children who speak only English or who speak English very well.

Increasing Rates of Poverty

Even more disturbing, according to the National Center for Children in Poverty, 12.8 million children, or 17.5 percent, live in families whose incomes fall below the poverty line (annual income of $20,000 or less for a family of four). This number represents an increase of 1.2 million children between 2000 and 2006. Thirty-nine percent, or more than 28 million of the nation's children, lived in low-income homes (annual income of $41,000 for a family of four) in 2006. For children living in cities, the poverty rate is much higher, presenting a greater challenge to urban schools. In addition, the National Center estimates that the actual number of children in poverty is higher than reported, given flaws that have been identified in the way that poverty is calculated. The number of children not covered by health insurance is estimated to be 8.7 million, an increase of 600,000 between 2005 and 2006 (Fass and Cauthen 2007).

Disparity in School Funding

The 2008 *Education Week* report "Quality Counts" grades the nation and the states' educational outcomes and policies. The report gives the grade of C+ to the nation overall in the area of school finance; only one state, West Virginia, earns the grade of A, and one, New Jersey, the grade of A–. The grades are based on measures of equity among state school districts and per-pupil spending. According to the report, the national average for adjusted per-pupil expenditures in 2005 was $7,372, with average per-pupil expenditures ranging from $12,429 in the District of Columbia to $5,463 in Utah (p. 57).

In the United States, each state has its own school funding system, with schools in a few states funded entirely by the state while schools in other states rely at least partially on local funding. Even in states where public funding is "equalized" by the state, schools in more affluent areas often have more resources because parents can afford to provide what the schools cannot. The Education Trust studies state funding for education periodically. In its 2004 study, the Education Trust found that "in 25 of the 49 states studied, the highest poverty school districts get fewer resources than the lowest-poverty districts" (Carey 2004, 2). According to Kevin Carey (2004), "School funding experts generally agree that high-poverty schools need more resources to meet the same standards" as schools with lower rates of poverty (p. 2). Under No Child Left Behind, Congress set a funding standard that would have states provide districts with "additional funding per low-income student equal to 40 percent of the average per student amount" (p. 3), but when that formula is applied, the disparity is even greater, with "the highest-poverty schools in 36 states receiving fewer cost-adjusted dollars that the lowest-poverty districts" (p. 5).

In a later study, Carey and Marguerite Roza (2008) compared two schools that serve primarily students who come from low-income families. One of the schools, in Virginia, spends more than twice as much per student ($14,040) as the other, in North Carolina ($6,773). Even though their student populations are similar, student performance at the Virginia school exceeds the state standards in mathematics and science, while student performance at the North Carolina school falls below the state average. The higher funding at the Virginia school ensures more experienced teachers; more books, computers, and instructional materials; and smaller classes so that teachers have time to meet the needs of individual students. The researchers found that it is not only state funding that is inequitable. Since federal funds are allocated at least partially on the amount of state funding a school has, the Virginia school receives more federal funding than the North Carolina school, exacerbating the disparity between the funding of the two neighboring states.

Highly Qualified Teachers

One of the provisions of No Child Left Behind is that all teachers should be "highly qualified"; they should be fully certified to teach the grade levels or subjects that they teach. "Quality Counts" also presents data that describe states' efforts to recruit high quality teachers and provide the professional development they need to help them become even better. In explaining why the 2008 report focuses on teaching, the executive summary of the report notes that "teaching matters more to student learning than any other school-related factor" (p. 8); a subsequent analysis of the data on teaching finds that "a few good teachers in a row can raise students' achievement significantly" (p. 20). But just being certified may not be enough for teachers to be effective; the factors that characterize effective teaching or a clear understanding of how teaching affects student learning have been elusive. It is interesting that in a half-century of efforts at the national level in the United States to reform education, and in the extensive research that has been conducted on education during that time, so little has been learned about teaching effectiveness or how to prepare teachers to be effective. Bess Keller, author of the analysis of the data on teaching, notes that only a handful of states gather data on teachers and teaching in ways that can be linked to student achievement data.

After this half-century of scrutiny of public education in the United States, as well as the efforts over that time to improve the quality of education, educational quality as measured by student achievement falls far short of what was envisioned in the optimistic goals set by the America 2000, the Goals 2000, and the NCLB legislation. The National Assessment of Educational Progress (NAEP) measures student achievement across the nation annually in reading and mathematics at the fourth and eighth grade levels. Each year the National Center for Education Statistics (NCES) publishes "The Nation's Report Card," an analysis of the data from the NAEP. Scores from the NAEP are organized into four levels: below basic, basic, proficient, and advanced, with proficient as the level of performance envisioned for all children. NAEP defines proficient as denoting "solid academic performance. Students reaching this level have demonstrated competency over challenging subject matter." Analysis of data from the 2007 administration of the NAEP finds that only 31.7 percent of fourth-graders and 29.2 percent of eighth-graders demonstrated proficiency (proficient and advanced levels) in reading, and only 38.6 percent of fourth-graders and 31 percent of eighth-graders scored at the proficient or advanced level in mathematics (National Center for Education Statistics 2008).

Interestingly, the same NAEP data show that while in some states the achievement gap between children living in poverty and their peers from more affluent families narrowed slightly between 2006 and 2007, in both reading and math, the gap has remained fairly constant nationally. At the fourth grade level in math, for example, the difference between the average scores of children eligible for free lunch (i.e., living in poverty) and those not eligible for free lunch has remained the same, 24 points, since 2003 (National Center for Education Statistics 2008). Tables of data from NAEP can be found in Chapter 6.

The 2007 report cards also report on the white-black and white-Hispanic achievement gaps, comparing them from 1990 to 2007. According to the mathematics report, "significant score gaps persisted between White students and their Black and Hispanic peers" with no significant differences between the gaps in 1990 and 2007 (p. 27).

Jonathan Kozol has chronicled inequity and the effects of inequity in U.S. schools in a number of books and articles. According to Kozol (2005), many people believe that

> the great extremes of racial isolation that were matters of grave national significance some thirty-five or forty years ago have gradually but steadily diminished in more recent years. The truth, unhappily, is that the trend, for well over a decade now, has been precisely the reverse. Schools that were already deeply segregated over twenty-five or thirty years ago are no less segregated now, while thousands of other schools around the country that had been integrated either voluntarily or by the force of law have since been rapidly resegregating.

According to researchers Gary Orfield and Chungmei Lee (2007) of the UCLA Civil Rights Project, "The country's rapidly growing population of Latino and black students is more segregated than they have been since the 1960s and we are going backward faster in the areas where integration was most far-reaching" (p. 4). Activists for racial equality attribute the widening of the achievement gaps to this resegregation and the unwillingness of the Justice Department and the Supreme Court to pursue desegregation and increased equity for minority children, particularly those in poverty. In support of their contention, these activists cite the 2007 Supreme Court decision in *Parents Involved in Community Schools v. Seattle School District No. 1 et al.* (551 US ___ 2007). In their ruling in this case, the Court barred using race as a determining factor in assigning children to schools to achieve racial balance. The Court acknowledged that there are advantages to integration, but it severely limited the ways that school districts may achieve integration. The ruling effectively stops many school districts whose efforts toward voluntary integration have involved assignment of children to school on the basis of race, and those districts are challenged to find ways to integrate schools without the consideration of race.

In half a century of school reform efforts for equity and quality, there have been some gains. Children with disabilities, girls, English language learners, and children who are members of racial and ethnic minorities have gained rights under the law; unfortunately, those rights, which are not always evident in the real world of schools, are being eroded (Orfield, Eaton, and the Harvard Project on School Desegregation 1996). All children have made some gains in achievement in reading and mathematics; however, with only about a third of the nation's children demonstrating proficiency, and persistent achievement gaps between children in poverty and their more affluent peers, and between black and Hispanic children and their white peers, there definitely is work to be done.

References

Abramson, L. 2007. "Sputnik Left Legacy for U.S. Science Education." NPR's *All Things Considered*. September 30. http://npr.org/templates/story/story/pho?storyid=14829195.

Anderson, R. C., E. H. Hiebert, J. A. Scott, and I. A. G. Wilkinson. 1985. *Becoming a Nation of Readers: The Report of the Commission on Reading.* Champaign, IL: Center for the Study of Reading.

Barnett, W. S. 2002. "The Battle over Head Start: What the Research Shows." Paper presented at Congressional Science and Public Policy briefing on the impact of Head Start, September 13.

Batalova, J. 2006. "Spotlight on Limited English Proficient Students in the United States." US in Focus. Migration Policy Institute. http://www.migrationinformation.org/USfo6us/display.cfm?ID=373.

Brown Foundation for Educational Equity, Excellence and Research. http://brownvboard.org/foundation.

Brown v. Board of Education, 347 U.S. 483 (1954) (USSC+). http://www.nationalcenter.org/brown.html.

Brown v. Board of Education, 349 U.S. 294 (1955) (USSC+). http://www.nationalcenter.org/cc0725.htm.

Callahan, R. E. 1962. *Education and the Cult of Efficiency.* Chicago: University of Chicago Press.

Carey, K. 2004. *The Funding Gap 2004: Many States Still Shortchange Low-Income and Minority Students.* Washington, DC: The Education Trust.

Carey, K., and M. Roza. 2008. *School Funding's Tragic Flaw.* Seattle, WA: Education Sector, Center on Reinventing Public Education.

Cavanaugh, S., and D. J. Hoff. 2008. "Schools Found Likely to Miss NCLB Targets." *Education Week online,* September 25. http://www.edweek.org/ew/articles/2008/09/25/06ayp.h28.html?tmp=1754231223.

Center for Public Education. 2007. "At-a-Glance: Changing Demographics." *Practical Information and Analysis about Public Education.* http://www.centerforpubliceducation.org/site/c.kjJXJ5MPIwE/b.3633965/Diversity.

Center for Public Education. 2008. "School Context: What is the Racial and Ethnic Makeup of our Schools?" *Practical Information and Analysis about Public Education.* http://www.centerforpubliceducation.org/site/c.kjJXJ5MPIwE/b.3523701/k.5B61/School_context_What_is_the_racial_and_ethnic_make_up_of_our_schools.htm#national.

Fass, S., and N. K. Cauthen. 2007. *Who are America's Poor Children? The Official Story.* New York: National Center for Children in Poverty.

Franklin, Benjamin. 1749. "Proposals Relating to the Education of Youth in Pensilvania." http://www.archives.upenn.edu/primdocs/1749proposals.html.

Fullan, M. 2007. *The New Meaning of Educational Change,* 4th ed. New York: Teachers College Press.

Garces, E., D. Thomas, and J. Currie. 2000. "Longer Term Effects of Head Start." http://www.econ.ucla.edu/people/papers/Currie/Currie139.pdf.

Goals 2000 History. n.d. http://www.ed.gov/pubs/G2KReforming/g2ch1.html.

Grindle, M. S. 2004. *Despite the Odds: The Contentious Politics of Education Reform.* Princeton, NJ: Princeton University Press.

Hanna, J. 2005. "The Elementary and Secondary Education Act: 40 Years Later." *News Features & Releases.* Harvard Graduate School of Education. http://www.gse.harvard.edu/news_events/features/2005/08/esea0819.html.

Horn, C. L., and M. Kurlaender. 2006. *The End of Keyes—Resegregation Trends and Achievement in Denver Public Schools.* Cambridge, MA: The Civil Rights Project at Harvard University. http://www.civilrightsproject.ucla.edu/research/deseg/denver–4_5_06.pdf.

International Association for the Evaluation of Educational Achievement. 2007. "Brief History of IEA." http://www.iea.nl/brief_history_of_iea.html.

Jefferson, Thomas. 1779. *A Bill for the More General Diffusion of Knowledge.* http://oll.libertyfund.org/?option=com_staticxt&staticfile=show.php%3Ftitle=755&chapter=86186&layout=html&Itemid=27.

Kozol, J. 2005. "Still Separate, Still Unequal: America's Educational Apartheid." *Harper's Magazine 311* (1864). www.mindfully.org/Reform/2005/American-Apartheid-Education1sep05.htm.

Lipman, P. 2004. *High Stakes Education: Inequality, Globalization, and Urban School Reform.* New York: Routledge Falmer.

Lowe, R. 2004. "The Strange History of School Desegregation." *Rethinking Schools* 18 (3). http://www.rethinkingschools.org/archive/18_03/stra183.shtml.

Lowe, R. 2007. "Backpedaling Toward Plessy." *Rethinking Schools* 22 (1): 14–17.

NASA. 2007. "Sputnik and The Dawn of the Space Age." http://history.nasa.gov/sputnik/.

National Center for Educational Statistics. 2008. *The Nation's Report Card: Mathematics 2007.* Washington, DC: U.S. Department of Education.

National Center for Educational Statistics. 2008. *The Nation's Report Card: Reading 2007.* Washington, DC: U.S. Department of Education.

National Commission on Excellence in Education. 1983. "A Nation at Risk: The Imperative for Education Reform." Washington, DC: U.S. Department of Education. http://ed.gov/pubs/NatAtRisk/risk.html.

National Education Goals Panel. November 1993. "Promises to Keep: Creating High Standards for American Students." Washington, DC: National Education Goals Panel. http://www.ed.gov/legislation/GOALS2000/TheAct/sec102.html.

The National Commission on Excellence in Education. 1983. "A Nation at Risk: The Imperative for Educational Reform." http://www.ed.gov/pubs/NatAtRisk/index.html.

Noguera, P. 2003. *City Schools and the American Dream: Reclaiming the Promise of Public Education*. New York: Teachers College Press.

Orenstein, P. 1994. *School Girls: Young Women, Self-Esteem, and the Confidence Gap*. New York: Doubleday.

Orfield, G., S. Eaton, and the Harvard Project on School Desegregation. 1996. *Dismantling Desegregation: The Quiet Reversal of Brown v. Board of Education*. New York: The New Press.

Orfield, G., and C. Lee. 2007. *Historic Reversals, Accelerating Resegregation, and the Need for New Integration Strategies*. Los Angeles: The Civil Rights Project, UCLA.

Pardini, P. 2002. "The History of Special Education." *Rethinking Schools* 16 (3). http://www.rethinkingschools.org/archive/16_03/Hist163.shtml.

Rose, L. C., and A. M. Gallup. 2007. "The 39th Annual Phi Delta Kappa/Gallup Poll of the Public's Attitudes toward the Public Schools." *Phi Delta Kappan* 89 (1): 33–48.

Rotberg, I. C. 2004. "Preface." In *Balancing Change and Tradition in Global Education Reform*, edited by I. C. Rotberg, vii–ix. New York: Rowman and Littlefield Education.

Sadker, M., and D. Sadker. 1995. *Failing at Fairness: How Our Schools Cheat Girls*. New York: Scribner.

Shannon, P. 2004. "What's the Problem for which *No Child Left Behind* is the Solution?" In *Saving Our Schools: The Case for Public Education Saying No to "No Child Left Behind,"* edited by K. Goodman, P. Shannon, Y. Goodman, and R. Rapoport, 12–26. Berkeley, CA: RDR Books.

Spalding, E. 2000. "Performance Assessment and the New Standards Project: A Story of Serendipitous Success." *Phi Delta Kappan* 81 (10): 758–764.

Street, P. 2005. *Segregated Schools: Educational Apartheid in Post-Civil Rights America*. New York: Routledge.

Tyack, D., and L. Cuban. 2001. "Progress or Regress?" In *The Jossey-Bass Reader on School Reform*, 5–42. San Francisco: Jossey-Bass.

U.S. Census Bureau. 2005. *School Enrollment—Social and Economic Characteristics of Students: October 2003*. Washington, DC: U.S. Department of Commerce Economics and Statistics Administration.

U.S. Department of Education. 2007. "The Federal Role in Education." http://www.ed.gov/about/overview/fed/role.html.

Valentin, I. 1997. "Title IX: A Brief History." *25 Years of Title IX Digest.* Newton, MA: Women's Educational Equity Act (WEEA) Resource Center at EDC. http://www2.edc.org/GDI/publications_SR/t9digest.pdf.

Vinovskis, M. A. 1998. *Overseeing the Nation's Report Card: The Creation and Evolution of the National Assessment Governing Board.* Washington, DC: National Assessment Governing Board.

Vinovskis, M. A. 1999. *The Road to Charlottesville: The 1989 Education Summit.* Washington, DC: National Education Goals Panel.

2

Problems, Controversies, and Solutions

Since the 1950s, there has been an ongoing critique of public education in the United States. Problems have been identified in nearly every aspect of schooling, and calls for school reform have come from nearly every sector of U.S. society. The problems identified in public education generally fall under the larger headings of equity and quality described in Chapter 1. Indeed, one of the most serious problems associated with public education in the United States today is that in the aggregate, its student achievement is not competitive with that of other developed nations. Even though student achievement in the United States seems to be improving slightly overall, there is a persistent gap between the achievement of white and Asian students and that of African American and Hispanic students that is as large today as it was in the 1970s. According to an analysis of National Assessment of Educational Progress (NAEP) data by Manhattan Institute Senior Fellows Abigail Thernstrom and Stephan Thernstrom (2003), there is a four-year skills gap. "By twelfth grade," the Thernstroms assert, "on average, black students are four years behind those who are white or Asian. Hispanics don't do much better" (p. 12). In other words, if average white and Asian students are achieving at the 12th grade level, on average their African American and Hispanic peers are achieving at the eighth grade level.

Proposals for solutions have come from many different directions—education professionals, psychologists, neurologists and brain researchers, the business community, politicians, parents, and the general public. Each of the calls and solutions for educational reform has brought with it a philosophical perspective and a political agenda that extended beyond the face value of those calls and solutions. Nearly every proposed solution has also generated controversy or backlash that has affected its implementation.

The myriad solutions proposed to address the problems represent not only a range of political and philosophical perspectives but also a wide range of scale. Solutions range from the introduction of specific teaching strategies in individual classrooms to those that call for comprehensive school reform at the national level. There are solutions that are characterized as "top-down," mandated by the federal or state government or by school administrators, with penalties for noncompliance, and there are approaches that are "bottom-up," those initiated by teachers seeking solutions to the problems they face on a day-to-day basis in their schools and classrooms. Some solutions attempt to apply business practices to education, while others begin with what neuroscience is learning about the brain. This chapter describes a wide range of proposed solutions, the political or philosophical perspectives they represent or that are associated with them, and controversies they have generated.

Curriculum and Teaching Models

There are many models of curriculum and teaching that have been adopted by schools as part of their reform efforts with the goal of improving student achievement. They represent a wide variety of educational philosophies and theories, and like most other aspects of schooling, each of them has proponents and critics. Each of the models described here links curriculum (content) and teaching (what teachers do to facilitate learning).

Direct Instruction

Direct Instruction (DI), according to the Web site of the National Institute for Direct Instruction (NIFDI), is "a model for teaching that emphasizes well-developed and carefully planned lessons designed around small learning increments and clearly defined and prescribed teaching tasks" (NIFDI n.d.). DI, a behaviorist (stimulus-response) approach to learning, uses prescribed curriculum and lessons that are scripted; teachers read the scripts and elicit responses from students as part of the lessons. The student responses are scripted as well, and teachers cue students to provide the correct responses. Proponents of scripted DI assert that the lessons and their sequences are carefully researched; skills and concepts are broken down into their smallest components and taught in the prescribed sequence. According to the developers of DI, teacher creativity and autonomy are not necessary parts of the teaching and learning process, and the scripts ensure that teachers pace their instruction appropriately and that what teachers say and do with their students results in learning.

DI was developed by Siegfried Engelmann and Wesley Becker, education professors at the University of Oregon and directors of NIFDI. They and their colleagues claim that DI results in improved student achievement in nearly all curriculum areas, and they cite an analysis of studies of DI by the American Institutes for Research that claims to show that DI not only improved student achievement in academics but also improved children's self esteem and behavior (NIFDI).

Another program based on scripted direct instruction is Success for All, developed at Johns Hopkins University by Robert Slavin. Success for All is a program for teaching reading; it was named one of only two programs rated "moderately strong evidence of positive effects" by the American Institutes for Research. The other such program was Engelmann and Becker's DI. The Success for All program is currently in place in 1,200 schools, and more than 30 external studies of Success for All have supported its effectiveness (Success for All 2008).

Critics of DI argue that DI does not address individual children's learning needs, that it promotes memorization and rote learning rather than concept development and thinking, and that it deskills teachers. Many educators and cognitive psychologists believe that rote memorization does not result in real learning; students who memorize information may not be able to use or critique that information. Experienced teachers believe and research in cognitive psychology supports the notion that children learn in many different ways and at different times. For these teachers and psychologists, teaching in only one way may leave out students whose learning needs do not match the prescribed methods or sequence of DI. They argue that it makes no sense to present the same lessons to students who may already know the content and those who are not ready to learn that content, either because of development or because of a lack of prerequisite learning.

Critics of DI believe that classroom teachers who know their students are in the best position to plan for their instruction; they can address the students' learning needs and preferences, and they can determine the appropriate time for teaching content. Classroom teachers can also connect the content of lessons to their students' lives outside school, making the lessons culturally and personally relevant to students. Critics describe DI lessons as culturally irrelevant and inappropriate for many urban and inner city children, and they cite studies (see Ryder, Sekulski, and Silberg 2003) that showed student achievement to be lower in classrooms where teachers use DI than in non-DI classrooms.

Integrated Curriculum

Many educators believe that it is important for students to connect what they learn in one curriculum area to what they learn in other areas, and they cite research in cognitive psychology and neuroscience that defines learning as a process of connecting learning in meaningful ways. They argue that the world is not divided into subject areas, and integrating the curriculum has the potential to make what children learn more authentic and relevant to their experiences in the real world. Educators often call integrated curriculum "theme study," in which the curriculum is organized around themes or big questions, rather than a sequence of discrete skills and concepts. The theme provides a context for learning specific skills and concepts.

An example of integrated curriculum might be a unit organized around the theme of the westward movement in the United States. In this unit, children would study the plants and animals along the Oregon Trail (science); they would learn about the land formations from east to west in the United States (geography); they would read real accounts of traveling on the Oregon Trail in the form of journal entries (history); and they would calculate distance and the amount of provisions necessary for such a trip (mathematics). They might even write "journals" of someone's experiences along the Oregon Trail (creative writing) or paint a mural of life on the Oregon Trail (art). According to Sam Hausfather (1995), a teacher researcher, "thematic instruction incorporates processes that involve focusing on meaning to make sense of the world and relying on one's intelligence to solve problems and discover relationships" (p. 3). While the focus of these classrooms may be themes or "big questions," there is still skill, strategy, and concept teaching and learning going on. Instead of teaching skills, strategies, and concepts as separate modules of learning, however, teachers teach them and students learn them in the context of themes that provide opportunities for authentic application and for developing critical thinking.

The U.S. Department of Education's NCLB newsletter (Ashby 2007), *The Achiever*, showcased a public elementary school in Oklahoma City that integrates the arts throughout the curriculum. Integrating the arts "is moving students beyond the rudimentary practices of memorization and recitation by providing a myriad of creative channels for learning the same subject matter" (p. 3). Linwood Elementary School is part of Oklahoma A+ Schools, a network of schools in Oklahoma modeled after North Carolina's A+ Schools Program. In an evaluation of the North Carolina A+ Schools, researchers found that the program has positive effects on students, teachers, schools, and communities, including an enriched school environment, increased equity, improved student achievement, and greater parent and community involvement (Nelson 2001). The results at Linwood Elementary School are similar, including high student achievement. Linwood serves an ethnically, racially, and linguistically diverse population of students, 92 percent of whom qualify for free or reduced-price lunches. According to Nicole Ashby (2007), Linwood "has exceeded the state's targets by at least a 40-percentage point margin" with 92 percent of fourth-graders demonstrating proficiency in reading compared to the Oklahoma City average of 74 percent, and 85 percent proficiency in mathematics compared to 66 percent citywide in 2006 (p. 3). The A+ Schools model also draws on and enacts multiple intelligence theory, described below.

Proponents of "back to basics" education often are critical of curriculum integration. They express concern that children may not focus on learning the skills and concepts that they need to know when learning is organized around themes or the curriculum is integrated. Critics believe that skills and concepts should be taught in a specific sequence, a sequence that may be difficult, if not impossible, to follow when the skills and concepts are integrated or taught as part of a theme study. Critics also argue that teachers spend an inordinate amount of time integrating the curriculum, sometimes focusing on planning elaborate activities to teach what might otherwise be considered simple skill lessons. Further, religious conservatives express concern about such methods of organizing teaching and learning because, they believe, themes often involve the teaching of values that should be left to parents and religious institutions.

Multiple Intelligences

Multiple intelligences is a theory developed and researched by Howard Gardner, Harvard University psychologist, that challenges the definition of intelligence as measured by traditional intelligence tests as too narrow. Instead, Gardner (2003) proposed that each individual possesses an array of intelligences, which he defines as biopsychological potentials. Based on interviews with people from all walks of life and on research about the brain, Gardner originally proposed seven different intelligences; his continued research identified three more intelligences. Each of the intelligences Gardner has identified use different parts of the brain. The intelligences include linguistic intelligence, logical-mathematical intelligence, musical intelligence, bodily kinesthetic intelligence, spatial intelligence, interpersonal intelligence, intrapersonal intelligence, naturalistic intelligence, existential intelligence, and moral intelligence (Smith 2002). Further, Gardner's work challenges the traditional theory that intelligence is something that people are born with; instead, he believes, and his research supports, the idea that intelligences are developed through life experiences. In other words, intelligence is not static; schools can help children raise their levels of these intelligences. The application of Gardner's multiple intelligences in schools requires that curriculum be designed and teaching be planned to provide learning experiences that develop all of the intelligences.

The Key Learning Community (Kunkel 2007) in Indianapolis, Indiana, is a school organized around Howard Gardner's theory of multiple intelligences. The word "community" is part of the name of the school, explains Key principal Christine Kunkel, because of the staff's "belief in the power of collaboration. We teach students how to work with others on projects, how to network with people out in the neighborhoods, and how to talk to one another when there is a dispute" (p. 207), evidence of Gardner's interpersonal intelligence at work. Students at Key have opportunities within "regular classes"—language arts, mathematics, science, social studies, music, the arts—and special classes to develop their intelligences through project-based learning and presentations of those projects, and they participate in Mentor and Apprenticeship programs with professionals and practitioners who work in areas of interest to the students. Students at the Key Learning Community document their learning through video portfolios that allow them, their parents, and their teachers to view the development of their intelligences, their academic achievement, and their interests over the time they spend at the school.

Kunkel reports that the school "boasts the highest graduation rate" among public high schools in Indianapolis, with 89 percent of its 2006 graduates going on to college. She also notes that some of the program's most important outcomes, which include self-knowledge and self-confidence, interpersonal skills, and leadership, cannot be measured by traditional tests or presented quantitatively.

Another school organized around multiple intelligences is the Gardner School in Vancouver, Washington. At the Gardner School, children are not grouped by age; instead, the school builds diverse learning communities in which each child is viewed as an individual with individual talents, strengths, and learning needs. The mission of the Gardner School includes "teaching to the uniqueness of each mind," and the curriculum at the Gardner School, an independent pre-kindergarten through eighth grade school, is "emergent," emerging from and responding to the interests of the children (Gardner School 2008).

Critics of multiple intelligences theory argue that Gardner's work has not been tested empirically and that Gardner's intelligences do correlate with what is traditionally tested as intelligence. Proponents of traditional measurements of intelligence also express concern that multiple intelligences cannot be measured. But supporters of multiple intelligences see the theory as the impetus for educators to view their students in a very different light. Instead of asking *whether* their students are "smart," multiple intelligences theory provides the basis for educators to assume that all of their students are "smart," and to look, instead, at their students' intelligence profiles to learn which of their students' intelligences are already developed. This knowledge can lead to teaching that will develop intelligences that are not yet fully developed as well as to targeting teaching at those intelligences that are developed.

Brain-Based Education

Brain-based education, a concept that has been developing since the 1980s, has a simple definition. According to Eric Jensen, proponent of brain-based education, it is the application of research about the brain to the teaching and learning process. Jensen has argued for more than 20 years that education should take advantage of the huge strides made in research on how the brain works, as well as help educators learn about how to apply that research in schools and classrooms.

Neurologist and middle school teacher Judy Willis (2008) cautioned that the connections between brain research and education have not all been made yet, but she also says, "We do need to take some temporary leaps of faith across the parts of the bridge that are not yet sturdy and try interventions before the research is complete" (p. 426). According to Willis, in finding ways to apply brain research to teaching, there "will be important challenges to meet, but the next decade will reward us with extraordinary opportunities" (p. 427).

While they may be taking "leaps of faith," proponents of brain-based education have proposed principles for educators to consider when implementing brain research in schools and classrooms. Each of the principles is based on interpretations of findings about the brain, some of them fairly certain, but others fairly tentative. In their seminal text, *Making Connections: Teaching and the Human Brain*, Renate Caine and Geoffrey Caine (1991) stated that the guiding principle of brain-based teaching should be to understand that "brain research establishes and confirms that multiple complex and concrete experiences are essential for meaningful learning and teaching" (p. 5). According to Caine and Caine (1991), to reflect the research on the brain and learning, teachers should plan and implement "lifelike, enriching, and appropriate experiences for learners" and "ensure that students process experiences in such a way as to increase the extraction of meaning" (p. 8). In other words, based on what is known about the brain and learning, it is complex, real-world experiences that lead to real learning. In a brain-based classroom, children are engaged in projects that are hands-on and authentic. Instead of reading about recycling and learning to say, "Reduce, reuse, recycle," for example, children would be engaged in designing and conducting a recycling project as they research how the materials they gather can be reused and recycled.

Other researchers have described the importance of the learning environment as a key finding of brain research. According to Marilee Sprenger (1999), brain research suggested that learning environments should allow children to interact socially as well as to interact with the environment itself. Learning environments should be enriched, and they should present challenges and offer opportunities for play.

Other researchers, including psychologists and neuroscientists, believe that it is too early to design educational interventions based on current findings of brain research. According to Robert J. Sternberg (2008), "Someday, brain science may give us conclusions that clearly point in one direction or another. We are not there yet. For the most part, the brain metaphor is comforting and may even be useful. But it does not provide us with unequivocal conclusions that lead to one educational practice versus another" (p. 419).

Differentiated Instruction

According to Tracey Hall (2002), senior research scientist at the National Center on Accessing the General Curriculum, "Differentiated instruction applies an approach to teaching and learning so that students have multiple options for taking in information and making sense of ideas" (p. 2). When teachers differentiate instruction, they purposely plan lessons that address the interests, learning styles, and needs of the individual students in their classrooms with the purpose of helping each child learn and succeed. Teachers can differentiate instruction in several different ways to meet the varied learning needs, styles, and preferences of their students.

Carol Ann Tomlinson (2000) listed four elements of differentiated instruction—content, process, product, and learning environment. Teachers can differentiate *content* in a variety of ways, such as providing instructional materials at a variety of levels, providing reading materials or other content information in audio or video form, and teaching small group lessons to either supplement or extend learning as students' needs warrant.

Teachers who differentiate *process* provide a variety of learning activities from which they and children may choose. These could include small and large group teaching, cooperative group learning, learning centers, manipulatives or other materials for hands-on learning, and opportunities for students to pursue areas of personal interest related to the content.

Differentiating *products* could take the form of allowing students to demonstrate their learning in different ways, allowing students the choice of working alone or with a partner to create a product that documents the learning, and providing rubrics for judging the products that communicate clearly what the expectations are for the learning.

Providing a differentiated learning environment can include arranging a classroom so that there are areas where students who need quiet can work and also areas for group work, allowing students who need to move to learn the space they need and the calm and quiet that other students need, and having a variety of learning materials that reflect diversity.

Tomlinson and Amy Germundson (2007) compared differentiated instruction to playing jazz with its improvisation, its intent to create personal connections, and ultimately, the music it makes. They say, "The teacher who uses differentiation in practice says, 'Whatever it takes to ensure success for each student, I'm willing to try.' In those moments of purpose, sensitivity, and improvisation, jazz happens" (p. 29).

While there have been no large-scale studies of differentiated instruction, smaller studies have documented its value to children's learning. Several studies of differentiated instruction in reading, for example, show that in addition to children's reading ability improving, their attitude toward reading also improved (Baumgartner, Lipowski, and Rush 2003). A study of differentiated learning in a high school showed that after five years of differentiating instruction, the average student's reading level increased more than two years (Fisher and Frey 2001).

Critics of differentiated instruction cite the difficulty of differentiating effectively as a drawback. Teaching each lesson in a variety of ways to meet students' perceived learning styles and preferences, according to the critics, has not been proven effective by research. Other critics, often educational researchers, label differentiated instruction a fad, citing the lack of empirical evidence of learning styles themselves, and argue that even if such styles exist, little real assessment of learning styles precedes differentiated instruction (Stahl 1999).

Assessment and Accountability

Documenting or assessing students' learning is an important element of education reform. It is important to know what students are learning for a number of reasons. Assessment can be used to give students feedback about their learning. Information from assessments can help teachers understand what their students are learning and what they still need to know; teachers can use that information to plan for teaching that addresses the needs that are identified through the assessment. Assessment information can be used to make decisions about the effectiveness of programs, schools, and school districts.

There are many ways to document student learning. At the classroom level, teachers use tests and quizzes, observations of their students, performance-based assessments, portfolios of student work, and standardized tests. Each of these forms of assessment has the potential to provide information about student learning. Many educators believe that the best assessment programs include a variety of assessment tools to be able to create as complete a profile of student learning as possible.

Experts in assessment and evaluation describe the best assessment programs as including "multiple measures" of student learning, an array of assessment tools that offer the opportunity to view a student's learning from many different perspectives over a period of time, rather than at one point in time.

Tests and Quizzes

Classroom-level tests and quizzes are most often designed by teachers or provided as part of the supporting materials with textbooks. Tests and quizzes, which typically have a set of questions, each with a "right" answer, can provide information about how students are learning and understanding facts and knowledge. While they are not always easy to design, they are usually fairly easy to score; answers are right or wrong. Tests and quizzes are easy to evaluate, but they provide limited information about students' learning because of the kinds of content that can be addressed in a test or quiz and because they give a "snapshot" view of student learning, a view at only one point in time.

Observations of Students

Observation of students can provide information to teachers not only about what students are learning, but also about how they are learning. Teachers can observe students' strengths and weaknesses, the processes and strategies that students use, and the ways that students interact with other students. Observation is most effective as an assessment strategy when teachers gather their observations and record them in a systematic way.

Observations rarely generate scores; instead, they provide qualitative information about students' learning. Observations are valuable because they can provide information about children's learning processes and interactions, but they are time-consuming and difficult to analyze and aggregate. Because it is difficult to analyze and aggregate observation data, observations usually do not provide information that can be used to evaluate progress of groups of children or programs.

Performance-Based Assessments and Portfolios of Student Work

Performance-based assessments have the potential for teachers to understand how their students use skills, knowledge, and concepts in the context of solving a problem or designing a product, project, or performance. Performance-based assessments are often called "authentic" because they require students to apply skills, knowledge, and concepts in real-world situations. Such assessments don't have one correct answer; instead, teachers use rubrics or scoring guides to judge each student's performance.

A performance-based assessment task, for example, might ask an elementary student to pretend that she is planning a pizza party for her class. She will need to decide how many and what kinds of pizza to order and to calculate how much the pizza will cost. As part of the assessment, she might be expected to survey her classmates about the kinds of pizza they like as well as how many pieces they would eat; organizing that information into a graph or table might also be a part of the task. She might also be asked to decide from a set of menus which pizza restaurant to order the pizza from and to justify her decision in writing. A task like this could provide information about how the child gathers information; how she organizes information in graphs or tables; how she performs mathematical operations such as addition, multiplication, and division; how she applies them; and how she explains her thinking.

Portfolios are collections of samples of students' work. Because work samples from various times throughout a school year or even throughout a students' school career can be included in them, portfolios have the potential to show how students' learning develops over time. Many schools use portfolios of students' writing to document how their students grow as writers; pieces of writing are selected for inclusion in portfolios by both teachers and students. Schools that use portfolios often have specific criteria for the pieces to be included in portfolios; they might include writing in a specific set of genres (expository writing, narrative writing, persuasive writing, poetry), or pieces of writing in the various stages of the writing process (prewriting, first drafts that are unedited, edited pieces, and final pieces). Students are often asked to review their own portfolios and reflect on their own progress; teachers may evaluate students' portfolios through a standard rubric or scoring guide.

Performance-based assessments and portfolios have the advantage of documenting students' learning through products and processes that are engaging for students and that are part of the teaching and learning process, rather than taking time from it. A further advantage of portfolios is that they can include samples of everyday work rather than work that is developed just for assessment. However, scoring or rating of performance-based assessments and portfolios requires thoughtful judgment on the part of teachers; if performance-based assessments or portfolios are used as part of student evaluation across classrooms or schools, teachers must be trained to judge them consistently so that ratings are comparable. This consistent judgment provides a measure that testing experts call interrater reliability—the assurance that a score determined by one "rater" will be the same as the score determined by any other "rater." Without the training of "raters," scores from performance assessments may provide information only to classroom teachers; they have little value for judging the effectiveness of schools or programs.

Standardized Tests

Standardized achievement tests are administered by most schools to gather information about students' learning that can be compared to standards, to rank students relative to their learning, or to provide information about groups of children or programs. What makes standardized tests "standardized" is that they consist of a set of questions or items that are administered to all children at a particular grade level under standard conditions—at the same time of year, with the same instructions, the same time constraints, and the same method of responding (usually "bubbling in" answers on an answer sheet that can be scanned). Such standardized testing is required under No Child Left Behind.

Standardized tests can provide information about individual children's learning, but they are more appropriately used to provide information about the learning of groups of children, whole schools, and whole school districts. They are limited, however, like other tests and quizzes, in the kinds of information that they can provide. Critics of standardized testing argue that the most important learning outcomes—thinking processes, problem solving, and applying skills and concepts appropriately—are not well documented or measured by standardized tests.

Further, standardized test scores are often misinterpreted and misused. Some school districts use test scores as the only measure to decide whether children pass to the next grade. Critics argue that test scores often don't provide information about the most important learning outcomes, so multiple assessment results should be used to make such decisions. Research on tests and student achievement has found that the largest factors in a child's test score are the socioeconomic status of her family and her parents' level of education. When school districts use standardized test scores to evaluate the quality of teachers or as a way to grade schools, the teacher and school evaluations may only reflect what students bring with them to school, not the quality of their school experience.

Currently, No Child Left Behind (NCLB) requires schools to administer standardized tests to all children in grades three through eight, and at one point in high school, typically 10th grade. Those scores, aggregated for entire schools and disaggregated by children's race, ethnicity, first language, and disability, are used to determine schools' progress toward having all children proficient in reading, language arts, and mathematics by the year 2014. Individual states determine appropriate levels of progress for schools, what NCLB terms "adequate yearly progress," and schools that do not demonstrate adequate yearly progress are identified and penalized. Schools that fail to make adequate yearly progress for several years are labeled failing schools, and school districts may even close failing schools.

Critics of NCLB's accountability requirements decry what they call the misuse of standardized testing. Under NCLB, standardized test scores are used to make what educators call "high stakes" decisions about individual children, and they are used to make "high stakes" decisions about schools. FairTest, the National Center for Fair and Open Testing, is a nonprofit watchdog on testing in schools. FairTest argues that

> standardized tests, especially norm-referenced multiple choice tests, are harmful to children and to education; [and that] basing high-stakes decisions on standardized tests (high school graduation, advancement, etc.) is bad educational practice while basing decisions about teachers and schools on test results damages education. (FairTest n.d.)

FairTest's full explanation of the harmful effects of "high-stakes" testing is found in Chapter 6.

Critics of NCLB accountability also cite the standardized testing requirement as responsible for a narrowing of the curriculum. Since standardized test scores are reported only for reading, language arts, and mathematics, these critics say, schools have reduced the amount of time children spend learning about subjects and curriculum areas that are not tested. In a study of the impact of NCLB on instructional time in elementary schools by the Center on Education Policy (McMurrer 2008), findings confirmed that the curriculum in many schools has indeed been narrowed. The study found that 44 percent of elementary schools increased instructional time for English language arts, including reading, and mathematics. To accommodate these increases, schools reported decreasing time for social studies, science, art, music, and physical education. One-fifth of the schools surveyed also decreased time for recess or eliminated it altogether.

Options for Alternative Schooling

A number of school reformers have suggested that it is not only curriculum, teaching, and assessment that should be reformed and improved. Rather, they recommend, the very organization of schooling should be reinvented to meet the needs of the changing and diverse population of children served by schools in the United States, as well as the expectations of the children's families. In addition, some reformers argue that "one size fits all" schools really fit no one, and they propose that parents have choices in the kinds of schools their children attend. Such options include charter schools, magnet or themed schools, single-sex schools, educational vouchers, tuition tax credits and scholarships, and home schooling. These options are intended to allow children and their parents to select schools or forms of schooling that meet their individual preferences, to offer competition to public schools, and to address the issues of quality or equity that provide the impetus for education reform in the United States. Schools of choice are most often found in urban school districts.

Small Schools

At a time when schools have become larger, more bureaucratic, and less personal, small schools, small learning communities, and schools within schools have been proposed as formats for addressing some of the problems students face in large high schools, especially those that serve low-income students. Small schools typically have student populations of less than 400; small learning communities and schools within schools sometimes divide larger high schools into small units within a larger building. Small learning communities and schools within schools typically have the autonomy that small schools have for organization, curriculum, and teaching, although they may share facilities within a larger school. Because these schools are smaller, teachers and administrators know individual students, and as a result, there is more student accountability for learning, attendance, and discipline. Many small schools, small learning communities, and schools within schools have themes or particular curriculum focuses.

Tobin McAndrews and Wendell Anderson (2002) identified a number of benefits of small schools that include higher student achievement and lower drop-out rates than comparable students in large high schools; a greater sense of belonging and higher student social and academic self-esteem; higher attendance and graduation rates; fewer discipline problems; and lower administrative costs. They caution, however, that just reducing the size of a school is not enough to reap the benefits. Instead, they argue, rigorous academic programs must accompany the creation of small nurturing environments to produce positive results in student learning.

In their evaluation of 75 small schools opened between 2002 and 2005 as part of the New Century High Schools Initiative in New York City, Eileen Foley, Allan Klinge, and Elizabeth Reisner found benefits similar to those identified by McAndrews and Anderson. In their study, Foley, Klinge, and Reisner (2007) found that 18 percent more New Century High Schools students graduated on time than comparable students in larger New York City high schools (78.2 percent versus 60.6 percent). The researchers also found that students in the small schools benefited from "close student-teacher relationships and adult mentoring of youth, the extension of student learning outside the regular school setting and school day, and the use of data to track student performance" (p. ii). In addition to the New Century High Schools in New York City, small schools networks have been created in other urban school districts, including Oakland, Los Angeles, Houston, Chicago, Cincinnati, Baltimore, and Boston, according to the Small Schools Project of the Coalition for Essential Schools.

Magnet and Themed Schools

Magnet schools are public schools that are part of local school districts and that have curriculums or themes intended to attract students. Such themes include fine arts, technology, mathematics and science, ecology, foreign language immersion, performing arts, military science, and agricultural science. Magnet schools were first proposed as a means of voluntary desegregation. The curriculum and instructional programs at magnet schools are designed to draw both minority and nonminority students to help achieve racial balance and diversity, and most magnet schools continue to have diversity as one of their goals. Typically, magnet schools draw students from across entire school districts or entire regions of school districts rather than from specific attendance areas as neighborhood schools do. While magnet schools are typically locally funded at the same level as other schools in their school districts, states have often been ordered by courts to provide desegregation funds to supplement local funds as part of desegregation remedies. In addition, there are funds allocated for magnet schools in the Elementary and Secondary Education Act (ESEA), No Child Left Behind (NCLB). Part C of that law provides for magnet school funding, as well as information about application for the funds and permissible uses of the funds.

There have been many evaluations of student achievement in magnet schools, Adam Gamoran (1996), a sociologist, conducted a study that compared magnet high school student achievement with the achievement of peers in comprehensive public high schools, private Catholic high schools, and private nonreligious schools. His findings showed that students in magnet high schools outperformed their peers in other high schools in reading, science, and social studies. In mathematics, the students in private Catholic high schools performed better. Another study of student performance in magnet schools that compared magnet school students in St. Louis to their non-magnet school peers found that "magnet students substantially outperform[ed] non-magnet students on state assessments in reading, mathematics, social studies, and science" (Yu and Taylor 1997, 19). There are also studies that found that attending a magnet school did not result in higher student achievement, but no studies have found magnet schools to have negative effects.

The main drawback of magnet and themed schools is that they typically require higher levels of funding to operate than neighborhood schools. Extra funding is required to support the special programs offered with more specialized teachers, facilities, and materials. In many school districts where systems of magnet schools were part of desegregation orders or plans, the magnet schools were dismantled or returned to neighborhood schools once school districts were no longer responsible for desegregation and the higher levels of funding available to them because desegregation orders were withdrawn.

Single-Sex Education

Single-sex education has reemerged as an option for schools. Single-sex education is generally defined as schools or classrooms where boys and girls are assigned based on gender—boys are in classrooms or schools attended only by boys, girls with only girls. While there have been same-sex parochial and private schools, nearly all public schools have traditionally been coeducational. But new research in psychology and neurology has shown that there are real physical differences between boys and girls, differences that affect how they learn. According to Leonard Sax, a psychologist and physician who is promoting single-sex education based on research he has conducted, the number of single-sex classrooms increased by more than 10 times between the 2000–2001 and 2005–2006 school years (Sax 2005).

While Sax believes that single-sex education has the potential to improve learning for both boys and girls, he argues that just separating students by gender is not enough to bring about improved learning. Teachers and administrators must understand the differences between boys and girls and learn how to teach them effectively. Sax (2005) explained, "In the past decade, however, good research has demonstrated that there are, in fact, hard-wired differences in the ways girls and boys learn, and that there are evidence-based techniques that can exploit those differences."

He recommends much more research be conducted, and that, for now at least, single-sex education should be a choice for parents to make, rather than a requirement for all children. It is interesting to note that although Sax claims to have conducted research about single-sex classrooms, none has been published or reviewed.

In its 2005 review of studies of single-sex education at the elementary and secondary level, the U.S. Department of Education, Fred Mael, and colleagues found that although there are few studies of single-sex public schools in general, or public or private elementary or middle schools, there are trends worth noting. According to the researchers, most of the studies showed single-sex education to have positive results in terms of academic achievement and socio-emotional development, both "current and long term" (p. xvii). These researchers call for more systematic and scientific research, both to better understand the results of single-sex schooling and to understand the costs and benefits of single-sex schools. David Sadker and Karen Zittleman (2004), who have conducted many studies of single-sex education, particularly for girls, recommended caution when considering single-sex schools. Their research, conducted in parochial schools for girls, found that the benefits of those schools may be related to factors other than their segregation by sex (p. 9).

Aricka Flowers, in an article published by the Heartland Institute in Chicago, reported that the U.S. Department of Education gave schools and school districts the go-ahead to open single-sex schools and classrooms in November 2006. Flowers (2007) noted that "critics [of single-sex schooling] worry that single-sex classes and schools do not adequately reflect the real world." Children who experience only single-sex classrooms and schools may not be prepared for workplaces, other educational settings, and society in general. Others are concerned that single-sex schools or classrooms are discriminatory; the American Civil Liberties Union has filed a number of lawsuits in school districts planning single-sex schools, claiming that single-sex schools violate the equal protection clause of the U.S. Constitution.

Charter Schools

One option parents have for school choice is charter schools. According to U.S. Charter Schools, "Charter schools are nonsectarian public school of choice that operate with freedom from many of the regulations that apply to traditional public schools"

(Overview). The state of Minnesota enacted the first charter law in 1991, and since then, 40 states, Puerto Rico, and the District of Columbia have enacted laws to establish and regulate charter schools. In general, charter schools are granted their charters, or contracts, to operate by states, local school boards, or other state-established chartering agencies or sponsors that include, in some states, universities. Typically, state laws allow only a specific number of charter schools to be opened within the state. Charters are given for a period of three to five years, and they may be renewed. While charter schools are exempt from many policies of the school districts in which they are located, charter schools are accountable to their chartering agencies, whether those are states, local school districts, or universities, for student achievement and for fiscal responsibility.

Charter schools are generally governed by boards that are independent of local school districts or states; the governing boards or agencies they represent may be for-profit or not-for-profit. Many charter schools are organized around principles or themes that are different from those typically represented by public schools; these include themes similar to magnet schools, such as Montessori, technology, foreign language immersion, fine arts, and expeditionary learning. Most often, charter schools are located within urban school districts, and they may be considered "limited enrollment," having specific requirements for enrollment, i.e., test scores. In 2008, according to U.S. Charter Schools, there were more than 3,500 charter schools across the United States and Puerto Rico, and more than 1 million children were enrolled in them (U.S. Charter Schools).

Analysis of the demographics of the 150 charter schools that participated in the 2003 National Assessment of Educational Progress (NAEP) showed that, "in comparison to other public schools, higher percentages of charter school fourth-grade students are Black" (National Center for Education Statistics 2003), suggesting that minority families are more likely to take advantage of the opportunity to attend charter schools. This same study showed that the performance in both reading and mathematics of fourth-graders attending charter schools "was not measurably different" from the performance of fourth grade students with "similar racial/ethnic backgrounds" in other public schools. There have been many other studies of charter school performance (Braun, Jenkins, and Griggs 2006; Hoxby 2004a; Hoxby 2004b; Roy and Mishel 2005), with little agreement about whether charter schools offer advantages in terms of improved student learning.

Educational Vouchers, Tuition Tax Credits, and Scholarships

Educational vouchers are generally public grants that allow low-income parents to send their children to public or private schools of their choice; there are also some privately funded voucher programs, with one such program in Arizona. In the Milwaukee, Wisconsin, educational voucher program, the largest and longest running in the United States, voucher schools receive $6,501 for each full-time student enrolled. In the 2006–2007 school year, 17,410 Milwaukee students participated in the program, according to *Rethinking Schools Online* (2002). In an *ERIC Digest* on educational vouchers, Margaret Hadderman explained that although the provisions of voucher programs vary from state to state, in general, a child would qualify for a voucher when the school he would normally attend has been labeled a failing school. Hadderman (2000) described several studies of voucher programs that report parent and student satisfaction with their experiences in voucher-funded schools; at the same time, studies of student achievement are inconclusive (p. 3). There have been a number of lawsuits testing the constitutionality of vouchers being used for parochial schools or schools with religious affiliation, but none of them seems to have set a national legal precedent. Some states allow vouchers to be used in parochial schools or schools with religious affiliations, while others do not.

Similar to vouchers in terms of providing financial support for children to attend schools of choice is the tuition tax credit. Currently, Minnesota and Iowa have limited tax credits for education expenses that include private school tuition, and several other states are considering them. According to the Center for Education Reform (2008), "School tax credits refund expenses made toward education up to a fixed figure. . . . The qualifying criteria cover educational expenses such as tutoring, texts, and computers, and in states that have them so far, private school tuition." The amount of tax credit or deduction allowed and the specific expenses that qualify for tax credits or deductions are determined by state law. Among the organizations calling for the institution of such tax credits is the Mackinac Center for Public Policy, a Michigan organization committed to the privatization of education.

At least five states have public scholarship programs that provide funding for special needs students to attend private schools that provide instructional programs that more closely meet their needs. In these states, parents apply directly to the state for scholar-ships, rather than depending on their school districts to determine when a placement outside the school district might better serve their children. The Bush administration has proposed provid-ing scholarships also to children who attend schools labeled as "failing." These scholarships would allow the students to attend private schools instead of their "failing" public schools.

There are many proponents and supporters of charter schools, vouchers, and other options for school choice. Abigail Thernstrom, a commissioner of the U.S. Commission on Civil Rights and senior fellow at the Manhattan Institute in New York, and Stephan Thernstrom (2003), a Harvard University professor and senior fellow at the Manhattan Institute, argued that charter schools, which can be "radically different" from traditional pub-lic schools, have the potential to close the racial achievement gap (p. 273). These researchers believe that public school systems and teacher unions preserve the mediocrity they argue is prevalent in most public schools, and that charter schools, without the con-straints of those traditions, can provide incentives for creativity and innovation, as well as motivation for excellence. The Thern-stroms are also proponents of vouchers, asserting that they allow low-income families the same power to choose schools for their children that middle-class parents have by virtue of their ability to choose where they live.

Business leaders and conservative politicians support options for school choice for many reasons, not the least of which is that they believe that school choice has the potential to spur compe-tition in the "school marketplace." For them, public school sys-tems should not have a monopoly on education. Viewing schools as businesses whose product is student achievement, business leaders argue that competition for students can drive education reform, make public schools more efficient, and, like private busi-nesses, lead to the closing of schools that do not show improving student achievement.

Others, including researcher and public policy analyst Ken-neth J. Saltman (2007) of DePaul University, argued that vouchers, tax credits and deductions, and charter schools, like other choice options, serve the purposes of dismantling U.S. public education and supporting the role of for-profit corporations in privatizing the nation's schools. He asserts that privatization subverts the tradi-tional purpose of public education—that of developing a citizenry prepared to participate actively in the democratic process. Saltman and many other educators argue that a free public education is critical to the democratic process, that public education should not be privatized, and that doing so has the potential to further undermine the equity that a free public education can provide.

Still other critics assert that charter schools and other choice options work against equity in education. They argue that schools of choice do not serve all children, that choices are not always available to the children most in need of them, and that choices such as vouchers offer false hope to the families most in need of high-quality education. Charter and magnet schools may have entrance requirements such as high test scores; they may not serve special education and other high-needs children. Critics of such choice plans argue that many parents of children most in need of high-quality options have little information about such choices, do not advocate for or act as agents on behalf of their children, or simply do not have access to choice options because of barriers such as transportation. In many cases, vouchers do not provide enough money to pay full tuition at high-quality private schools, and private schools that do serve voucher students are often unregulated and sometimes of questionable quality.

Critics of choice programs also argue that magnet schools, charter schools, and voucher programs take the best and most capable students from regular public schools, leaving the public schools to educate those children with the highest needs, often the most difficult to teach. Charter schools and vouchers also take funding from public schools coffers, critics assert, decreasing the funds available for regular public schools.

Still others decry choice, particularly when vouchers or tax credits are used to pay for children to attend parochial schools or other schools with religious affiliations, as a violation of the U.S. Constitution's separation of church and state. They believe that such schools should not be supported in any way by public funds. The courts have sometimes concurred. In Arizona in May 2008, the state supreme court struck down the state's voucher program, citing the state prohibition against using public funds to support religious institutions.

Home Schooling

One other choice option that seems to be gaining in popularity is home schooling. According to Mark Penn, author of *Microtrends: The Small Forces Behind Tomorrow's Big Changes* (2007), the number of home-schooled children increased nearly 30 percent between 1999 and 2003, the last year that the National Center for Education Statistics (NCES) did a census of children who were home-schooled. Penn (2007) argued that "home-schooled kids in America actually outnumber charter school and voucher students *combined*" (p. 295). States vary in their regulation of home schooling, from some that do not require parents to notify the state at all of their children's home schooling to some states that require standardized testing and the use of a state-approved curriculum for home-schooled children.

In studies of home-schooled student achievement reported in 2001 by the Home School Legal Defense Association, "home schoolers outperformed their public school peers by 30 to 37 percentile points across all subjects" (p. 1). The studies also found no achievement gaps between minority and nonminority children or between genders; they also found little variance that could be attributed to parents' levels of education, even though many parents who homeschool their children have had no teacher education (p. 4).

Comprehensive School Reform

Many educators and researchers have long believed, echoing "A Nation at Risk," that all components of a school or school district must be addressed together to bring about real change in the performance of the schools and the learning of the children in them. Recognizing that schools and school districts are systems in which each component affects and is affected by each other component is key to such comprehensive reform. Peter Senge (1990) of the Massachusetts Institute of Technology, used the phrase "systems-thinking" to explain that in systems, one "can only understand the system . . . by contemplating the whole, not any individual part of the pattern" (p. 7). In a systems-thinking approach to school reform, all components of a school or school district must be examined as a whole, not as separate pieces of the educational puzzle.

Beginning in the 1960s, researchers and educators began to investigate and develop models for comprehensive school reform. The models in general were generated in two different ways. One of those ways was to begin with a set of theoretical principles and determine how a school could be organized and operated if it were aligned with those principles. Yale child psychiatrist James

Comer developed a model of school reform based on accepted principles of child development and sociological research on the relationship between school and family, particularly the importance of that relationship for minority and low-income families. Beginning with those principles and that research, Comer and his associates designed a model of school organization and management. That model will be described further below.

The other way school reform models have been developed is through research on and evaluation of the components of effective schools. A number of researchers responded to the Coleman study (see Chapter 1) by designing studies that sought to verify that effective schools existed; in other words, they looked for schools that outperformed other comparable schools even when controlling for the "outside of school" factors identified by Coleman as having the most effect on the quality of children's learning. These studies did confirm the existence of some effective schools, and researchers began to study the effective schools to look for commonalities among them. In the late 1970s and early 1980s, researchers identified characteristics that were common to the effective schools they had studied, and a number of models of comprehensive school reform were developed based on the redesign of schools around those characteristics (Mace-Matluck 1987). Some of those models are described below.

The Yale School Development Program

The comprehensive school reform process developed by James Comer is called the Yale School Development Program (SDP). The implementation of SDP is a five-year cycle of work to "replace traditional school organization and management with an operating system that works for schools and the students they serve" (Yale School Development Program Staff 2004, 18). The SDP, based on children's six developmental pathways—physical, cognitive, psychological, language, social, and ethical—seeks not only to raise student achievement but also, as the program vision states, "to create a just and fair society in which all children have the support for development that will allow them to become positive and successful contributors in family, work, and civic life" (p. 18). In his description of the SDP model, Charles Payne (1991) compared Comer's basic principles to those of John Dewey, summing up the underlying philosophy of SDP thus: "If the adults in a child's life behave as if they are in a community, children are likely to develop into healthier adults, and part of that development will be expressed in intellectual growth" (p. 12). Dewey, considered one of the most influential educators in the United States in the 20th century, believed that education should be child-centered and responsive to each individual child as a member of a learning community that includes adults who model for children what it means to be a learning community member.

SDP is built on an organizational structure within each school of three teams made up of administrators, teachers, support staff, students, and parents. In the school reform process, these teams develop and implement a comprehensive school plan that includes goals for teaching, learning, and assessment, as well as vehicles for sharing information about the school with the entire community. The process is cyclic; it includes professional development for teachers and other school staff to support the curriculum and teaching addressed in the school plan as well as revision to the plan based on analysis of the information generated by periodic and ongoing assessment of both student learning and other program goals.

Over its life of more than 40 years, the SDP has been implemented in many urban schools and schools that serve children from low-income families throughout the United States. During that time, many external evaluations have been conducted on the effects of SDP in schools. Christina Ramirez-Smith (1995), for example, described the implementation of the SDP in an inner-city elementary school in Newport News, Virginia, that resulted in a 67 percent increase in student test scores and "a spirit of unity" among school personnel, parents, and students (p. 19). Testimonials from other schools report similar results. More importantly, the SDP staff of the Yale Child Study Center has engaged in systematic analysis of data about the implementation and outcomes of the SDP on an ongoing basis, and there have also been external evaluations of schools involved in SDP. Internal evaluations of elementary and middle schools that have fully implemented the SDP have shown gains in student achievement that were significantly greater than comparable schools in the same school districts not implementing the SDP. These studies also show improvement in students' attendance rates, behavior, and self-concept, as well as school climate and parent participation (Haynes, Emmons, Gebreyesus, and Ben-Avie 1996). Thomas Cook, H. D. Hunt, and Robert Murphy (2000) studied the effects of SDP on an elementary school in Chicago and found results that were similar to those of SDP's internal analyses.

Accelerated Schools

Accelerated Schools is a comprehensive school reform process similar to the SDP in that it is based on developing a school community that takes responsibility for the learning of children. In addition to the community of parents, children, and school personnel envisioned by the SDP, however, the Accelerated Schools extends the notion of community to include local businesses and service organizations. Accelerated Schools focuses on the social, emotional, and academic needs of each child through a governance model that includes the entire community. Begun in 1986 by Henry Levin of Stanford University, Accelerated Schools begins with the strengths of children (rather than their deficits or weaknesses), is intentionally flexible to implement within a wide variety of school contexts, and builds the capacity of teachers (Siegle 2006).

In Accelerated Schools, all school personnel, parents, and community members serve on teams that plan for, implement, and evaluate the results of the implementation of initiatives that address problems that the teams identify in the schools. Because the implementation of Accelerated Schools is unique to each school, each Accelerated School works on its own priorities. One school, for instance, with a problem with student attendance might have a team that works to address the attendance issue. Another school might have a team working on improving student behavior or mathematics achievement. What sets Accelerated Schools apart is that parents and community members are integral members of each improvement team.

The Accelerated Schools model seeks to transform schools and classrooms into powerful learning environments (PLEs) where learning is "authentic, interactive, learner-centered, inclusive, and continuous" (Finnan, Schnepel, and Anderson 2003, 392). In other words, teachers in Accelerated Schools are expected to provide the kinds of learning environments that are most often provided to gifted and high-achieving children and that most minority children and children living in poverty rarely experience. In a study of classrooms in schools where Accelerated Schools was being implemented, the researchers found a correlation between the degree of implementation of PLEs and higher student achievement. In other words, the more a classroom reflected the characteristics of a PLE, the higher was the achievement of students in that classroom.

Other studies have evaluated the overall effects of Accelerated Schools on achievement of at-risk students. A study by Howard Bloom, Sandra Ham, Laura Melton, and Julieanne O'Brien (2001) of third-graders' achievement in reading and mathematics in schools implementing Accelerated Schools followed the schools through their first five years of implementation. The researchers noted that during their first three years of implementation of Accelerated Schools, the focus of the reform efforts was on school governance and school culture rather than on classroom practice. Consequently, "there were no positive impacts in the first two years, a slight decline in the third year—as schools began to modify their curriculum and instruction—and a gradual increase in the fourth and fifth years. The average third-grade reading and math scores in the fifth year exceeded the predicted levels by a statistically significant amount" (Bloom, Ham, Melton, and O'Brien 2001, 7). The researchers concluded that Accelerated Schools was successful in improving the achievement of at-risk students.

Effective Schools

The Effective Schools movement has a long history of shaping school reform efforts. The mission of Effective Schools is *Learning for All*, and Ronald Edmonds summed up its philosophy, when he said,

> We can, whenever and wherever we choose, successfully teach all children whose schooling is of interest to us. We already know more than we need to do that. Whether or not we do it must finally depend on how we feel about the fact that we haven't so far. (Lezotte n.d., 2)

The Effective Schools movement is organized around seven correlates: (1) instructional leadership, (2) clear and focused mission, (3) safe and orderly environment, (4) climate of high expectations, (5) frequent monitoring of student progress, (6) positive home-school relations, and (7) opportunity to learn and student time on task. These correlates were derived from years of research on schools that were effective in helping students achieve high levels of learning; the correlates are descriptors of those schools. A complete explanation of the correlates of effective schools is found in Chapter 6.

Although there is not a specific process for implementing Effective Schools that can be applied at all schools, school districts and schools that implement these correlates engage in a cyclic and recursive process that involves gathering and analyzing data about the extent to which each of the correlates is in place in their school or school district, planning for improvement of each of them, engaging in professional development to support their improvement, gathering and analyzing data about their improvement, and revisiting and revising the improvement plans relative to the data.

The main criticism of Effective Schools is that no specific process has been developed or is promoted by the proponents of Effective Schools that will lead schools to have the characteristics, and they can't be applied. Rather, the characteristics can serve only as goals for schools. Critics argue that schools need a process to reach the goals; without a process, Effective Schools cannot be viewed as a model. The correlates of effective schools, however, are evident in many other education reforms, including the No Child Left Behind legislation.

Outcome-Based Education

Outcome-Based Education (OBE) combines the correlates of Effective Schools with the alignment of a high-quality curriculum, an effective and efficient instructional program that leads students to mastery of the outcomes, and a program of formative and summative assessments to document that mastery. Built on a foundation that included work by Benjamin Bloom, OBE draws on notions of mastery of content rather than coverage of content. What is distinctive about OBE is that it requires a school or school district to focus completely on learning outcomes of significance, that is, what is important for students to know and be able to do. William G. Spady, a key proponent of OBE, "urge[d] schools to generate 'exit outcomes' based on the challenges and opportunities that students will face after graduation, and then to 'design down' from the outcomes for all other aspects of educational delivery" (McNeir 1993, 2). The philosophy of OBE, like Effective Schools, is that all students can learn, but that they learn in different ways and need different amounts of time to learn well. OBE requires schools and teachers to vary the instruction students receive and the amount of time students have to achieve the outcomes, rather than allowing time to be a determiner of learning. In other words, students' opportunities to learn continue until they achieve mastery, and mastery of outcomes is documented whenever it happens. In many cases, OBE school districts extended the school day and the school year to allow for the additional time students needed to master outcomes and demonstrate that mastery.

In OBE, students typically document their learning, not through paper and pencil, one-right-answer tests, but through projects and performances that allow them to apply the learning in a meaningful, real-world context. Examples of such assessments might be as simple as young children who are learning about money counting out sums of money with real coins or giving change as they play store; for older children, it might mean researching a character from history and preparing journal entries or letters about a historical event from that character's perspective.

OBE was adopted and implemented by many schools and school districts in the United States and promoted by several states. Schools and school districts that implemented OBE reported that student achievement increased, but no large-scale evaluations of OBE have been conducted. Because OBE did not rely on standardized achievement tests but rather locally developed outcomes, it would have been difficult to make comparisons of student achievement. Interestingly, there are many similarities between OBE and standards-based reforms.

In spite of its purported success, OBE generated controversy, particularly among political and Christian conservatives. The critics of OBE, including Phyllis Schlafly, raised several concerns, among them that the "exit outcomes" of many OBE school districts included values that had the potential to conflict with conservative Christian morals and values. Other critics were concerned with the notion that "all children can learn," believing that it is the responsibility of schools to rank students, or in Spady's words, "to sort and select" students. Interestingly, while few schools in the United States would currently own up to implementing OBE, OBE is being implemented widely outside the United States, primarily in Africa, New Zealand, and Australia. A discussion of such an OBE implementation is included in Chapter 3.

Business Models Applied to School Reform

Several business models have been applied to comprehensive school reform. In general, the business models in education are based on the premise that student learning is the product of schools, with families, the general public, and business community considered the consumers of this product. These models evaluate schools in terms of their productivity, and they view competition as key to motivating schools to be successful. Some of the models include Total Quality Management, the Baldridge Model, and Management by Objective.

Total Quality Management

Total Quality Management (TQM), a model developed by W. Edwards Deming, author and business consultant, has as its foundation the development of shared organizational goals and aims. Combined with the principles of Effective Schools, it was applied to schools as Total Quality Schools. According to National School Services, an organization that has promoted and supported the model, Total Quality Schools is "a focused plan for continuous school improvement . . . that involves the whole school community in all aspects of improvement" (National School Services). The Total Quality Schools Process (TQSP) involves several phases that include learning the principles of TQSP; gathering and analyzing data about the current state of the school or school district, both to identify needs that should be addressed and to establish a baseline against which improvements can be measured; developing a strategic plan to address the needs identified; providing training and professional development to implement the plan; and evaluating the effects of the plan by comparing new data with baseline data. Key to the TQSP is Deming's principle of requiring statistical evidence of quality; the challenge in schools is to determine how to generate and analyze statistical evidence about the goals and aims of the school and school district.

The Baldrige Model

The Baldrige model is also based on Deming's Total Quality Management principles, but it extends the TQM model by adding specific criteria for implementation of "quality" in nearly every aspect of a school district. These criteria, the Malcolm Baldrige Criteria for Performance Excellence, provide benchmarks for schools as they seek to improve. According to the Web site of the Montgomery County (Maryland) Public Schools, a school district that has won awards for its improvement and its student achievement, school personnel credit the implementation of the Baldrige process for their results (Montgomery County Public Schools 2006). Using the "Plan Do Study Act" process (similar to the TQSP), schools plan for improvement. In Baldrige schools, teachers teach children the "Plan Do Study Act" process to help the students set goals for and assess their own learning. The Baldrige model provides a set of strategies and processes for improvement at the leadership, classroom, and student levels, as well as recommendations for parents and parent involvement. At the classroom level, for example, Baldrige begins by establishing a culture that is characterized by acceptance and trust, and teachers make children partners in the development of quality through personal goal setting. Teachers use a set of "teaching tools" that focus on quality, they lead their students in gathering and analyzing data about their own learning, and teachers themselves gather and analyze data to document student progress and to plan for their teaching (Montgomery County Public Schools 2006).

Critics of applying business models to education argue that the business metaphor is not appropriate for education because the purpose of schooling is very different from that of business. Many educators believe that schools exist to socialize students into American society and to create an educated citizenry who are prepared to participate actively in U.S. democracy, not to support U.S. competition in the global marketplace. With this purpose, students and student achievement are not products to be marketed; rather they are participants in education. Critics also decry the push for competition between and among publicly funded schools; instead, they believe that all public schools should be adequately funded and have the resources they need to provide a high-quality education for all children in the United States.

Standards-Based Education

Since the federal government began requiring states to adopt or develop standards and assessments that document students' progress toward meeting those standards in the 1990s, schools and school districts have focused their reform efforts on helping students meet the standards and demonstrate that on state assessments. Many schools have worked to align their curricula with state and national standards, develop local assessments that document student achievement of the standards, and refine teaching so that children experience success relative to the standards. They use data from student assessments to further refine the curriculum and the quality of teaching.

No Child Left Behind (NCLB) builds accountability for results into the teaching and learning process. NCLB requires not only that students participate in state assessments but also that they make progress each year toward proficiency in those assessments. Schools are expected to show what NCLB terms "adequate yearly progress" (AYP) toward the goal of all students demonstrating proficiency in reading and mathematics by the year 2014. Schools must not only show that most of their students are making progress in the aggregate; NCLB requires them to break down the achievement data by groups that include race, families' income level, English language proficiency, and special education. The great strength of NCLB is the expectation that it communicates that all students can and will learn to high standards, and that schools are accountable for finding strategies to ensure the learning of all students.

As schools seek to have their students meet the standards for AYP, many of them have turned to a number of strategies that have been termed "standards-based education." Interestingly, standards-based education includes strategies developed earlier as part of other comprehensive school reform models, like the Comer model and OBE. Evidence of other models can be found in the alignment and mapping of curriculum; designing instruction to lead to achievement of standards; raising expectations for all children to meet the standards; checking, assessing, and analyzing children's work relative to the standards; and developing and using benchmark assessments.

Unlike other standards-based reform initiatives, NCLB includes standards for teacher quality. According to the law, teachers are expected to be what the law terms "highly qualified." To be considered highly qualified, teachers must have a bachelor's degree, state certification, and proof that they "know each subject they teach" (U.S. Department of Education 2004). While the law requires that all teachers in all schools be highly qualified by the 2005–2006 school year, some flexibility has been added to the regulations in terms of the length of time experienced teachers had to demonstrate that they were highly qualified; some flexibility has also been added for rural and small school districts where the size of the district dictates that teachers, especially at the high school level, teach more than one subject. At the same time, NCLB requires schools to notify parents if their children have teachers who are not highly qualified. Research shows the importance of effective teaching to children's learning; setting and enforcing standards of teacher quality are critical for raising student achievement.

NCLB adds to standards-based education stringent accountability measures. The achievement of all students in third through eighth grade, and at one point in high school, must be evaluated each year through tests that have been determined by their states to measure progress toward state standards. The law includes penalties for schools where students, both in the aggregate (all together) and disaggregated (analyzed by race, gender, poverty, first language, disability), do not demonstrate AYP for three years in a row, up to and including closing the school or reconstituting it. Such schools are labeled "failing," and they are required to notify parents of that status. Parents of children in schools that are failing may transfer their children to schools that are not failing; children in a failing school are also entitled to individual tutoring, usually provided by independent contractors who are not school employees and often not certified teachers; and in some cases, they are eligible for vouchers to attend private schools.

In its report of a nationwide series of dialogues on standards and standards-based education, McREL (Mid-continent Research for Education and Learning) (Goodwin 2003) found that "the public appears to have an entirely different agenda for school reform than most educators and policymakers. As a result, even if schools succeed in boosting test scores and avoiding sanctions, they could nonetheless fail to increase public satisfaction with or support for public schools" (p. 7). McREL conducted focus groups with members of the general public about "where people stand on standards-based education," and among its findings are the following:

- Standards are meaningless without tests, but accountability should be based on more than just test scores;
- True accountability makes schools more responsive to parents and communities, not to outside officials;
- Parents and students are a crucial yet often missing part of most accountability systems; and
- The biggest problems with public schools have little to do with standards or academics. (p. 2)

In other words, participants in these focus groups agree that standards and accountability are important to school reform, but they disagree with the way NCLB uses standards and testing. They see NCLB as making local school districts and schools responsible to state and federal governments, but these participants believe instead that schools and school districts should be accountable and responsive to students, parents, and their local communities. When queried about the problems they see in public schools, participants' concerns were less about academics and much more about character, values, and safety in schools.

The U.S. Department of Education has publicized a few successes that it attributes to No Child Left Behind, but critics look at how the NCLB funds are distributed, the amount of money required to implement the provisions of the law compared to the amount of money allocated, and the impossible goal of all children demonstrating proficiency by 2014 as major flaws in the law. NCLB funding is supposed to provide services to the children most in need, but critics say that is not how the funds have been distributed.

> According to Mary Kusler, the assistant director of government relations for the American Association of School Administrators, . . . under the current formula, districts with high enrollments and relatively low poverty rates receive more money per Title I pupil than districts with small enrollments and high poverty rates. (Hoff 2007, 18)

Critics of NCLB often call the law an "unfunded mandate," arguing that the amount of money states and school districts must spend to meet the requirements of the law is far more than is being provided by the federal government. The National Education Association (NEA) and several states filed a lawsuit against the U.S. Department of Education in 2005 "simply asking the Bush administration to allow parents to spend hard-earned tax dollars on their children's classrooms—not bureaucracy, paperwork and testing companies" (NEA 2008). A January 8, 2008, ruling by the United States Court of Appeals for the Sixth Circuit agreed with the plaintiffs that states and school districts should not be expected to spend state or local money to implement the requirements of NCLB, but how that ruling will affect the implementation of the law is not yet clear. What is clear is that NCLB has not been fully funded; the full amount of funds allocated for NCLB has never been appropriated by Congress or even earmarked in the president's budget.

Other critics argue that the goal of all students to be proficient by 2014 is impractical, if not impossible, and that by 2014, nearly all schools in the United States, even those currently considered high performing, will be labeled "failing." In their study of the impact of adequate yearly progress on schools in the Great Lakes states, Edward Wiley, William Mathis, and David Garcia (2005) projected that as many as 95 percent of schools in Illinois, Indiana, Michigan, Minnesota, Ohio, and Wisconsin will have been labeled failing by 2013. Studies of California schools have come to the same conclusion (Cavanaugh and Hoff 2008). Some public policy analysts even believe that declaring so many schools failing is the intent of the underlying philosophy of the law. Saltman (2007) asserted that "Clearly, NCLB is designed to accomplish the implementation of privatization and deregulation in ways that open action could not" (p. 7).

The Call for New Kinds of Reforms in Education

Nel Noddings (2007) believes that "most reform movements, paradoxically, have been flawed by moral shortcomings," even when they are "started on high moral ground" (p. 79). Children's achievement in school depends only partly on what happens in school. According to Noddings, "Success in school is largely dependent on social and economic factors over which schools have no control" (p. 81). She argues that until the United States is willing to commit to improving the social and economic conditions in which so many children live, reform efforts will fail.

The Forum for Education and Democracy, convened by prominent educators, educational researchers, and education reformers, released a report, "Democracy at Risk: The Need for a New Federal Policy in Education" (Darling-Hammond, Wood, and Glenn 2008), that calls for an approach to education reform aimed at both equity and quality. The vision of the Forum for a new federal policy includes a real commitment to high-quality curriculum for all children; serious financial investment in teaching, both in training for new teachers and in professional development for those already teaching in schools; and equalizing resources so that all children attend schools that have quality teachers, the materials and textbooks they need, and school buildings that are safe and in good repair. Further, the report suggests four new priorities for education at the federal level: they are "paying off the educational debt," a debt that has accrued for poor and minority children because of the many years of inequity in education and in society in general that they have experienced; developing skilled educators who are professionals and are viewed as such; supporting educational research and real innovation; and engaging, involving, and educating local communities in playing out these strategies to reach the vision of a free, universal public education system that provides real opportunities for learning and advancement for *all* children.

The challenge of reforming education in the United States is not that there are no solutions—there are just no easy solutions. There are many reform efforts that have shown success in raising student achievement. Whether schools succeed in closing the achievement gap and helping all students learn well in school will depend on how the social and economic issues in our country are addressed; schools and teachers having the resources and latitude to make changes necessary to improve curriculum and teaching; and the commitment of the general public, parents, teachers, school administrators, and students to improvement.

References

A+ Schools Program. n.d. "Research and Results." Greensboro, NC. http://aplus-schools.uncg.edu/overviewofkeyfindings.pdf.

Ashby, N. 2007. "Arts Integration at Oklahoma School Provides Multiple Paths for Learning." *The Achiever* 6 (6): 1, 3–4.

Baumgartner, T., M. Lipowski, and C. Rush. 2003. "Increasing Reading Achievement of Primary and Middle School Students through Differentiated Instruction." PhD diss., Saint Xavier University, Chicago.

Bloom, H. S., S. Ham, L. Melton, and J. O'Brien. 2001. "Evaluating the Accelerated Schools Approach: A Look at Early Implementation and Impacts on Student Achievement in Eight Elementary Schools." New York: Manpower Demonstration Research Corporation. ERIC Document Reproduction Service No. ED 460791.

Braun, H., F. Jenkins, and W. Griggs. 2006. *A Closer Look at Charter Schools Using Hierarchical Linear Modeling*. Washington, DC: National Center for Educational Statistics.

Caine, R. N., and G. Caine. 1991. *Making Connections: Teaching and the Human Brain.* Alexandria, VA: Association for Supervision and Curriculum Development.

Carr, J. F., and D. E. Harris. 2001. *Succeeding with Standards: Linking Curriculum, Assessment, and Action Planning.* Alexandria, VA: Association for Supervision and Curriculum Development.

Cavanaugh, S., and D. J. Hoff. 2008. "Schools Found Likely to Miss NCLB Targets." *Education Week Online,* September 25. http://www.edweek.org/ew/articles/2008/09/25/06ayp.h28.html?tmp=1754231223.

Center for Education Reform. 2008. "Just the FAQs—Tuition Tax Credits and Tax Deductions." http://www.edreform.com/index.cfm?fuseAction=document&documentID=59.

Cook, T. D., H. D. Hunt, and R. F. Murphy. 2000. "Comer's School Development Program in Chicago: A Theory-Based Evaluation." *American Educational Research Journal* 37 (2): 535–597.

Darling-Hammond, L., G. Wood, and B. Glenn. 2008. "Democracy at Risk: The Need for a New Federal Policy in Education." Athens, OH: Forum for Education and Democracy.

FairTest. *K-12 Testing.* http://www.fairtest.org/k–12.

Finnan, C., K. C. Schnepel, and L. W. Anderson. 2003. "Powerful Learning Environments: The Critical Link Between School and Classroom Cultures." *Journal of Education for Students Placed at Risk* 8 (4): 391–418.

Fisher, D., and N. Frey. 2001. "Access to the Core Curriculum: Critical Ingredients for Students." *Remedial and Special Education* 22 (3): 148–157.

Flowers, A. 2007. "Single-Sex Public Schools OK: Education Department." Chicago: Heartland Institute. http://www.heartland.org/Article.cfm?artid=20434.

Foley, E. M., A. Klinge, and E. R. Reisner. 2007. *Evaluation of New Century High Schools: Profile of an Initiative to Create and Sustain Small Successful High Schools.* Washington, DC: Policy Studies Associates, Inc.

Gamoran, A. 1996. "Do Magnet Schools Boost Student Achievement?" *Educational Leadership* 54 (2): 42–46.

Gardner, H. 2003. "Multiple Intelligences after Twenty Years." Paper presented at the American Educational Research Association Annual Meeting, Chicago. http://www.pz.harvard.edu/PIs/HG_MI_after_20_years.pdf.

Gardner School Web site. 2008. http://www.gardnerschool.org/.

Goodwin, B. 2003. "Digging Deeper: Where Does the Public Stand on Standards-based Education?" Issues Brief. Aurora, CO: Mid-Continent Research for Education and Learning.

Hadderman, M. 2000. "Educational Vouchers." *ERIC Digest* 137. Eugene, OR: ERIC Clearinghouse on Educational Management.

Hall, T. 2002. "Differentiated Instruction." Wakefield, MA: National Center on Accessing the General Curriculum. http://www.cast.org/publications/ncac/ncac_diffinstruc.html.

Hausfather, S. 1995. "Creating a Theme Study Classroom around 'Big' Questions: Opportunities and Constraints." Paper presented at the annual meeting of the National Council for the Social Studies, Chicago, Illinois. (ERIC Document Reproduction Service No. ED 291711).

Haynes, N. M., C. L. Emmons, S. Gebreyesus, and M. Ben-Avie. 1996. "The School Development Program Evaluation Process." In *Rallying the Whole Village: The Comer Process for Reforming Education*, edited by E. T. Joyner, J. P. Comer, and M. Ben-Avie, 123–146. New York: Teachers College, Columbia University.

Hoff, D. J. 2007. "Usually Contentious Title Formula is No NCLB Barrier." *Education Week* 27 (14): 18–19.

Home School Legal Defense Association. 2001. *Home Schooling Achievement*. Purcellville, VA.

Hoxby, C. 2004a. *A Straightforward Comparison of Charter Schools and Regular Public Schools in the US*. Cambridge, MA: National Bureau of Economic Research.

Hoxby, C. 2004b. *Achievement in Charter Schools and Regular Public Schools in the US: Understanding the Differences*. Cambridge, MA: Taubman Center for State and Local Government, Kennedy School of Government.

Jensen, E. 1998. *Teaching with the Brain in Mind*. Alexandria, VA: Association for Supervision and Curriculum Development.

Jensen, E. 2008. "Principles of Brain-Based Learning." http://www.brainexpo.com/BBLearn/principles.asp.

Jensen, E. C. 2008. "A Fresh Look at Brain-Based Education." *Phi Delta Kappan* 89 (6): 409–417.

Kunkel, C. 2007. "The Power of Key: Celebrating 20 Years of Innovation at the Key Learning Community." *Phi Delta Kappan* 89 (3): 204–209.

Lake, K. 2001. "Integrated Curriculum." *School Improvement Research Series (SIRS): Research You Can Use*. Portland, OR: Northwest Regional Educational Laboratory. http://www.nwrel.org/scpd/sirs/8/c016.html.

Lezotte, L. W. n.d. "Revolutionary and Evolutionary: The Effective Schools Movement." http://www.effectiveschools.com/images/stories/RevEv.pdf.

Lezotte, L. W. 1991. *Correlates of Effective Schools: The First and Second Generation*. Okemos, MI: Effective Schools Products, Ltd.

Mace-Matluck, B. 1987. *The Effective Schools Movement: Its History and Context*. Austin, TX: Southwest Educational Development Lab (ERIC Document Reproduction Service No. ED304781).

Mael, F., A. Alonso, D. Gibson, K. Rogers, and M. Smith. 2005. "Single-Sex Versus Coeducational Schooling: A Systematic Review." Washington, DC: U.S. Department of Education, Office of Planning, Evaluation and Policy Development, Policy and Program Studies Service. http://www.ed.gov/rschstat/eval/other/single-sex/single-sex.pdf.

McAndrews, T., and W. Anderson. 2002. "Schools Within Schools." *ERIC Digest* 154. Eugene, OR: ERIC Clearinghouse on Educational Management (ERIC Document Reproduction Service No. ED461915).

McMurrer, J. 2008. "Instructional Time in Elementary Schools: A Closer Look at Changes for Specific Subjects." *From the Capital to the Classroom: Year 5 of the No Child Left Behind Act*. Washington, DC: Center on Education Policy.

McNeir, G. 1993. "Outcome-Based Education." *ERIC Digest* 85. http://eric.uoregon.edu/publications/digests/digest085.html.

Montgomery County Public Schools. 2006. "Baldrige Education Criteria for Performance Excellence." http://www.montgomeryschoolsmd.org/info/baldrige.

National Center for Education Statistics. 2003. "Executive Summary, America's Charter Schools." *The Nation's Report Card*. Washington, DC: Institute for Educational Sciences, U.S. Department of Education. http://nces.ed.gov/nationsreportcard/studies/charter/2005456.asp.

National School Services. n.d. "The Total Quality School Process." http://www.n-s-s.com/tqsp.htm.

NEA. 2008. "Stand Up for Children: *Pontiac v. Spellings*." *Issues in Education*. http://www.nea.org:80/home/10675.htm.

Nelson, C. A. 2001. *The Arts and Education Reform: Lessons from a Four-Year Pilot of the A+ Schools Program*. Greensboro, NC: A+ Schools Program. http://aplus-schools.uncg.edu/overviewofkeyfindings.pdf.

NIFDI. n.d. "What is Direct Instruction?" Eugene, OR. www.nifdi.org.

Noddings, N. 2007. *When School Reform Goes Wrong*. New York: Teachers College Press.

O'Shea, M. R. 2005. *From Standards to Success*. Alexandria, VA: Association for Supervision and Curriculum Development.

Payne, C. 1991. "The Comer Intervention Model and School Reform in Chicago: Implications of Two Models of Change." *Urban Education* 26 (8): 8–24.

Penn, M. J. 2007. *Microtrends: The Small Forces Behind Tomorrow's Big Changes*. New York: Twelve.

Ramirez-Smith, C. 1995. "Stopping the Cycle of Failure: The Comer Model." *Educational Leadership* 52 (5): 14–19.

Rossell, C. 2005. "Whatever Happened to Magnet Schools." *Education Next* 4 (3). http://www.hoover.org/publications/ednext/3220691. html.

Roy, J., and L. Mishel. 2005. *Advantage None: Reexamining Hoxby's Findings of Charter School Benefits*. Washington, DC: Economic Policy Institute.

Ryder, R. J., J. L. Sekulski, and A. Silberg. 2003. *Results of Direct Instruction Reading Program Evaluation Longitudinal Results: First Through Third Grade 2000–2003*. Milwaukee: University of Wisconsin.

Sadker, D., and K. Zittleman. 2004. "Single Sex Schools: A Good Idea Gone Wrong?" *Christian Science Monitor*, April 8. http://www.sadker. org/PDF/SingleSexSchools.pdf.

Saltman, K. J. 2007. *Capitalizing on Disaster: Taking and Breaking Public Schools*. Boulder, CO: Paradigm.

Sax, L. 2005. "The Promise and Peril of Single-Sex *Public* Education: Mr. Chips Meets Snoop Dogg." *Education Week*, March 2. http://www. singlesexschools.org/edweek.html.

Senge, P. M. 1990. *The Fifth Discipline: The Art & Practice of the Learning Organization*. New York: Doubleday.

Siegle, D. 2006. "The Last Word: An Interview with Gene Chasin, CEO of Accelerated Schools Plus." *Journal of Advanced Academics* 18 (1): 146–154.

Small Schools Project Web site. http://www.smallschoolsproject.org.

Smith, M. K. 2002. "Howard Gardner and Multiple Intelligences." *The Encyclopedia of Informal Education*. http://www.infed.org/ thinkers/gardner.htm.

Sprenger, M. 1999. *Learning & Memory: The Brain in Action*. Alexandria, VA: Association for Supervision and Curriculum Development.

Stahl, S. A. 1999. "Different Strokes for Different Folks? A Critique of Learning Styles." *American Educator* (Fall). http://www.aft.org/pubs-reports/american_educator/fall99/DiffStrokes.pdf.

Sternberg, R. J. 2008. "The Answer Depends on the Question: A Reply to Eric Jensen." *Phi Delta Kappan* 89 (6): 418–420.

"Struggle Against Vouchers Continues in Milwaukee and Across Nation." 2002. *Rethinking Schools Online*. http://www.rethinkingschools. org/special_reports/voucher_report/index.shtml.

Success for All Foundation. 2008. "Programs Excluded by Reading First Top List of Research-Based Programs." Baltimore, MD. http://www.successforall.net/press/press_csrq.htm.

Thernstrom, A., and S. Thernstrom. 2003. *No Excuses: Closing the Racial Gap in Learning.* New York: Simon & Schuster.

Tienken, C., and M. Wilson. 2001. "Using State Standards and Tests to Improve Instruction." *Practical Assessment, Research & Evaluation* 7 (13). http://PAREonline.net.getvn.asp?v=7&n=13.

Tomlinson, C. A. 2000. "Differentiation of Instruction in the Elementary Grades." *ERIC Digest.* Champaign, IL: ERIC Clearinghouse on Elementary and Early Childhood Education (ERIC Document Reproduction Service No. ED 443572).

Tomlinson, C. A., and A. Germundson. 2007. "Teaching as Jazz." *Educational Leadership* 64 (8): 27–31.

U.S. Charter Schools. n.d. "History." http://www.uscharterschools.org/pub/uscs_docs/o/history.htm.

U.S. Charter Schools. n.d. "Overview." http://www.uscharterschools.org/pub/uscs_docs/o/index.htm.

U.S. Department of Education. 2004. "Fact Sheet: New *No Child Left Behind* Flexibility: Highly Qualified Teachers." http://www.ed.gov/nclb/methods/teachers/hqtflexibility.html.

U.S. Department of Education. 2002. "Part C: Magnet School Assistance." http://www.ed.gov/policy/elsec/leg/esea02/pg65.html.

Wasley, P. 2002. "Small Classes, Small Schools: The Time is Now." *Educational Leadership* 59 (5): 6–10.

Watkins, D., and W. A. Kritsonis. 2008. "Aristotle, Philosophy, and the *Ways of Knowing through the Realms of Meaning:* A National Study on Integrating a Postmodernist Approach to Education and Student Academic Achievement." *National Forum of Applied Educational Research Journal* 21 (8) (ERIC Document Reproduction Service No. ED 499545).

"What is a Magnet School?" n.d. *Public School Review.* http://www.publicschoolreview.com/articles/2.

Wiley, E. W., W. J. Mathis, and D. R. Garcia. 2005. "Executive Summary." *The Impact of the Adequate Yearly Progress Requirement of the Federal 'No Child Left Behind' Act on Schools in the Great Lakes Region.* Tempe, AZ: Education Policy Studies Laboratory. http://epsl.asu.edu/epru/documents/EPSL-0509-109-EPRU-exec.pdf.

Willis, J. 2008. "Building a Bridge from Neuroscience to the Classroom." *Phi Delta Kappan* 89 (6): 424–427.

Yale School Development Program Staff. 2004. "Essential Understandings of the Yale School Development Program." In *Transforming School Leadership and Management to Support Student Learning and Development*, edited by E. T. Joyner, J. P. Comer, and M. Ben-Avie, 15–23. Thousand Oaks, CA: Corwin.

Yu, C., and W. L. Taylor. 1997. *Difficult Choices: Do Magnet Schools Serve Children in Need?* Washington, DC: Citizens' Commission on Civil Rights.

3

Education Reform — A Global Enterprise

Since the 1950s, advances in technology have brought about monumental changes throughout the world. Live satellite television and real-time video have brought events and everyday life in other parts of the world into our homes when they are happening. The time it takes to travel long distances has decreased, resulting in much more international travel, and increases in international travel have reduced the cost of such travel, which in turn allows for more. Computer technology has greatly increased the speed and ease of global communication, creating opportunities for increased cross-cultural interaction and exchange of culture and making the world smaller and much more interconnected. According to John Engler and James Hunt (2004), "Globalization is a fact, not an ideology" (p. 199).

Economies also have become more interconnected; indeed, in the 21st century, national economies have been superseded by a global economy in which events in one region of the world affect the economic situation throughout the world. Multinational businesses and industries compete globally for skilled workers and for profits. Education is viewed by many as a factor in this economic competition, and educational competition itself has taken on the stature of an Olympic event, making education reform an international enterprise.

The United States began to compare the quality of its education system with that of other countries after the launch of Sputnik I in 1957, based on the judgment that the U.S.S.R. was ahead in the "space race" because of superior education in mathematics and science. Shortly after that, in 1959, the International Association for the Evaluation of Educational Achievement (IEA), an international group of scholars that included Benjamin Bloom, began the first study that compared the learning of students internationally. Data for this Pilot Twelve-Country Study were gathered between 1959 and 1962 from 13-year-old students in the areas of reading comprehension, mathematics, science, geography, and nonverbal ability. Interestingly, the study found that the differences in academic achievement at that time were larger among students within each country studied than between the countries. More importantly for the researchers who conducted the study, the study demonstrated that is was possible to evaluate educational outcomes across cultures and languages, setting the stage for regular international evaluations that compare student learning.

The IEA has gone on to conduct periodic studies that compare education internationally. The two latest studies are the Trends in International Mathematics and Science Study (TIMSS) in 2003, and the Progress in International Reading Literacy Study (PIRLS) in 2006. In the TIMMS study of fourth grade students, the average score was 495; the average score of U.S. fourth graders was 518, significantly above the international average. The U.S. students scored better than the students from 13 of the other 24 countries in the study; students from 11 countries scored better than U.S. fourth graders. Compared to students in the other Organization for Economic Co-operation and Development (OECD) member countries in the study, U.S. fourth graders performed better than fourth graders in Australia, Italy, New Zealand, Norway, and Scotland, and were outperformed by fourth graders from Belgium-Flemish, England, Hungary, Japan, and the Netherlands (Gonzales et al., 2004). Table 1 in Chapter 6 shows the rankings of the 24 countries in the study. The 2003 TIMMS also studied eighth grade mathematics achievement. U.S. eighth graders scored 504, again significantly higher than the average score of 466, performing better than their peers in 25 of the 44 countries participating in the study (Gonzales et al., 2004). See Table 2 in Chapter 6 for the average scores of eighth graders by country.

The 2006 PIRLS study of fourth grade reading achievement compares the reading comprehension of children in the United States with their peers in 44 other countries or jurisdictions around the world. The study found that the average score for U.S. fourth graders was 540, higher than students from 22 other countries or jurisdictions, and lower than students from 10 other countries or jurisdictions. The report of the study presents the data by background characteristics, finding that girls scored higher than boys in the United States and all other countries, except for two where there was no difference in the average scores of girls and boys.

In considering racial and ethnic backgrounds of U.S. fourth graders, the study found that the scores for white, non-Hispanic students; Asian, non-Hispanic students; and non-Hispanic students classified as "other" were significantly higher than scores for black, non-Hispanic; Hispanic; and American Indian/Alaskan Native, non-Hispanic students. In other words, the scores represented a significant gap in reading comprehension achievement between white and Asian students on the one hand and Black, Hispanic, and American Indian/Alaskan Native students on the other (Baer et al., 2007).

The report of the 2006 PIRLS study also compares the reading comprehension of U.S. fourth graders in 2006 with that of U.S. fourth graders in 2001, finding no measurable difference between the 2001 and 2006 scores (Baer et al., 2007). In other words, in spite of all the effort to improve reading through No Child Left Behind, no such improvement was shown by the PIRLS.

In 2006, the latest Program in International Student Assessment, or PISA, was conducted by the OECD. That study compared achievement of 15-year-old students in reading, mathematics, and science. The average score of students in the United States ranked 21st of the 30 countries included in the assessment. In mathematics, U.S. students ranked 25th. (Scores for U.S. students in reading were not included in the report because of a problem with testing.) Table 5 in Chapter 6 shows the rankings of the scores for all of the countries that participated in the assessment.

The OECD also gathers data about a number of societal and economic factors related to educational achievement and compares them across the countries that participated in PISA. Interestingly, the data show that diversity is increasing in nearly all of the participant countries. When comparing rates of poverty among the schoolchildren of countries participating in the study, the study found that 22 percent of the children enrolled in schools in the United States live in families whose income is below the poverty line, a rate higher than any other OECD country except Mexico. This is an especially important statistic to consider because the United States ranks 45th out of 55 countries in the PISA measure of equity. This means that students from different socioeconomic or racial backgrounds have large disparities in average scores. According to Linda Darling-Hammond and Wood George (2008), in the PISA reading, mathematics, and science assessments, "The distance between the average score for Asian and white students, on the one hand, and Hispanic and Latino students, on the other, is equal to the distance between the United States average and that of the highest scoring nations" (p. 8).

There is little agreement about what these comparisons of student achievement mean, but Gerald Bracey (2007) points out that there are students in the United States whose performance on these tests *is* the highest in the world. His reanalysis of the PIRLS and TIMSS data at the fourth grade level shows that students who attend the 13 percent of U.S. schools with fewer than 10 percent of their students considered living in poverty have the highest average score on the PIRLS—589. Schools with between 10 and 25 percent of their populations living in poverty also scored higher than any other country, with an average score of 567; 17 percent of U.S. fourth graders attend schools with such levels of poverty. Bracey's reanalysis shows similar results in fourth grade science on the TIMSS, with the same groups of students earning the highest scores. On the TIMSS mathematics test, these groups scored just below fourth graders from Singapore and Hong Kong. On the other hand, U.S. schools where 75 percent or more of the students live in poverty scored significantly below the international average on all three measures; 20 percent of U.S. fourth grade students attend schools where 75 percent or more of their student populations live in poverty. In other words, socioeconomic status is not evenly distributed across schools in the United States, and how well U.S. students perform on the tests depends to a large extent on the percentage of children living in poverty in their schools.

The United Nations Educational, Scientific and Cultural Organization (UNESCO) gathers and compares statistics about education around the world and reports those statistics in its annual *Global Education Digest*. The digest compares education funding as a percentage of GDP, the value of all goods and services produced by a country in a given year. According to the International Monetary Fund database, the United States had the highest GDP of any country in the world in 2007—$13,843,825 million—which also typically is used as a measure of standard of living. The per capita GDP for the United States in 2007 was $45,845.477 (International Monetary Fund 2008). The Global Education Digest (UNESCO 2007) reports that the United States spent public funds totaling 5.6 percent of the GDP on public education in 2005.

Since education has been so closely linked to economic growth and competition in the global marketplace, almost every country in the world is involved in some way in the reform of education. While every country has conditions that make its education system unique, there is also much that can be learned from the strategies that are being used around the world to reform education systems and to increase student achievement. The next section of this chapter describes education reform and how it is progressing in South Africa, Finland, China, France, and Chile. These countries were selected because they represent developed and developing countries, different regions of the world, and widely varying cultures. They have addressed or are grappling with some of the same issues that schools and school districts in the United States face as they seek to reform education.

Education Reform in South Africa

The challenges facing South Africa in developing a system of education that provides real opportunities for all children to learn are great. The obstacles to effective schools there are monumental, and in the short time since the beginning of the dismantling of legal racial segregation there, great strides have been made in policy, if not in practice. It is interesting to consider how the process of education reform is unfolding there.

In 1948, South Africa officially enacted apartheid, institutionalizing the racial segregation that had characterized every aspect of South African society for 350 years. Apartheid officially assigned South Africans to one of four racial groups—Black (Africans), Colored (mixed race), White, and Indian/Asian. Apartheid relegated Black South Africans, the majority of the population, to tribally based "homelands," areas with few resources and few opportunities to earn a living, or rural townships that grew up around cities to house Black workers who served as labor for White enterprises. (Black South Africans were not allowed to live in the cities.) Black South Africans were only allowed to vote in their tribal homelands, even if that was not where they resided.

Apartheid also affected education. During apartheid, public education programs and schools in South Africa were administered through a network of 15 education departments, 14 of them divided along regional and racial lines, with the 15th a national department whose responsibility was to oversee the other

14 departments. Education during apartheid in South Africa could only be characterized by the most extreme racial segregation, with students allowed to attend public schools as well as institutions of higher education that served only their own race. There was gross inequity in educational resources, including funding, school facilities, teacher quality, and class size. Schools for White children had far more resources and much higher levels of funding—as much as three and a half times higher—than schools for Black children.

Schools in South Africa followed a national curriculum, outlined in the national exam system required of all students; needless to say, the national curriculum reflected the White majority's interests (Kruse 1996). The language of education was primarily Afrikaans, and rarely did Black children experience education in their native languages. The White European-centered curriculum ensured that Black children learned "about how inferior they [were] because of studying battles where whites beat blacks" (Murphy 1992, 269). According to Edward Fiske and Helen Ladd (2005), public policy researchers, "The rationale for such inequity was a matter of public record. Blacks were given poor education so as to keep them out of the modern sector of the economy and to ensure a steady supply of cheap labor, particularly for the agricultural, mining and domestic service sectors" (p. 2). In other words, the gross inequities in South African public education were intentional and a matter of public policy.

To compound the intentional undereducation of Black children, in the 1990s, Black schools were often sites of civil unrest. Many closed as students vandalized them. And many students went on strike, and eventually quit school, in support of the African National Congress (ANC), the party of Nelson Mandela, who went on to be the first president of the Government of National Unity in 1994.

With the election of the Government of National Unity in 1994, apartheid officially ended, and the new government began with a new understanding that declared all South Africans to be equal under the law and entitled to the same rights. One of those rights under the South African constitution is education. The Reconstruction and Development Programme (RDP) developed by the ANC to shape the transition from the former apartheid government to a democracy included provisions for education under the heading of "Developing Our Human Resources." This section of the RDP formed the basis for education reform in South Africa.

As part of undoing the legacy of apartheid, South Africa was challenged by the new government to create a system of education that both integrated the schools and provided a larger measure of equity. The RDP links improvement in education with economic development of the country.

The new government published a "White Paper on Education and Training" in 1995 "which describes the first steps in policy formation by the Ministry of Education in the Government of National Unity" (Department of Education). The white paper described the reorganization of education in South Africa into a single national system with a national Ministry of Education responsible for setting policy and developing guidelines and structures that lead to the reform envisioned by the ANC and in the RDP, and nine new provincial education departments, all responsible for implementing education policy. Local school governing boards were to be elected and given the responsibility for running the local schools. In theory, the schools in each province would be racially integrated and provided with the resources to implement the learner-centered, culturally responsive, critical thinking curriculum envisioned in the white paper.

In 1995, the Ministry of Education adopted a National Qualifications Framework, a system of testing and certification of student qualifications that is organized around three "bands" of education—General Education and Training, Further Education and Training, and Higher Education and Training—that extend from grade 0 through doctoral education. General Education and Training begins at grade 0, which is not mandatory, and goes through grade 9. The South African Schools Act of 1996 made education mandatory from grade 1 or the age of seven through grade 9 or the age of 15; successful completion of this band results in a general education certificate.

The South Africa Ministry of Education adopted outcome-based education as a strategy for reforming its schools and improving student learning to support the National Qualifications Framework. Outcome-based education was adopted in part because it represents equity and social change. (See Chapter 2 for a description of outcome-based education.) Outcome-based education had been implemented with some success (and much controversy) in some schools in other countries, including the United States, Canada, Australia, and New Zealand. William Spady, the self-proclaimed "father of outcome-based education," traveled around South Africa in 1997, explaining outcome-based education to policy makers, teachers, school administrators, and the general public.

In South Africa, outcome-based education was, on the one hand, hailed as an opportunity for real change, and on the other, a tremendous challenge because it requires sophisticated instructional knowledge that many teachers did not have, as well as instructional materials that many schools did not have available. Another issue that has been raised is that the adoption process was antithetical to the democratic process that the new government represented. Much of the value of outcome-based education lies in the participatory process of designing and determining outcomes that are significant and meaningful, as well as determining how learners would demonstrate that they had achieved the outcomes. However, most of that process was sidestepped in South Africa. When committees were convened, for example, to work on the design of outcomes and performance indicators, a specialist group from the Department of Education had already completed the work, and the committees were only invited to respond rather than to be actively involved in the design process.

Crain Soudien (1997), University of Cape Town professor and researcher, identified a further criticism of the process of the adoption of outcome-based education. He argued that

> Education was central to the discursive process of racial and cultural segregation in the "old" South Africa. What is called for in curriculum making in the new nation is a process that is more sensitive to the multiplicity of differences that have animated South Africa's 300-year long history and an interrogation of those differences. (p. 458)

In other words, when the Ministry of Education adopted outcome-based education, the implicit assumption was that one curriculum would be appropriate for all children in South Africa, regardless of their personal and cultural histories, at the same time that the new government was promoting a stance of recognizing and valuing diversity.

The Ministry of Education introduced a national curriculum framework in 1997 called Curriculum 2005 that explicitly described outcome-based education as the way the new curriculum would be implemented. Curriculum 2005 was begun in grade 1 in 1998, and in grade 7 in 2000. And in 2000, the Minister of Education appointed a committee to review and revise Curriculum 2005. Curriculum

2005 was revised to "streamline" the document and add specificity. The revised Curriculum 2005 provides outcomes and assessment standards by grade level, as well as examples of assessments and ways to organize learner data for teachers. What seems to be missing from the Curriculum 2005 document is a strong expectation for the professional development necessary for teachers to be able to organize their teaching to meet the learner outcomes and to design assessments that document the attainment of the outcomes.

William Spady himself criticized the South African implementation of outcome-based education. In a 2007 "letter" to the country published in the *South African Journal for Science and Technology*, Spady argued that there had been little understanding of or agreement with the basic notions of outcome-based education in South Africa. He asserted that little had happened to address the misunderstanding of outcome-based education between the time it was adopted in 1997 and 2007, and he called for South Africa to stop referring to outcome-based education.

South Africa faces a number of issues external to the schools that serve as barriers to ensuring high-quality education. Besides the social issues related to the ending of apartheid and official racial segregation, and to the beginning of a new, more inclusive government, there continue to be high levels of violence in schools, particularly sexual violence against girls, and high numbers of children who either are infected with HIV/AIDS or are affected by HIV/AIDS in their families.

Human Rights Watch (2001) investigated alleged cases of rape, sexual abuse, and sexual harassment in South African schools in 2000, as well as the government's response to gender violence in schools. The Human Rights Watch researchers found a high prevalence of sexual violence against girls in schools, both by other students and by teachers, and few efforts to address this sexual violence or to punish the perpetrators. Indeed, girls who had been victims of such violence were often ridiculed at their schools, and administrators did very little to support them when they returned to school after reporting sexual violence. Human Rights Watch found that these girls' experiences of sexual violence affected their school performance, up to and including leaving school, because of feeling unsafe there. The researchers found that there was no national and little provincial or school policy that was aimed at addressing sexual violence, nor was there any systematic monitoring of sexual violence in schools.

South Africa also has the highest incidence of HIV and AIDS of any country in the world (Human Rights Watch 2001). Six million of its 44 million people are infected with HIV, and according to a 2005 article in the *Los Angeles Times*, 40 percent of childhood deaths are the result of HIV and AIDS. At the Soweto primary school described in the article, one of every 10 children was orphaned due to their parents' deaths from HIV/AIDS. Many of those orphans were also abandoned by their relatives to live on the street. Schools are left to deal with the affects of HIV and AIDs that include orphaned children living in extreme poverty, children who do not attend school because of the affects of HIV and AIDS, children who are gravely ill attending school, teachers who are infected with HIV and AIDS, and even having to take the responsibility for funerals of children or parents who die of HIV and AIDS.

Even though equity is one of the goals of the national education system in South Africa, great disparity continues to characterize the schools. The majority of children attend schools that serve predominantly or exclusively one race, mainly because of traditional residential segregation. Because most of the schools levy fees, there is still great financial inequity. The poorest children, those whose families cannot afford to pay fees, attend schools that are underfunded, while the most affluent children attend schools where high fees support smaller class sizes, better teachers, and more resources for learning.

In 2006, the South African government instituted some "no-fee" schools, schools that were exempted by the Minister of Education from charging fees. In 2006, according to the South African Department of Education, there were 7,800 "no-fee" schools that served about 2.5 million children; in 2007, the number of children eligible for "no-fee" schools was increased to 5 million, and schools in more affluent areas were to be reimbursed for children whose families could not afford to pay the schools' fees (Gabade 2006).

In 2007, Statistics South Africa estimated the population of the country to be 47.9 million. People in South Africa are traditionally divided into four racial groups—White, African, Colored (mixed race), and Indian/Asian. The majority of the population—79.6 percent—is African (Black); 9.1 percent of the population is White; 8.9 percent is Colored; and 2.5 percent is Indian/Asian. Currently, there are 11 official languages in South Africa—Afrikaans, English, IsiNdebele, IsiXhosa, IsiZulu, Sepedi,

Sesotho, Setswana, SiSwati, Tshivenda, and Xitsonga (South Africa's Population 2008). Statistics from the International Monetary Fund list the 2007 GDP of South Africa at $282.630 million, and the per capita GDP at $5,906.491. In 2005, South Africa's total spending of public funds on education was 5.3 percent of its GDP (UNESCO 2007).

While South Africa has been working since the end of apartheid to improve the quality of its schools and the learning of its students, international comparisons show that South African students rank at the bottom of the countries included in both TIMSS and PIRLS. South African eighth grade students' mathematics performance ranked 38th—last—of the 38 countries in the 1999 TIMSS study, with an average score of 275; in 2003, they ranked 45th of the 45 countries in the study, with an average score of 264, significantly below 1999. In the 2006 PIRLS, South African fourth grade students ranked last of the 45 countries included in the study; South Africa had not participated in the previous PIRLS study.

Education Reform in Finland

In all international comparisons of student achievement in reading, mathematics, and science, student scores from Finland rank at the top. Ninety-nine percent of Finns are literate, and the school dropout rate in Finland is lower than 5 percent (Finkelstein 1995; Sahlberg 2006). Education is, according to many sources, a priority for the country, and Finland has by many accounts the finest school system in the world.

Finland's history is one of control from outside—alternatively by Sweden and Russia—and for Finland, being totally independent is a relatively recent development. But according to Andrew Hargreaves, Gábor Halász, and Beatriz Pont (2007), "Finns are driven by a common and articulately expressed social vision that connects a creative and prosperous future . . . to the people's sense of themselves as having a creative history and social identity" (p. 12). The country has one of the strongest economies in the world, with a GDP in 2007 of $245,013 million and an estimated per capita income of $46,601.865. Finland's public expenditures on education in 2005 totaled 6 percent of its GDP. The strength of the Finnish economy is notable particularly because it represents a recovery from near financial collapse in the 1990s. But Finland is not just about technology and making money; its social identity is also grounded in the arts and lifelong learning.

The Finnish education system today is the result of the tradition of free compulsory public education for all that was written into Finland's 1919 constitution. Children in Finland begin that compulsory primary education at age seven (later than any other developed country), although most recently, nearly 95 percent of all six-year-olds attend a noncompulsory preschool year (Sahlberg 2006). Since the early 1980s, education in Finland has been required for all children through age 17 or the completion of comprehensive school.

Primary schools in Finland extend through grade six, and lower secondary school includes grades seven through nine, with an optional 10th year available to students who wish to improve their academic preparation for upper secondary school. At the end of lower secondary school, children have the option of attending upper secondary school in a general education program, generally about three years, or a three-year basic vocational education that includes both general education and vocational training. According to Sahlberg (2006), more than 95 percent of the students completing compulsory education continue their educations beyond the ninth grade, continuing on to upper secondary school or the optional 10th year. The education options beyond compulsory education are designed to allow students to move from one to the other, should they desire to do so. Interestingly, even though upper secondary education is not compulsory, nearly all Finnish children complete one of the programs.

The upper secondary program is nongraded; that is, students do not attend classes organized by age-cohort. Rather, there is a great deal of choice for students when it comes to determining the content and the sequencing of their own educational programs. Completion of 75 courses in 18 subjects is needed to earn an upper secondary school diploma; only six of those courses are required subjects. Sahlberg (2006) noted that 90 percent of students who begin vocational education and 98 percent of students who begin upper general education stay in school to complete their programs. At the end of the upper secondary school, nearly all general education students take a National Matriculation Examination; it is a high-stakes examination in that the results are used to determine entrance into post-secondary education. The test is open to students from the vocational program as well, but according to Sahlberg, few of them actually take the test. Students who complete either the general education program or the vocational education program are eligible to go on to university or other post-secondary education that includes polytechnical schools.

Finland has national goals and standards for education, but it is left to local municipalities and individual schools and teachers to develop curriculum that helps students meet the goals and standards. According to Lea Houtsonen (2005), the curriculum is "based on a conception of learning which states that learning is a result of a pupil's active and focused actions aimed to process and interpret received information in interaction with other pupils, teachers and the environment" (p. 190). In other words, the Finnish instructional process is viewed as an active one, and the teacher's role in that process is as a facilitator and mentor, guiding students through experiences and interactions that shape learning. No standardized tests are administered to students during the compulsory education years in Finland; assessment and documentation of student learning is the responsibility of teachers. Student achievement is not viewed as competitive, and schools are not ranked or rated publicly in any way based on student achievement.

Finnish students spend much less time in school than their counterparts in other countries. According to Lawrence Baines (2007), the average number of hours students in developed countries spend in public school in a school year is 701. Finnish students, on the other hand, spend about 600 hours a school year in school. Students in the United States spend almost twice as much time in school—1,100 hours—as students in Finland.

Visitors to schools in Finland find teachers committed to the learning of their students and students engaged in learning—learning that is creative, requires high levels of thinking, and is relaxed and collaborative; teachers and students are on a first-name basis. The curriculum in Finnish schools includes "native language and literature, other languages, environmental study, civics, religion or ethics, history, social studies, mathematics, physics, chemistry, biology, geography, physical education, music, art, handicrafts, and home economics" (Korpela 2008). All students have religious instruction in their family's religion as part of their school curriculum; however, students who are not part of a religious group are exempted from this instruction. They study ethics instead. Many students participate in project-based learning that involves problems and issues in the real world outside their classrooms. But many others in Finland experience what might be considered conservative teaching techniques and strategies.

The Finnish commitment to a free public education that provides equal opportunities for all children extends to schools providing all of the necessary materials that children need to learn. Classes, especially at the primary school level, are typically small; many classrooms have fewer than 20 students, and primary schools average less than 300 students. This enables teachers and other school personnel to know each student personally and to have the time to intervene, should any learning difficulty arise.

All children in public schools are provided with free hot meals, school-based health care, and transportation to school if they live too far away to walk to school. Children with special learning needs are provided the support that they need in speech, reading, and mathematics. Interestingly, according to Sahlberg (2006), 40 percent of the students with special needs have such learning problems identified and addressed in primary school; by the time they reach lower secondary school, that percentage drops to 13 percent. In other words, early interventions are successful in helping students overcome those problems and go on without learning support.

Finland is a bilingual country; both Finnish and Swedish are its official languages, and instruction is provided in both of them. Students begin the study of a foreign language in their third year in school; instruction in the second official language (either Finnish or Swedish) begins in the seventh year of school. Instruction in Finnish as a second language is provided to immigrant students in Finland. These students participate in instruction in their own first language as well, because the Finns believe that proficiency in a child's native language helps them to learn Finnish and Swedish (Korpela 2008).

Teachers are highly respected in Finland, and they have high levels of autonomy and freedom in developing lessons and in teaching students. Korpela (2008) stated that "the Finnish system is based on a culture of trust, not on control, and teachers are active in developing their own work. With their own work, they set an example of lifelong learning" (p. 3). Teachers select their own books and determine the lessons that will meet the needs of each student. They also work collaboratively, designing curriculum and planning instruction (Gamerman 2008).

The quality of the teaching force in Finland is no accident. "Public education is seen as vital to the country's growth and security, and the shared high regard for educators who are seen as central to this generational mission, draws highly qualified candidates into the teaching profession" (Hargreaves, Halász, and Pont 2007, 14). A master's degree is required to enter the teaching profession, and teacher preparation programs are highly selective. According to W. Norton Grubb (2007), only about 10 percent of applicants are selected for teacher education. The curriculum of the teacher preparation program is standardized across the universities that provide it; in the four to five years it takes students to complete the program, they spend about half of each year in internships working with mentor teachers in classrooms. Pre-service teachers also learn how to develop curriculum so that they can participate actively in the curriculum process when they are working in schools (Houtsonen 2005). Finland invests in teacher candidates monetarily as well as in terms of high-quality preparation. University enrollment is free in Finland for students who qualify; teacher candidates are also paid while they are students.

The system of public education in Finland is decentralized, and decisions about individual schools are made locally. Principals and teachers share governance of schools, and they view one another as colleagues and professionals. Principals must have been teachers before they become principals, and most principals continue to teach in classrooms even while they are principals. There is little hierarchy among the adults in Finnish schools (Korpela 2004). Students are also involved in governance and leadership, and they participate in developing action plans for reform at the school level.

Finland has been engaged in systemic reform of education since the 1970s, and, based on high levels of student achievement and participation in public education, that reform has been highly successful. Reform in Finland has progressed slowly and deliberately; it is integrally interwoven into the social and economic fabric of the country. However, Finland is facing a number of challenges as a nation that have the potential to affect its education system and the schools within it. One of these challenges is growth in diversity as membership in the European Union opens its borders to increased immigration; teachers and principals may need training to maintain the level of personal connection to students that characterizes their interaction with students when they work with a more diverse group of students. Another is the strain on the economy of Finland's welfare state as baby boomers retire. Some schools are already beginning to feel the constraints of reduced resources. In their evaluation of Finland's school leadership, Hargreaves, Halász, and Pont (2007) predict that the process that Finland has used to reform education since the 1970s can serve the country well as its schools adjust to changing students and economic conditions, even as they make recommendations for continued development of school leadership in Finland.

Probably the most important recommendation Hargreaves, Halász, and Pont (2007) make is not as much for Finland as it is for other countries working on education reform. The researchers suggest that Finland "articulate and share hitherto tacit knowledge about Finland's educational and economic success so that others can learn from it and it is organizationally more transferable" (p. 33).

Education Reform in China

China is the world's largest developing country, with a GDP in 2007 of $3,250,827 million in U.S. dollars and a per capita GDP, according to the International Monetary Fund, of $2,460.786 (compared to $45,845 in the United States), and it has the largest system of public education in the world. According to UNESCO (2007), in 2005, there were 112,739,964 children enrolled in primary schools and 100,631,925 in secondary schools in China, not including Hong Kong and Macao (pp. 82, 102). No data are available regarding the percentage of GDP that China spends on education.

The current system of education in China is the result of a series of reforms that have taken place over the last half-century as part of political and economic changes in China. Before 1949, education in China was available only to children of the elite; there was virtually no education for children of workers and peasants. By contrast, the UNESCO figures indicate that more than 99 percent of primary school–age children are enrolled in school.

After China's "Cultural Revolution," which for all practical purposes dismantled the educational system from 1966 to 1976, education in China was redeveloped as a decentralized system. Since 1986, nine years of education has been compulsory in China. Although the law stipulated that the compulsory education be free for every citizen, funds were not allocated to support a free education. Funding for education was left up to local governments, and basic education, especially in rural areas, is funded by a mix of local revenues, donations, and income generated by tuition and commercial and industrial activities conducted by the schools (Cheng, 2004). The Chinese government announced in 2006 that it intended to eliminate all fees for the nine years of compulsory education for rural students by the end of 2007 (Xinhua News Agency 2006).

The decentralization of education funding, according to Iris Rotberg (2004), had positive and negative effects. On the positive side, the decentralization resulted in the generation of great local support for and ownership of education and schools, and enrollments increased greatly between the mid-1980s and mid-1990s. On the negative side, the local funding of basic education resulted in great disparity in the levels of funding for schools, and great disparity in the quality of the schools and the education children experienced in the schools. In 1988, the national government allowed local governments and schools to develop their own curricula and textbooks, creating even more diversity in Chinese schools.

Compulsory education in China is configured to include six years of primary school and three years of junior secondary school. Students can continue beyond the nine years of compulsory education to three years of senior secondary school if they qualify. To be able to attend senior secondary school, students must pass locally developed entrance examinations before they are admitted. Because of the decentralization, however, some regions have five years of primary school and three or four years of junior secondary school. There are also some urban schools that offer an additional year of senior secondary school to extend and enhance student learning at that level.

The latest reform in Chinese education began in the mid-1990s and led to the publication of new guidelines for curriculum, with the latest version completed in 2002. The reform has four purposes: further decentralization of the education system; a move from an "examination-oriented" education to what the Chinese Ministry of Education called a "quality education"; an increase in the amount of pre-service education required for new teachers and in the amount of education in teaching techniques; and more professional development for practicing teachers.

The decentralization, according to Betty Preus (2007), includes encouragement for local and state governments and teachers to develop and select textbooks. She reports, "China is also encouraging curriculum development at the state, local, and school levels and promoting a more flexible curriculum with choices for students" (p. 116). The Chinese reform agenda calls for local development of assessments that match and are aligned with locally developed curricula, rather than the standardized tests that have been used in the past.

Allowing choices for students also represents a shift in instruction. Chinese education has traditionally been teacher-directed, knowledge-based, and passive. Teachers make decisions about the knowledge children need, they provide that knowledge, and children "receive" and memorize that knowledge. The "quality education" promoted by the current reform is an effort to change instruction in schools from being teacher-directed to being learner-centered, to teaching practices that develop the whole child; that offer opportunities for hands-on learning; and that foster creativity, choice, and practical knowledge.

The call for reform is comprehensive and includes significant changes in teacher preparation. The new initiative requires that teacher preparation programs be increased in the short term to three years and eventually to four years. Teacher preparation programs have traditionally focused on developing the pre-service teachers' content knowledge—science, mathematics, or history, for example. That focus has shifted, and teacher preparation programs are including much more work on learning and practicing teaching strategies that support "quality education." Teacher preparation programs are modeling the kinds of teaching that the reform is promoting. University programs are working to build connections between university programs and schools, and pre-service teachers are having opportunities to practice the new teaching strategies they are learning in classrooms with students.

The reform initiative also includes changes in professional development for practicing teachers. Teachers in Chinese schools have traditionally been organized into teacher research groups that include both beginning and experienced teachers as well as pre-service teachers; the research groups have met on a regular basis to discuss ways to teach their subject areas. The focus of these research groups is changing from how to teach subjects to how to use new teaching strategies.

Chinese policy makers designed the "quality education" reform to reflect what they believe are the strengths of the educational system in the United States, the development of creativity and innovation. The Chinese authorities believe it is creativity and the ability to innovate that put and keeps the United States ahead in the global economy. Aibe Chen, associate professor and deputy director of the Department of Educational Administration at the Beijing Institute of Education, visited schools in the United States in 2001 to observe teachers and to learn about how U.S. children learn to be creative and to solve problems. In an interview with staffers of the Kappa Delta Pi Record, Chen acknowledged that while teachers and principals in China talk about "quality-oriented education," what is going on in their schools is "exam-oriented education." She said, "I know that we can find out what we need from schools in the United States and from your new education theory and practice. I want to introduce them to China to help our reform efforts" (Kappa Delta Pi Record 2002).

While there are many reports on the success of China's educational reform, China has not participated in TIMSS or PIRLS, and there are no data available that compare the academic performance of Chinese students to that of the rest of the world. Not all observers of education reform in China agree that the reforms there are succeeding. Willy Lam, an education policy analyst, wondered about China's real commitment to education reform as well as its ability to make it happen, arguing that in many of the western provinces of the country, there is not even a high-quality basic education available, much less opportunities for secondary education. According to Lam (2006), these schools depend on donations from foreign countries "to keep their poorly equipped schools running." Schooling comes after and is often supported by agriculture in some of these provinces, and "it is not uncommon for administrators in poor remote areas to ask students to . . . [spend] several hours a week working in factories" (p. 7). Lam (2006) also noted that there are other economic and cultural factors that impede the implementation of reform. Qualified teachers are reluctant to teach in rural areas where schools are poorly equipped and where there are few other qualified teachers. There is also gender discrimination, evidenced by parents who often do not send their daughters to school.

It is interesting to note that the reforms promoted for education in China and those in the United States are opposites. According to Preus (2007), as China has worked and is working toward learner-centered and decentralized education, the United States policy in No Child Left Behind is embracing the centralization and standardization that the Chinese believe is an impediment to their progress in the global economy.

Education Reform in France

France has a well-developed economy. According to the International Monetary Fund, France's 2007 GDP was $2,252,108 million. That translates into a per capita GDP of $41,511.154, clearly among the highest in the world. In 2005, France spent public funds on education totaling 5.4 percent of its GDP.

The education system in France has historically been a centralized one, reflected in the concept of equality, *egalité*, which has been a foundation of the country since the French Revolution. Even before the Revolution, "French" has not just been an indicator of national identity or citizenship. It also represents a cultural orientation, a legal identity, and a historical context. "French" under the law in France assumes that every citizen be treated identically, and "French" assumes a homogenous cultural perspective. Indeed, immigrants to France have been expected to assimilate and to adopt that cultural perspective, and schools historically have been a key element in that assimilation.

The school system in France is administered from the central Ministry of National Education, a cabinet-level agency in the national government, through a set of regional *académies*, administrative units that oversee schools in their regions. The heads of the *académies* are appointed by the Minister of Education, and the *académies* are funded through contract with the Ministry of Education. School development and reform are still "dominated" by national decisions, and an administrative reform of education in France has begun with the national government devolving some of the responsibility for oversight of education to the *academies* (Bonnet 2004). Most administrative responsibilities, however, are reserved for the national Ministry, including the hiring, administration, evaluation, and dismissal of the teaching staff, typically managed through the *académies*.

A national curriculum is used in all schools, both public and private. The curriculum specifies the subjects to be taught at each level of schooling, and teachers select textbooks from a list that has been approved by the Ministry of Education. In recent years, there has been some local adaptation of the national curriculum, according to Gerard Bonnet (2004), from the Department of Assessment and Forecasting in the French Ministry of Education, and teachers have considerable autonomy in determining how to teach.

Children begin school as preschoolers; preschool education is provided free of charge to all children from age two to age six. (In practice, most children begin preschool at age three; there are not enough places in publicly funded preschools for all two-year-olds.) Paul O'Brien (2007), an OECD staffer and the author of a working paper about the French education system, noted that by the 1990s, 100 percent of three-year-olds were enrolled in preschool. There has been a national curriculum for preschool since 1995; that curriculum includes beginning reading instruction. Compulsory education in France, however, does not begin until age six, when children enter primary or elementary school for grades one through five. After elementary school, children attend the lower secondary school or *collège* for four years, typically until age 15, although O'Brien (2007) noted that nearly one in three students has repeated at least one year of schooling up to this point and is older than 15. Compulsory education continues through age 16, which means that many students who complete *collège* must continue on for at least one year in the *lycée*. Students attend either a general and technological *lycée* or a vocational *lycée*, both of which provide a three-year program.

Traditionally in France, schools have been open six days a week, with no classes on Wednesday and Saturday classes meeting only in the morning. Recently, some schools have adjusted their schedules to eliminate classes on Saturday.

While children are in elementary school, teachers have the responsibility of assessing their progress periodically and continuously, but no high-stakes tests are administered. At the beginning of the school year, all eight-year-olds and 11-year-olds are administered national diagnostic tests to provide information for teachers as a basis for planning instruction, and samples of students are selected to participate in end-of-the-year testing. Fifteen-year-olds take a national test, and their scores on the test along with their grades from the two previous years make up their *diplôme national du brevet*. The *brevet*, once a credential required for continuing on into the *lycée*, is mostly a formality and no longer necessary for entrance into the *lycée*.

Students sit for a high-stakes national examination at the end of the *lycée*. This examination is the *baccalauréat*, or *bac*, as it is popularly called. There are three different types of *baccalauréat*. There is a general *baccalauréat*, usually for students going on to higher education; the *baccalauréat technologique* and the *baccalauréat professionelle* can lead either to higher education or to employment. O'Brien

(2007) noted that about 63 percent of French students have earned the *bac* in recent years; according to the Web site of the French Ministry of Education, in 2007, 54 percent of the students who passed the *bac* earned the general credential, 26 percent earned the technological, and 20 percent earned the professional. All three of the *bacs* entitle students to enter public universities in France. Because the *baccalauréats* are high-stakes tests, the curriculum in the *lycées* is geared toward preparing students for the tests.

There has been an effort in France to improve students' performance on the *bac*, and as in the United States, the press is eager to report on the tests. In July 2007, *le Figaro* reported that for the third year in a row, the percentage of students who passed the *bac* had increased. Of the 626,000 students who took the tests in 2007, 83.3 percent or 521,000 earned the credential. According to the article, the increase in the numbers of students passing the *bac* is an indication of the improving quality of French schools.

In France, besides the public schools, there are semiprivate schools, most of them parochial (Roman Catholic) schools. These schools also conform to the national regulations governing education, and they are funded almost entirely with public funds. The schools are required to use the national curriculum, and most of the teachers, like their counterparts in public, secular schools, are civil servants paid by the national government. There are also a very small number of schools that are truly private. These schools, which operate without any public funding, are not required to conform to national education regulations. The roster of private schools in France also includes about 450 schools referred to as *écoles hors contrat*, literally schools outside the contract, which have been founded by parents or teachers to offer curriculums or teaching methods that are different from those offered by the public schools (*Le Figaro* 2008a). The number of these small *écoles*, according to the newspaper article, is growing.

Education reform in France has generally consisted of administrative reform in the form of decentralization. According to Bonnet, the decentralization has not been very successful at the school level, since schools are not very strong as institutions. School personnel, especially in the elementary schools where there are no administrators on site, are not organized to make decisions or lead organizational or curricular changes. So even though the Ministry of Education has given the schools some authority to make changes, very little has changed in terms of the authority and autonomy of local schools.

School improvement efforts at the national level that began in 1982 identified education priority zones, *Zones d'éducation prioritaire* (ZEPs), geographic areas where schools show poor performance. The policy was updated in 1998 when education priority networks, *Réseaux d'éducation prioritaire* (REPs), were created to extend the benefits of such identification to additional schools. Schools identified as ZEPs and REPs are allocated more resources, including smaller class size; develop individual education plans for students; and offer incentives for teachers who are willing to teach in them, including higher pay and accelerated career development (O'Brien 2007). According to O'Brien (2007), in 2004 about one in five students in lower secondary schools, the *collèges*, were enrolled in a school that was either in a ZEP or a REP. O'Brien also reported that being named to the status of either ZEP or REP has stigmatized schools, and the program has shown very little effect in raising student achievement.

In 2006, the Ministry of Education again revised school improvement efforts to identify, among schools considered to be performing poorly, three different levels of need for improvement. Additional resources are allocated to these schools based on their levels of need for improvement. Along with some increased accountability for outcomes that are identified by the schools, the new policy allows schools to experiment with new teaching methods. The program, initiated during the 2006–2007 school year, has not been in force long enough to measure its effects (O'Brien 2007).

In recent years there have also been some efforts to improve student achievement in the form of helping struggling students to succeed at schools that are not part of ZEPs or REPs. Beginning in the 2006–2007 school year, for example, the Ministry of Education began the phase-in of an initiative called *programmes personnaliseés de réussite éducative* (personal programs for education success) at the elementary and *collège* levels. This program allows for the development of an individualized education plan for each child who is at risk (Ministre d'Education Nationale 2006).

All of this centralization results in a system of education that is standardized throughout the country, which clearly fits with the principle of equality traditionally espoused by the French and woven throughout the fabric of society in France. That traditional principle has been interpreted in public policy to mean that all people should be treated as if they were the same and had the same needs. "Cultural diversity," according to Guy Tchibozo

(2005), a professor at Louis Pasteur University in Strasbourg and educational researcher, "has long been ignored in public policies, especially in education policy" (p. 515).

Since 1993 and the establishment of the European Union, however, the population of France in general, and the school population in particular, has become far more diverse. Public policy in France has been slow to recognize the diversity, and slower yet to promote any changes in national policy or in schools to account for the diversity. An example of France's pace to address diversity is its response to the European Council's recognition of the legitimacy of regional languages. In 1998, countries in the European Council ratified the European Council Charter for Regional or Minority Languages. Although France was a signer of the charter, the French Constitution prohibited France from fully ratifying the charter or acting on it. It wasn't until 10 years later that the French Constitution was revised (in July 2008), and a new article, Article 75–1, was added to recognize officially regional languages in France.

Further evidence of France's position toward diversity is shown in its dealings with its increasing Muslim population. According to Patrick Simon (2003), from the French *Institut national d'études démographique,* the number of Muslims in France has tripled since 1994, with currently about 6 percent of the population identifying themselves as Muslim. The visibility of Muslims in France has become a political and educational issue, brought to the fore by a controversy over girls wearing the traditional headscarf in schools. French law bans any outward symbols of religion in schools, as part of its efforts toward public secularism. In 1989, an exception to that ban was approved so that Muslim girls could attend school wearing headscarves. That exception had been debated for more than 10 years when, in 2004, France adopted a new law that reinstated the ban. Members of the commission that recommended the reinstatement of the ban did so based on the belief that "the French educational system should be a neutral environment where the principles of secularism, republicanism, and citizenship are taught and reflected" (Hamilton, Simon, and Veniard 2004).

France's efforts at education reform have not produced significant improvement. According to UNESCO (2007) figures, in 2005 there were 4,015,490 children enrolled in primary schools in France, and 6,036,192 students enrolled in secondary schools. Data from the Program for International Student Assessment

(PISA) conducted in 2006 rank French 15-year-olds 19th in science and 17th in mathematics and reading of the 57 countries that participated in the test. (See Table 4 in Chapter 6 for more information.) In the two latest PIRLS (Progress in International Reading Literacy Study) conducted in 2001 and 2006, average scores of French fourth graders who took the test were 535 in 2001 and 522 in 2006. The 2006 scores ranked 27th and significantly below the average of the countries that participated in the test. According to a report on the reading progress of French children reported in *le Figaro* (2008b), 21.7 percent of French fourth graders had difficulty with the test, significantly more than in the previous administration of the same test.

Tchibozo (2005) speculated that France's reluctance to address diversity in schools may be one of the reasons that there are schools and children who are not succeeding academically. He attributes that reluctance to the French perspective on equality. According to him, it is not that French teachers haven't wanted to be bothered with accounting for cultural differences. He speculates that "taking into account cultural differences at school might have been perceived as a sign of inequity among pupils and students" (p. 515). Thus, even though France has become and is continuing to become more diverse, schools have yet to respond either in terms of providing more culturally appropriate teaching or in terms of supporting learning in their first languages.

Education Reform in Chile

In Chile, education reform has been in process for a number of years, and other Latin American countries have looked to Chile's reform as a model of what could be done to reform education. There have been two major education reform initiatives in Chile's recent history, both of which are still influencing the schools, and both of which, according to Robert McMeekin (2004), a researcher at the Center for Education Research and Development in Santiago, Chile, have had significant effects on teaching and on children and their learning. Yet another wave of reform is on the horizon, as Chile's new president Michelle Bachelet signed a new General Law of Education in 2007 that replaced the 1990 *Ley Orgánica Constitucional de Enseñanza* (L.O.C.E.) that codified education reforms enacted under General Augusto Pinochet.

The first wave of education reform in Chile took place during Pinochet's military government that was in power from 1973 to 1990. The reform during this period, enacted in 1980, was part of the "modernization" imposed on Chile by the military government that affected seven areas of Chile's society, including education, labor policies, and decentralization. The education "modernization" included several major initiatives: (1) a decentralization of the administration of public schools from the country's Ministry of Education to local authorities; (2) competition between private and public schools; (3) a nationwide voucher system financed through grants to public and private schools based on attendance; (4) revocation of teachers' civil service status; and (5) a national testing system to monitor the quality of schools (McMeekin 2004; Delannoy 2000). The modernization, according to Francoise Delannoy (2000), education specialist at the World Bank, was "driven by efficiency concerns: the search for greater responsiveness to local needs through market mechanisms," but the reforms also served to "fragment" and limit the power of labor unions.

Andrea Arango (2008), a research associate of the Council on Hemispheric Affairs, reported that when the decentralization took place, the federal contribution to education was reduced by 18 percent, forcing local municipalities to allocate local funds for schools. Wealthier municipalities could afford to fund their schools at higher levels than poorer ones, and the level of inequity that resulted has never been alleviated.

Because the reforms were enacted in the context of the Pinochet dictatorship, there was no opportunity for public debate and little public opposition to them—public opposition and dissent were not allowed during this time. But Delannoy (2000) argued that the way the reforms were enforced created resistance among the very people who were required to implement them—the teachers. At the same time that they were being asked to serve as enactors of the reform efforts, teachers found their salaries declining in the decade between 1980 and 1990 to about one-half of what they had been, and their working conditions were also declining. The teachers' salaries declined partly because Chile experienced an economic recession during this time, but also partly because of the reform.

Under the voucher system, still in force today, children are allowed to attend either public schools or private schools that are subsidized by the government. There is also the freedom to choose whether to attend a school in the children's own neighborhood or a school in another location, although there are no subsidies for transportation. Poor children whose families cannot afford to pay for transportation are forced to attend the schools in their own neighborhoods, regardless of their quality. Voucher payments go directly to the schools, public or private. The payments cover the full cost of education and are based on monthly attendance at the schools. Opponents of voucher plans often predict the demise of public schools, but in Chile that has not been the case. According to McMeekin (2004), "Even though private voucher-paid education provides 40 percent of voucher-supported primary and secondary education in Chile, municipally provided public education still accommodates over one-half of total enrollment" of primary and secondary school children (p. 88).

A democratic government was elected in 1990, and with that government came a new set of priorities for education that purportedly included equity and quality. The new government negotiated with the teachers, and in 1991, the labor policies of the Pinochet government that affected teachers were reversed. Teachers' salaries and working conditions were once again negotiated at the national level and tenure was restored.

The new government also began investing in teachers' professional training and in classrooms. The World Bank, in collaboration with the Chilean government, supported programs that supplied textbooks and classroom libraries, and professional development was provided that helped teachers to learn new teaching methods and strategies to network with their colleagues. Part of the World Bank–funded initiative was a program of competitive grants for school improvement plans, and many of the schools took advantage of this opportunity to work toward school improvement.

According to Delannoy (2000), all of this work helped to create a context of support among educators for the next round of reform, the "Full Day School" reform, which was enacted in 1996. This reform included four "pillars"—an extended school day, a new curriculum framework, teacher professionalism, and secondary school innovation.

Extending the school day meant that schools could no longer operate two shifts, and teachers would have to teach full time in one school rather than teach in different shifts at two or more schools. The reform initiative also included policy for developing the infrastructure necessary to eliminate double shifts—building new schools, for example.

The new curriculum includes objectives and minimum standards for primary and secondary schools; it was phased in and is now in place in Chile's schools. According to McMeekin (2004), the curriculum was operational in all schools and all subject areas by 2003. The national assessment, SIMCE, was revised to align with the new curriculum.

The teacher professionalism provisions of the new reform extended the professional development initiated soon after the democratic government took office in 1990. This area of the reform provides improved teacher preparation as well as professional development for in-service teachers. As part of the reform, teacher salaries increased more than 100 percent in real value over what they were in 1990 (McMeekin 2004).

Since 2003, children in Chile have been required to attend primary and secondary school; education is compulsory from age five through age 18. Currently, children may attend preschool, but the law to guarantee fully funded preschool for children ages two to five will not take effect until the end of Bachelet's presidency. Primary school begins at age five; it consists of eight grades. Secondary school is four years, and it is divided into two different formats beginning in 11th grade. One format is a scientific-humanities curriculum; students in this program select an academic major in science or humanities, and their courses in 11th and 12th grades reflect that major. The other format is technical-professional education; this program offers students the opportunity to take courses in trades such as mechanics and electricity to prepare them for work.

Ten percent of schoolchildren in Chile attend private schools that do not benefit from government funding. These schools are tuition-funded; they typically charge 10 times (or more) the per-pupil grant that publicly funded schools receive, obviously resulting in a huge disparity between private schools and those funded by the government. According to the *Economist* (2007), the education reform enacted and announced by President Bachelet includes a new superintendency at the national level; the person in that position will oversee the grants that fund the schools. "The superintendency should shine light on how local governments spend their education grants, and whether these reach the poorest schools." There has been considerable criticism of private, voucher-funded schools profiting from providing education, and the new reform requires that all government-funded private schools be operated by nonprofit organizations. As a further measure to address equity, this latest reform also prohibits schools that are publicly funded from selecting students by ability until they reach age 11; before this prohibition, publicly funded schools could set their own criteria for entrance and often were not willing to enroll children perceived to be slower learners.

In spite of the reform efforts to improve schools in Chile, the inequities of the education system have been documented in a wide variety of sources (*Economist* 2007; Claude 2008; Delannoy 2000). Those sources attribute the inequities to the decentralization and the voucher system. Arango's (2008) analysis of the current state of Chile's schools was that "Chilean education offers inherently unequal opportunities for students from low-income families, who consistently experience sub-standard educational achievements as a result of an ongoing bias in favor of privatization measures." Arango (2008) expresses concern that Bachelet's reform falls short of providing the equity and quality that children in Chile deserve, and she recommends that Bachelet "reassess the structure of Chile's education system and strive for a long-term overhaul of Pinochet-era divisions between rich and poor families."

The International Monetary Fund reported that Chile's 2007 GDP was $4,163,792 million; the per capita GDP for Chile was estimated to be $9,879.094. In 2005, Chile reported spending public funds equal to 3.3 percent of its GDP on education. UNESCO reports the enrollment of primary students in Chile in 2005 to be 1,720,951, and the enrollment of secondary students of 1,630,099, for a total of 3,351,050 students in Chile's primary and secondary schools. In the 2003 Trends in International Mathematics and Science Study, eighth grade scores from Chile ranked 38th out of the 44 countries that participated in the study, and well below the average score. Only Morocco, the Philippines, Botswana, Saudi Arabia, Ghana, and South Africa scored lower than Chile (Gonzales et al. 2004). Chile has come a long way in terms of education policy and is working to develop the infrastructure for academic achievement, but the Chilean education system has a long way to go to ensure that all children in Chile have the high-quality education that they deserve.

Lessons to be Learned

Each of the countries whose education reform efforts are described here faces very different economic and contextual issues, as well as different reform processes. Rotberg (2005a) argues that it is important to understand a country's education reform efforts within that country's economic and social context. According to her, "A country's priorities, values, and economic status ultimately play a major role in determining whether reforms can be implemented as planned" (p. 611).

Merilee Grindle (2004) noted that it is also important to understand the political context of reforms. She says,

> The task of moving from a recognition of problems and solutions to a situation in which political decision makers are willing to consider taking action to resolve them is not simply a matter of demonstrating the nature of the problem. For reform to get on national political agendas for action, it must have political salience as an issue and influential voices to promote it. (p. 44)

In other words, without political involvement, education reform issues do not rise to the level of national action. Grindle speculates that economic, social, and political factors came together around the world relative to education as a factor in the global economy in the 1990s, and she cites as evidence the emergence of education reform initiatives in every region of the world at that time.

In spite of the differences in social, economic, and political context among the countries involved in education reform, however, there is much that can be learned from the experiences of other countries. Rotberg (2005) says that there are "key trends" in global education reform, and how those trends are playing out in education reform can provide valuable lessons about how education systems can be improved. The trends she identifies involve educational equity, control of education, accountability, learning environments, and access to education. Other issues that can provide lessons in education reform include the preparation and professional development of teachers and the capacity of teachers and school leaders to make and sustain changes.

Lesson 1. Educational Equity

Most countries work to address equity in their education systems as part of education reform. But social, economic, and political contexts define equity and influence how equity is planned for and achieved. In South Africa, equity is a basic premise of the post-apartheid reform, not only for education but also for the government and the society. To begin to undo the inequities of apartheid, the government redistributed public funding and other resources for education, taking them away from some schools and giving them to others. At the same time, in an effort to keep more affluent children from leaving the public schools, the new government has allowed parents to make contributions to their children's schools. South Africa also has designated a large group of schools "fee free." These schools may not charge their students fees, and the government provides a higher level of financial support to them to make up for the loss of student fees.

In France, the principle of *égalité* means treating all citizens as if they are the same. Public funding for education is the same for all children whether they attend public or semiprivate schools. But for schools that are at risk, France provides additional funds and resources through its ZEPs and REPs.

In China, increasing equity means, at least in part, ensuring that all children have access to education. This has not always been the case, and there are still areas of China where access is limited because of extreme poverty. China's Ministry of Education announced "fee free" schools for children in rural areas where parents cannot afford to pay to send their children to school.

Chile has a voucher system that allows parents to choose from among an array of public and private schools for their children; the government pays the schools directly based on attendance. This voucher system was designed to improve access to schools and increase equity. Current reforms are aimed at improving equity by restricting schools' selective enrollment and requiring that schools be run by nonprofit organizations.

In the United States, the basic premise of the Elementary and Secondary Education Act has always been to provide compensatory education to children in poverty—to provide more education to them to help make up for the effects of poverty on their education. Some states have voucher systems, and all states have charter schools that allow for parent choice of schools for their children.

Finland's schools provide interventions for children with learning difficulties in the early grades. The result is that many of their learning difficulties are addressed successfully, and children go on to lower secondary school with no need for additional support. Finnish schools are bilingual, with instruction in Finnish and

Swedish, and there is also instruction in children's first languages if they are not Finnish or Swedish.

Lesson 2. Governance of Education

Many countries view the governance of education as an important issue in education reform. Governance and control of education in most countries are decentralized or moving toward decentralization. Decentralization and local control are seen as means of responding to the diverse educational needs of local communities.

Education in South Africa during apartheid, according to Jonathan Jansen (1999), was an "authoritarian and state-controlled system" (p. 43). With the end of apartheid, South Africa developed new policies and regulations for education; decentralization was part of the new platform.

In France, decentralization of the administration of education has been the centerpiece of education reform, with much of the administration of schools left to the *académies*. Individual teachers have autonomy in determining how to teach, but the curriculum is national, and the central Ministry of Education must approve textbooks.

The administration of Finland's schools is decentralized; school personnel make decisions about their own schools. Although there are national standards, individual schools determine their own budgets, their curriculum, and how they will teach. There is very little central control of education.

Pinochet decentralized the governance of education in Chile as part of his military government's "modernization." With decentralization came the responsibility of governing and funding schools, and many local governments were neither equipped to operate schools nor wealthy enough to fund them. Observers of education in Chile credit the decentralization with worsening the inequity between children from families in poverty and children from more affluent families.

The current reform of China's massive education system has decentralization as its centerpiece. Chinese officials are hoping that decentralization will promote innovation. Local schools have autonomy to develop curriculum, create or select their own textbooks, and design assessments that are aligned with their curriculums. Local schools also have responsibility for their own governance. Decentralization in China, however, like in Chile, has widened the resource gap among schools, because decentralization has meant that local communities have had to take a larger responsibility for funding the schools.

In contrast to these other countries, control of education in the United States is being centralized to a large extent through the accountability requirements of No Child Left Behind (NCLB) and other education legislation. Even though the majority of education funding in the United States comes from state and local revenues, school districts and schools are being required to enforce national standards and to have their results measured by standardized tests. At the same time, the U.S. government is decentralizing control for some by promoting school choice in the form of vouchers and charter schools that are exempt from much of the federal and state regulation governing schools.

Lesson 3. Accountability for Student Learning

Accountability and responsibility for student learning usually lie with teachers. In many countries, standardized testing of children is used as a way to hold teachers accountable, but "the United States has by far the most demanding test-based accountability requirements" (Rotberg 2005b). In the United States, No Child Left Behind mandates the use of standardized test scores to determine the quality of schools, and they are also used to sanction schools considered failing. Proponents of such accountability believe that it helps to increase equity, as all children are expected to learn to the same standards. But critics say that the testing does just the opposite, causing harm to the children who are most at risk. According to Yong Zhao (2007), University Distinguished Professor of Education at Michigan State University, "The clearly observed and indisputably identified effects are all undesirable: narrowing what students learn, teaching to tests, forcing teachers to cheat, and making schools find 'creative' ways to meet Adequate Yearly Progress (AYP) requirements" (p. 5).

Chile uses a standardized test, the SIMCE, to measure student progress toward meeting the goals of the national curriculum. School level data are reported publicly, and it is possible to compare the performance of schools. But the purpose of the test is not to sanction schools, but to understand their progress toward meeting national standards.

In Finland and France, student learning is documented through assessments created by teachers. In Finland, no high-stakes tests are administered; in France, students take a high-stakes test at the end of secondary school. Students in South Africa also take a high-stakes test, the Matric, at the end of secondary school.

China, on the other hand, according to Zhao (2007), is reforming evaluation and assessment. China's new policy "specifically forbids ranking school districts, schools, or individual students based on test results or making test results public" (p. 13). Instead, the Chinese policy calls for schools to develop alternatives to testing to document student learning.

Lesson 4. Quality of Learning Environments

One of the most important education reforms is creating school and classroom environments that contribute to high levels of learning. Some countries, China among them, "are trying to create more flexible learning environments and to produce the less easily measured skills of creativity and problem-solving, which are considered important in a knowledge-intensive, high-tech, global environment" (Stewart and Kagan 2005, 243). They believe that it is the flexible learning environments that they have observed in Western countries that contribute to the development of creativity and innovation.

Teachers in Finland and France have the autonomy to design their classrooms to meet the learning needs of the children in them. The United States, however, seems to be moving away from flexible learning environments. According to Rotberg (2005a), "the increasing emphasis on testing, more pressure on schools to raise scores, and strong incentives to 'teach to the test'" spur more teacher-directed, didactic methods of teaching (p. 615). The flexibility that is admired by other countries is giving way to more rigidity and standardization in U.S. classrooms.

Lesson 5. Access to Education

The United Nations has declared education to be a basic human right. Access to education ensures that right. Many countries have made increased access to education a part of education reform.

China has worked to increase access to education, both to basic education and to lower secondary school. Providing a "fee free" education to children whose families cannot afford to pay for school opens the door to education for children who could not participate in schooling. South Africa has also greatly increased access to education as a result of its reform. Under apartheid, there were many children who had no access to education or access only to a very poor-quality education. Integration, improving schools, ensuring adequate funding, and establishing "fee free" schools have increased access to schooling, particularly for black children.

Chile's voucher system has helped to increase access to schools of choice, and vouchers and charter schools in the United States have similarly increased access to higher-quality schools for some children. Desegregation in the United States also increased access to quality education for minority children.

The introduction of the vocational *baccalauréat* in France has increased the number of students earning the credential. Such differentiation provides access to higher education for students who might not have earned the general *baccalauréat*.

Lesson 6. Preparation and Professional Development of Teachers

Research has shown that the strongest influence on children's learning is the quality of the teachers they have. Many countries have made teacher preparation and teacher professional development priorities.

Teacher preparation in Finland is considered by many to be a model of excellence. Entrance into teacher preparation programs in Finland is highly selective. Finnish programs emphasize collaborative learning, and teacher candidates spend time working in classrooms with master teachers.

France, China, and South Africa have raised their standards for teacher preparation to increase the amount of coursework teachers must complete before they can begin teaching. China's teacher preparation program previously focused on learning content; the curriculum of its teacher preparation programs has changed to include more work on teaching methods. The coursework also provides opportunities for prospective teachers to experience the kinds of teaching strategies and methods they are expected to learn.

China's reform efforts also include professional development for teachers. Time is provided for experienced and novice teachers to collaborate and to work to improve their practice during the school day. Likewise, Chile has invested highly in teacher professional development as a means to educational reform.

In the United States, there are models of effective professional development that help teachers improve their practice. According to Ann Lieberman (2008), senior scholar at the Carnegie Foundation and professor emeritus from Columbia University, effective professional development has commonalities that include "opportunities to be engaged with a professional learning community of peers that expects, encourages, and supports continuous learning about teaching practice" (p. 215). Lieberman describes teacher networks and collaborative projects as creating the conditions for teacher learning.

Lesson 7. Capacity of Teachers and School Leaders to Change

Many education reformers believe that the extent to which reforms will be implemented and sustained depends on the capacity of teachers and school leaders to actually carry them out. Capacity involves the knowledge and skills necessary to put the reforms in place; it also involves believing in the potential of the reforms to lead to improvement. Chile's plan for education reform after democracy was restored, for example, included professional development that gave teachers the opportunity to network, to learn new teaching methods, and to learn how to collaborate with their colleagues, all of which would be important in the next stage of education reform.

In Finland, teacher preparation programs include academic preparation in the development of curriculum as well as opportunities to work with mentor teachers on developing curriculum and conducting research so that they are prepared to participate in this work when they become teachers.

South Africa, on the other hand, attempted to adopt outcome-based education without gaining the support of teachers or providing them with the professional development they would need to put it in place in their schools and classrooms. Outcome-based education is based on thinking about teaching and learning in an entirely new way, and it requires fairly sophisticated knowledge of instructional theory and skills in teaching that the majority of teachers did not have. Consequently, not only has outcome-based education not been implemented, but also teachers have actively resisted its implementation.

In the United States, No Child Left Behind was developed without the consensus of teachers and school leaders. Many educators, among them researchers and education theorists, believe that the mandates of NCLB run counter to the findings of research and to best practice. There have been few efforts to change those beliefs, and many teachers resist the mandates of NCLB.

Globalization and Education

So what does globalization mean for teaching and learning and the reform of education? Much of the discourse about globalization is about economics and work. But Marcelo Suárez-Orozco (2005), professor of globalization and education at New York University, argues that globalization should be about "demographic and cultural transformations." He says that such transformation calls for a different kind of education, "an education for lifelong cognitive, behavioral, and relational engagement with the world" (p. 212).

Some theorists predict that globalization will threaten our democratic society and our system of public education. Alan Reid, professor of education at the University of South Australia, thinks that public education will be even more important to democracy in a global society. According to Reid (2005),

> The scale and urgency of the challenges to democracy point to an enlarged role for public schools in a globalizing world. Public schools represent the only spaces in our society where young people from a wide range of cultures, experiences, and backgrounds can learn with and from one another on a systematic basis, developing the understanding, respect, and tolerance that is the life-blood of a cosmopolitan democracy. (p. 291)

Classrooms then become laboratories where students experiment with and hone their interpersonal, intercultural skills as they learn the knowledge and skills that they will need to create, live in, and be productive citizens in the cosmopolitan democracy.

Joel Spring (2007) proposes that education be organized to achieve a new purpose in the global society. He argues that the purpose of education should be to prepare students to live a long and happy life, and that the goal of education reform in the global society should be to create equality of opportunity for all students to learn what they need to live a long and happy life.

Spring (2007) proposed a curriculum to prepare students to be active agents in creating a global society that values living long and happy lives. Similar to Reid (2005), Spring (2007) said that education should lead "students to understand that human social interactions create new knowledge and institutions, and that people have the power to bring about social change" (p. 83). The curriculum focuses on human rights and environmental education, as well as seeing the world and society from and valuing many different perspectives. Spring envisions the classroom for this new kind of education as a biosphere that would allow students to experience the environment even as they learn about it and learn to "live" in it with their peers. Spring's proposal, like Reid's, views education as a vehicle to a new society, one in which there is understanding, respect, and tolerance.

Educators in the global society will have to be facilitators of learning, learners along with their students, and models of learning. Their work "will henceforth be tending to the cognitive skills, interpersonal sensibilities, and cultural sophistication of young people whose lives will be engaged in local context yet suffused with larger transnational realities" (Suárez-Orozco 2005, 210).

Obviously, the development of such educational institutions will require change and reform and is not without risk. Ciaran Sugrue (2008) said that

> Risk and uncertainty are a persistent presence, all the more real in a globalised world that hurtles headlong into the future at increasing velocity so that "going forward" can rapidly become a blind leap of faith that jettisons past and present, ignoring the "lessons" they proffer. (p. 220)

But we can't afford to ignore the lessons of the past and present reforms. Sugrue (2008) said that there are also important lessons to learn about the *process* of reform. First, reform must be situated in society, society must be taken into account in any reform effort, and it might be society that should be changed. Second, it is individual and collective motivation to accomplish something, not mandates or external accountability, that leads to real change. Third, an expanded idea of research and creating new knowledge that includes communities not only builds a research base but also builds a base of support for change. Fourth, teachers are key to reform, and they must be respected as professionals.

External forms of accountability interfere with teachers' professionalism. And last, reform must lead to equity and social justice if it is to be sustained.

Education in the United States and in the world may very well be in crisis, but it is often a crisis that creates new opportunities, new leaders, new ideas, and new solutions. How we deal with the crisis will depend on how well we have learned from the work of reformers before us.

References

Arango, A. 2008. *The Failings of Chile's Education System: Institutionalized Inequality and a Preference for the Affluent.* Washington, DC: Council on Hemispheric Affairs.

Baer, J., S. Baldo, K. Ayotte, and P. J. Green. 2007. *The Reading Literacy of U.S. Fourth-Grade Students in an International Context: Results from the 2001 and 2006 Progress in International Reading Literacy Study (PIRLS).* (NCES 2008–017). Washington, DC: National Center for Education Statistics, Institute of Education Sciences, U.S. Department of Education.

Baines, L. 2007. "Learning from the World: Achieving More by Doing Less." *Phi Delta Kappan* 89 (2): 98–104.

Bonnet, G. 2004. "France: Diverse Populations, Centralized Administration." In *Balancing Change and Tradition in Global Education Reform*, edited by I. C. Rotberg, 127–152. New York: Rowman & Littlefield Education.

Bracey, G. W. 2007. "The First Time 'Everything Changed.'" *Phi Delta Kappan* 89 (2): 119–136.

Bracey, G. W. 2002. "Test Scores, Creativity, and Global Competitiveness." *Phi Delta Kappan* 83 (10): 738–739.

Cheng, K. 2004. "China: Turning the Bad Master into a Good Servant." In *Balancing Change and Tradition in Global Education Reform*, edited by I. C. Rotberg, 5–29. New York: Rowman & Littlefield Education.

Claude, M. 2006. "Educational Reform in Chile." *Upside Down World,* June 14. http://upsidedownworld.org/main/content/view/322/34/.

Darling-Hammond, L., and G. Wood. 2008. *Democracy at Risk: The Need for a New Federal Policy in Education.* Athens, OH: Forum for Education and Democracy.

Delannoy, F. 2000. "Education Reforms in Chile, 1980–98: A Lesson in Pragmatism." *Country Studies: Education Reform and Management Publication Series* 1 (1). World Bank.

Department of Education. 1995. "White paper on Education and Training." Cape Town: Parliament of the Republic of South Africa.

The Economist. 2007. "Playground Harmony." December 13. http://www.economist.com/PrinterFriendly.cfm?story_id=10286281.

Engler, J. M., and J. B. Hunt, Jr. 2004. "Preparing Our Students for Work and Citizenship in the Global Age." *Phi Delta Kappan* 86 (3): 197–199.

Finkelstein, L. B. 1995. "Finland's Lessons." *Education Week*, October 18. http://www.edweek.org/ew/articles/1995/10/18/07finkel.h15.html.

Fiske, E. B., and H. F. Ladd. 2005. "Racial Equity in Education: How Far Has South Africa Come?" Working Paper Series SAN05–03, Terry Sanford Institute of Public Policy, Duke University, Durham, NC.

Gabade, T. 2006. "Free Schooling for Five Million." http://www.southafrica.info/about/education/schooling–231106.htm.

Gamerman, E. 2008. "What Makes Finnish Kids So Smart?" *Wall Street Journal*, February 28. http://online.wsj.com/article/SB120425355065601997.html?mod=fpa_mostpop.

Gardner, W. 2008. "Lessons from Finland: The Way to Education Excellence." *Providence Journal*, February 27. http://www.commondreams.org/archive/2008/02/27/7330/.

Gonzales, P., J. C. Guzman, L. Partelow, E. Pahlke, L. Jocelyn, D. Kastberg, and T. Williams. 2004. *Highlights from the Trends in International Mathematics and Science Study (TIMSS) 2003* (NCES 2005–005). U.S. Department of Education, National Center for Education Statistics. Washington, DC: U.S. Government Printing Office.

Grindle, M. S. 2004. *The Contentious Politics of Education Reform*. Princeton, NJ: Princeton University Press.

Grubb, W. N. 2007. "Dynamic Inequality and Intervention: Lessons from a Small Country." *Phi Delta Kappan* 89 (2): 105–114.

Hamilton, K., P. Simon, and C. Veniard. 2004. "The Challenge of French Diversity." *Migration Source*, November. http://www.migrationinformation.org/feature/print.cfm?ID=266.

Hargreaves, A., G. Halász, and B. Pont. 2007. "School Leadership for Systemic Improvement in Finland: A Case Study Report for the OECD Activity Improving School Leadership." http://www.oecd.org/dataoecd/43/17/39928629.pdf.

Houtsonen, L. 2005. "Developments in Teacher Training in Finland: Emerging Models of Geography Education." *International Research in Geographical and Environmental Education* 13 (2): 190–196.

Human Rights Watch. 2001. *Scared at School: Sexual Violence against Girls in South African Schools*. New York.

International Monetary Fund. 2008. *World Economic Outlook Database, April 2008: Nominal GDP List for the World and the European Union.* Data for the year 2007. http://www.imf.org/external/pubs/ft/weo/2008/01/weodata/index.aspx.

Jansen, J. D. 1999. "Globalization, Curriculum and the Third World State: In Dialogue with Michael Apple." *Current Issues in Comparative Education* 1 (2): 42–47.

Jansen, J., and N. Taylor. 2003. "Educational Changes in South Africa 1994–2003: Case Studies in Large-Scale Education Reform." *Education Reform and Management Publication Series* II (1). World Bank.

Kagan, S. L., and V. Stewart. 2005. "Introduction: A New World View: Education in a Global Era." *Phi Delta Kappan* 87 (3): 185–187.

Kappa Delta Pi Record. 2002. "Education Reform in China: An Interview with Aibe Chen." Winter. http://findarticles.com/p/articles/mi_qa4009/is_200201/ai_n9072424/print?tag=atBody.col1.

Korpela, S. 2004. "The Finnish School—A Source of Skills and Well-being: A Day at the Strömberg Lower Comprehensive School." http://virtual.finland.fi/netcomm/news/showarticle.asp?intNWSAID=30625.

Korpela, S. 2008. "Free Schooling for All: The Finnish School System Supports Lifelong Learning." http://virtual.finland.fi/netcomm/news/showarticle.asp?intNWSAID=41557.

Kruse, D. 1996. "Fish Hoek Middle School: Issues of Education Reform in South Africa." Paper presented at the annual conference of the National Middle School Association Annual Conference, Baltimore, Maryland.

Lam, W. 2006. "Perpetual Challenges to China's Education Reform." *China Brief* VI (24): 6–8.

Le Figaro. 2007. "Bac: la cuvée 2007 est encore meilleure." July 11.

Le Figaro. 2008a. "Quelque 450 établissements hors contrat scolarisent 45,000 élèves." January 8.

Le Figaro. 2008b. "Les Européens peinent á apprendre a lire á l'école." July 22.

Lieberman, A. 2008. "How Do Teachers Learn to Lead?" In *The Future of Educational Change: International Perspectives*, edited by C. Sugrue, 204–218. New York: Routledge.

McMeekin, R. W. 2004. "Chile: Vouchers and Beyond." In *Balancing Change and Tradition in Global Education Reform*, edited by I. C. Rotberg, 83–107. New York: Rowman & Littlefield Education.

Ministre d'education nationale. 2006. "Programmes personnalisés de réussite éducative." *Bulletin Officiel*. http://www.education.gouv.fr/bo/2006/31/MENE0601969C.htm.

Mullis, I. V. S., M. O. Martin, A. M. Kennedy, and P. Foy. 2007. *IEA's Progress in International Reading Literacy Study in Primary School in 40 Countries.* Chestnut Hill, MA: TIMSS & PIRLS International Study Center, Boston College.

Murphy, J. T. 1992. "Apartheid's Legacy to Black Children." *Phi Delta Kappan* 73 (5): 367–374.

O'Brien, P. 2007. "Enhancing Incentives to Improve Performance in the Education System in France." Economics Department Working Paper No. 570, Organization for Economic Co-operation and Development, Paris.

Preus, B. 2007. "Educational Trends in China and the United States: Proverbial Pendulum or Potential for Balance?" *Phi Delta Kappan* 89 (2): 115–118.

Reid, A. 2005. "Rethinking the Democratic Purposes of Public Schooling." In *Globalizing Education: Policies, Pedagogies, & Politics,* edited by M. W. Apple, J. Kenway, and M. Singh, 281–296. New York: Peter Lang.

Rotberg, I. C., ed. 2004. *Balancing Change and Tradition in Global Education Reform.* New York: Rowman & Littlefield Education.

Rotberg, I. C. 2005a. "Tradeoffs, Societal Values, and School Reform." *Phi Delta Kappan* 86 (8): 611–618.

Rotberg, I. C. 2005b. "The Bigger Picture." *Education Week,* February 9. http://www.edweek.org/ew/articles/2005/02/09/22rotberg.h24.html.

Sahlberg, P. 2006. "Raising the Bar: How Finland Responds to the Twin Challenge of Secondary Education." *Profesorado. Revista de curriculum y formacíon del profesorado* 10 (1): 1–24. http://www.see-educoop.net/education_in/pdf/Raising%20the%20Bar%202006.pdf.

Simon, P. 2003. "French Muslims, Government Grapple With Integration Pains." *Migration Information Source,* August 1. http://www.migrationinformation.org/feature/print.cfm?ID=153.

Singh, A. 2005. "Towards a Theory of National Consciousness: Values and Beliefs in Education as a Contribution to 'Cultural Capital' in Post-Apartheid South Africa." *Journal of Asian and African Studies* 40 (5): 323–343.

Soudien, C. 1997. "Transformation and Outcomes-based Education in South Africa: Opportunities and Challenges." *Journal of Negro Education* 66 (4): 449–459.

"South Africa's Population." 2008. South Africa.info. http://www.southafrica.info/about/people/population.htm.

Spady, W. 2007. "It's Time to End the Decade of Confusion about OBE in South Africa." *South African Journal for Science and*

Technology. http://edulibpretoria.files.wordpress.com/2008/08/spadyobeconfusionpaper.pdf.

Spring, J. 2007. *A New Paradigm for Global School Systems: Education for a Long and Happy Life.* Mahwah, NJ: Lawrence Erlbaum.

Stewart, V., and S. L. Kagan. 2005. "Conclusion: A New World View: Education in a Global Era." *Phi Delta Kappan* 87 (3): 241–245.

Suárez-Orozco, M. M. 2005. "Rethinking Education in the Global Era." *Phi Delta Kappan* 89 (3): 209–212.

Sugrue, C. 2008. *The Future of Educational Change: International Perspectives.* New York: Routledge.

Tchibozo, G. 2005. "The Recognition of Cultural Diversity in the French Educational Context: A Literature Review." Paper presented at the annual meeting of the Association for Teacher Education in Europe, Amsterdam. http://www.atee2005.nl/download/papers/18_ab.pdf.

Tye, K. A. 2003. "Global Education as a Worldwide Movement." *Phi Delta Kappan* 85 (2): 165–168.

UNESCO. 2007. *Global Education Digest: Comparing Education Statistics Across the World.* Montreal.

Xinhua News Agency. 2006. "China Adopts Amendment to Compulsory Education Law." June 30. http://china.org.cn/english/MATERIAL/173281.htm.

Young, E. 2008. "Focus on Global Education." *Phi Delta Kappan* 89 (5): 349–353.

Zhao, Y. 2007. "Education in the Flat World." *Edge* 2 (4).

4

Chronology

This chapter provides a timeline of events, court cases, legislation, publications, public meetings, and public addresses that relate to the reform of education in the United States. The timeline begins with the *Brown v. Board of Education* Supreme Court decision and the launch of Sputnik I because they were instrumental in bringing about education reform on a national scale in the United States.

1954   The United States Supreme Court rules in *Brown v. Topeka (KS) Board of Education* (347 U.S. 483) that providing separate schools for white and black children is not legal and orders that schools in the United States be desegregated. This decision effectively overturns *Plessy v. Ferguson* (163 U.S. 537, 1896), which decreed that the provision of separate but equal schools was constitutional.

1955   The United States Supreme Court rules in *Brown v. Board of Education II* (349 U.S. 294) that schools be desegregated "with all deliberate speed" in response to states having made little progress in dismantling separate school systems and integrating schools.

1957   The Soviet Union is successful in launching Sputnik I, a satellite, into orbit around the earth. The launch begins the space race and serves as the impetus for international comparisons of academic achievement and calls to reform U.S. education in science and mathematics.

1958   The National Education Defense Act (NDEA), the first legislation to call for and support education reform in the United States at the federal government level, is enacted by Congress in response to the "crisis" in education identified as a result of the launch of Sputnik I. The law provides funding for reform of mathematics and science teaching in schools, support for professional development for teachers, and funding for school libraries.

1959   The first international study of student achievement is begun by the International Association for the Evaluation of Educational Achievement (IEA). The Pilot Twelve-Country Study samples the achievement of 13-year-olds in 12 countries in the areas of mathematics, reading comprehension, geography, science, and nonverbal ability. The findings of the study are published in 1962. More important than the findings, the IEA asserts, is that the study shows that international comparisons of student achievement is possible.

1964   President Lyndon B. Johnson signs the Civil Rights Act into law. The law prohibits racial discrimination in public places and facilities and businesses in the United States, racial discrimination in employment and housing, and segregation of schools. The Civil Rights Act invalidates the Jim Crow laws in southern states, and although it was initially intended to aid African Americans, the law includes women and whites. The law also creates the Equal Employment Opportunity Commission, and it sets the stage for other legislation and court cases aimed at equality of opportunity.

1965   Project Head Start begins under the auspices of the Office of Economic Opportunity. This preschool program, part of President Lyndon Johnson's War on Poverty, is intended to help children in poverty develop the skills necessary to begin school academically on par with their more affluent peers. Project Head Start, later administered by the U.S. Department of Health and Human Services, provides services not only in education, but also in nutrition, parent involvement, and health to young children and their families.

1965   The Elementary and Secondary Education Act (ESEA), P.L. 89–10, is signed into law. A part of President

Johnson's War on Poverty, ESEA is based on the premise that children from low-income families need more educational services to be successful in school. ESEA, designed by President Johnson's commissioner of education Francis Keppel, is the first federal legislation to provide funding for K-12 education. In addition to direct services to children, ESEA allocates funding for teacher professional development, instructional materials, and parent involvement in schools.

1966   Recognizing the gaps that exist in the education of students who travel with their parents for work and the need for compensatory education for them, the Elementary and Secondary Education Act is amended to include children of migrant farm workers. Funds are allocated specifically to provide education programs that help to fill the gaps in their educations as they move from school to school.

1966   The Coleman Report, "Equality in Educational Opportunity," is issued. This report, developed by James Coleman, an educational sociologist, and others, was commissioned by Congress to assess the state of K-12 education in the United States. The Coleman report is controversial in its finding that the effects of schooling are not as strong as socioeconomic status on the quality of children's learning. The report also finds that African American children who attend integrated schools where the majority of children are white have higher academic achievement than African American children who attend schools that have a majority population of minority students.

1968   The Elementary and Secondary Education Act adds Title VII, the Bilingual Education Act, to provide assistance for school districts that serve children who have limited English-speaking ability (LESA). Funds under Title VII are provided to school districts in the form of grants. Interestingly, no appropriation is made for Title VII; funding will have to wait until 1969.

1970   The Experimental Schools Program (ESP) is announced by President Richard Nixon. ESP is a program that promotes "comprehensive school reform." Under the program, school districts can apply for grants to support their comprehensive school reform efforts. Nixon

	also proposes an organization to conduct research about education, the National Institute of Education.
1972	The National Institute of Education (NIE) begins operation. NIE is to become the Office of Educational Research and Improvement (OERI) in 1979 under Secretary of Education William Bennett.
1972	Title IX of the Education Amendments of 1972 is signed into law. Title IX states, "No person in the United States shall, on the basis of sex, be excluded from participation in, be denied the benefits of, or be subjected to discrimination under any education program or activity receiving Federal financial assistance" (Section 1681a). Initially, Title IX is used to address high school and college or university sports for girls and women, although the law does not specifically address sports.
1974	Women's Educational Equity Act (WEEA) is signed into law as Title IVA of the Elementary and Secondary Education Act. WEEA awards grants and contracts to operate programs that promote educational equity for women and girls. WEEA also establishes the Women's Equity Resource Center to provide technical assistance to grantees and to disseminate nationally the models it develops.
1974	P.L. 94–142, the Education of All Handicapped Children Act, is enacted by Congress and signed into law by President Gerald Ford. This law requires that all children and adults with disabilities, ages 3 to 21, be educated in "the least restrictive environment" to the maximum extent appropriate. This means that children and adults who have disabilities are to be educated in regular classrooms as much as is possible, given their disabilities. The law also requires a specific process be followed for identification and evaluation of children with disabilities. It includes provisions for notifying and involving parents in decisions about special education services to their children, and requires that an Individual Education Plan (IEP) be developed for each child who qualifies for special education services. The IEP outlines the specific services a child is entitled to, the objectives of the services provided, who will provide the services and the amount of time or proportion of the school day the services will be provided,

accommodations required for the child in the regular classroom, and how the child's progress toward meeting the objectives will be measured. The IEP process includes provisions for annual review of the IEP.

1981 The National Commission on Excellence in Education is established by Congress to "review and synthesize the data and scholarly literature on the quality of learning and teaching in the nation's schools, colleges, and universities, both public and private, with special concern for the educational experience of teen-age youth" (20 U.S.C. 1233a). The commission is further charged with comparing education programs in the United States with those of other countries, to investigate programs that are recognized as leading to "uncommon success" in preparing students for post-secondary education, and to hold hearings on what should be done to improve schools in general.

1983 The National Commission on Excellence in Education releases its landmark report, "A Nation at Risk." The report, in the form of a letter to the nation, describes the quality of U.S. education as jeopardizing our national security. The report includes a list of reforms that should be put in place by schools and challenges the nation's educators, parents, and students to work together to improve education in the United States.

1985 At its annual summer meeting in Boise, Idaho, the National Governors' Association sets seven education reform tasks in response to concern about the economy and the role of education in supporting the work force and global competitiveness. The seven education reform tasks are (1) creating a more highly professional teaching force; (2) strengthening school leadership and management; (3) promoting greater parent involvement and choice in their children's education; (4) helping at-risk children and youth meet higher educational standards; (5) making better and more effective use of new technologies in education; (6) making better use of the resources invested in school facilities; and (7) strengthening the mission and effectiveness of colleges and universities.

Tennessee governor Lamar Alexander announces the formation of seven task forces, each to investigate one of the seven education reform tasks (Currence 1985).

1988 The Jacob Javits Gifted and Talented Students Education Act is added to the reauthorization of ESEA (Elementary and Secondary Education Act). The Jacob Javits Gifted and Talented Students Education Act is the only federal education legislation that addresses the education of gifted and talented students. The law does not provide direct aid to local gifted education programs. Instead, funding under this law supports research in gifted and talented education and the identification of innovative and demonstration programs for gifted and talented students. The law is particularly aimed at serving students who might otherwise be underrepresented in gifted and talented programs, such as economically disadvantaged children, children who are limited English-proficient, and children who are disabled. The law also provides for the establishment and ongoing operations of the National Research Center on the Gifted and Talented.

1989 The state governors meet with President George Herbert Walker Bush in the first National Education Summit to discuss education reform and set six national goals to improve education in the United States by the year 2000. The goals, based on the premise that all children can learn, address school readiness, high school graduation rate, general student achievement and citizenship, achievement in science and mathematics, adult literacy and lifelong learning, and safe and drug-free schools. The president and governors challenge all Americans to participate in achieving the goals to maintain both a healthy economy and our democracy.

1990 The six national education goals are announced by President Bush in his State of the Union address. The six goals are intended to serve as a framework for education reform. The goals are

Goal 1. Readiness for School: By the year 2000, all children in America will start school ready to learn.

Goal 2. High School Completion: By the year 2000, the high school graduation rate will increase to at least 90 percent.

Goal 3. Student Achievement and Citizenship: By the year 2000, American students will leave grades four, eight, and twelve having demonstrated competency in challenging subject matter including English, mathematics, science, history, and geography; and every school in America will ensure that all students learn to use their minds well, so they may be prepared for responsible citizenship, further learning, and productive employment in our modern economy.

Goal 4. Science and Mathematics: By the year 2000, U.S. students will be first in the world in science and mathematics achievement.

Goal 5. Adult Literacy and Lifelong Learning: By the year 2000, every adult American will be literate and will possess the knowledge and skills necessary to compete in a global economy and exercise the rights and responsibilities of citizenship.

Goal 6. Safe, Disciplined, and Drug-Free Schools: By the year 2000, every school in America will be free of drugs and violence and will offer a disciplined environment conducive to learning. Schools, families, and communities must work together to counteract negative social influences and create safe and orderly schools (Vinovskis 1999).

1990   Congress establishes a National Education Goals Panel as an independent agency in the executive branch of the federal government. The purposes of the panel are: (1) to build a national consensus for educational improvement; (2) to report on progress toward achieving the national goals set forth by the president, the nation's governors, and Congress; and (3) to review and certify the standards states develop for achieving the goals and the criteria states set for meeting the standards. The National Education Goals Panel is made up of governors, members of the Bush administration, legislators, and members of Congress.

1990   The Secretary of Labor appoints a commission, the Secretary's Commission on Achieving Necessary Skills (SCANS), to identify skills needed for work. In particular, the Secretary charges SCANS to define the skills needed for employment; propose acceptable levels of proficiency; suggest ways to assess proficiency; and develop a strategy to disseminate that information to schools, businesses, and homes in the United States.

1990 The New Standards Project (NSP) begins. The New Standards Project is a consortium of states and urban school districts chaired by Lauren Resnick of the University of Pittsburg Learning, Research, and Development Center and Marc Tucker from the National Center on Education and the Economy in Washington, D.C. The purpose of NSP is to create a system of standards for student learning and to design performance assessments and portfolios that allow students to demonstrate that they meet those standards. During the years the NSP exists, thousands of educators around the country are involved in creating such assessments through the NSP.

1990 The Individuals with Disabilities Education Act (IDEA) is signed into law. IDEA takes the place of P.L. 94–142, the Education of All Handicapped Children Act, and is seen both as an education and a civil rights law. Under the law, all children, ages 3 through 21, are entitled to a free, appropriate public education. IDEA provides funding for states whose special education policies and procedures meet at least the minimum outlined in the law. Although the law does not require that states participate, all states do.

1991 The National Education Goals Panel releases its first report, "The National Education Goals Report: Building a Nation of Learners," on progress toward meeting the six national education goals. The report echoes calls for improved student achievement, but it also reports that high school graduation rates are 83 percent, the highest ever in the history of the United States. The panel reports that it is difficult to evaluate progress toward meeting the goals because data on many of the goals are not readily available and the data that are available may not be reliable for making such judgments. To address this problem, the panel calls for more testing and the gathering of more data relative specifically to the goals.

1991 President Bush announces "American 2000: A National Strategy" aimed at reaching the national goals by

2000. The strategy has four parts: (1) improving the schools and making them accountable for their work through the setting of "world class standards" in five curriculum areas—English, mathematics, science, history, and geography; (2) creating a "new generation of American Schools," schools that are invented to "meet the demands of a new century"; (3) creating a nation of life-long learners (adults who are no longer in school); and (4) creating communities that support learning and are committed to the success of their schools. American 2000 recommends the creation and use of an American Achievement Test that will be used to hold schools accountable for improved student learning.

1991 Congress establishes the National Council on Education Standards and Testing (NCEST) at the request of Education Secretary Lamar Alexander. NCEST is established to, along with the National Education Goals Panel, monitor the process of developing national standards and a system of national testing.

1991 The SCANS report, "What Work Requires of Schools: A SCANS Report for America 2000," is released. The report identifies competencies and foundational skills needed for success in the workplace and proposes minimum skills that should be required of students in schools, with the intent of informing the development of learning standards. The SCANS report becomes a resource for many school districts for revising and developing curriculum.

1992 *How Schools Shortchange Girls*, the landmark study of gender equity in schools, is published by David and Myra Sadker. The book documents how schools and classrooms are organized and how teachers teach in ways that are detrimental to the learning of girls and to their self-esteem as learners.

1993 The National Education Goals Panel calls for the development and institution of national curriculum standards in its report, "Promises to Keep: Creating High Standards for American Students." National curriculum standards would include both content and performance standards. Content standards would define the knowledge and skills that children should learn in eight subject areas: English, mathematics, science, history, citizenship/civics, geography, foreign languages, and fine arts. Performance standards would, according to the report, "provide tools to determine whether content standards are met." They would determine "the evidence required and the quality of student performance that would be considered acceptable to demonstrate that content standards had been met." Such standards would create a curriculum that, if required, would be used by schools across the country, and children throughout the country would be expected to learn the same knowledge and skills and be held to the same expectations in terms of the quality of that learning. The idea of national curriculum standards represents a huge departure from the control and administration of education that had been reserved for the states in the U.S. Constitution.

1994   President Bill Clinton signs the Goals 2000: Educate America Act (P.L. 103–227) into law. In addition to the original six goals set by the nation's governors and President Bush, Goals 2000 includes two new goals. The new goals address teacher education and professional development and parental participation in education. Goals 2000 also adds foreign languages, the arts, economics, and civics and government to the five core subject areas in which students should demonstrate competency.

Unlike American 2000, Goals 2000 provides resources to states and communities for school improvement; the law also provides grants for pre-service teacher education and professional development for practicing teachers. The Goals 2000: Educate America Act establishes the National Education Standards and Improvement Council to oversee the development of and certify content, student performance, and opportunity to learn standards, as well as assessment systems submitted by states. (Opportunity to learn standards describe the educational resources— facilities and learning environment, quality of teachers, professional development for teachers, instructional materials, and so on, required for schools to ensure that students meet the content and performance standards.) To complement the School to Work Opportunity Act of 1994 (P.L. 103–239), Goals 2000 also creates a National Skill Standards Board to support the development of occupational standards, assessments, and certification of skills in specific occupational areas.

1996 Goals 2000: Educate America Act is amended in President Clinton's budget bill to eliminate opportunity to learn standards. Opportunity to learn standards are eliminated because they are viewed by some legislators as intruding on the states' and local school districts' rights to administer education programs, and by others as opportunities for particular political agendas to be promoted. Still others believe setting opportunity to learn standards at the federal level would require the federal government to provide funding for all schools to be able to meet the opportunity to learn standards. The amendments also eliminate the National Education Standards and Improvement Council, which has not yet been convened and is viewed as unnecessary because its purpose is nearly identical to work already being done by the National Education Goals Panel and the National Council on Education Standards and Testing.

1996 The second National Education Summit is held in Palisades, New York. Forty-one governors and business and community leaders meet, and most affirm their support for "new, world-class" academic standards in core subject areas, high-quality assessments, and accountability for schools in meeting the standards. A few of the governors as well as some business leaders, including the CEO of IBM, disagree with the idea of national standards, arguing instead that education standards should be set locally. Conference participants also call for increased and improved use of technology in meeting academic standards. Business leaders agree to consider academic standards in deciding where to locate new business facilities. While leaders of the National Education Association and some other educators participate in the summit, only a few teachers are invited. The National School Boards Association and the National Parent Teacher Association complain because they are not invited to the summit and they believe that they should be included in the national discussion about standards and their implementation.

1997   IDEA (Individuals with Disabilities Education Act) is reauthorized with some important amendments. The new law, P.L. 105–17, expands the definition of children with disabilities to include children between the ages of three and nine who have developmental delays. It provides a process for mediating disputes between parents and schools and school districts, and requires that mediation occur. The law also provides for additional grants for programs for infants and toddlers with disabilities, and additional funding for technology, parent training, and professional development for teachers.

1997   In his State of the Union address, President Clinton calls for every state to adopt high national standards, "representing what all our students must know to succeed in the knowledge economy of the 21st century," and he asks that states "shape the curriculum to reflect these standards, and train teachers to lift students up to them" (Clinton 1997). He also argues for the development of a national test to evaluate the progress of all fourth grade students in reading and all eighth grade students in mathematics every year. President Clinton, in effect, in arguing for a national test, is calling for a national curriculum. This is significant because up until now, states have been mandated to develop their own standards and assessments to measure students' progress toward meeting those state standards.

1999   A third National Education Summit is held. Participants in the summit, including governors, educators, and business leaders, identify three challenges for U.S. education. The challenges are improving teacher quality, helping all students reach high standards, and holding all schools accountable. Participants agree to support their states in addressing the challenges.

2001   The fourth National Education Summit, held in Palisades, New York, again focuses on raising standards for student achievement. The business, government, and education leaders call for the improvement of teaching, the expansion of testing and accountability, and continuing public support as ways to increase student achievement.

2002 President George W. Bush signs the latest reauthorization of the Elementary and Secondary Education Act into law. This new authorization, named No Child Left Behind (NCLB; P.L. 107–110), requires states to hold all schools accountable for making progress toward proficient performance of state curriculum standards through annual testing of all students grades three through eight in reading and mathematics by the 2005–2006 school year. Beginning in the 2007–2008 school year, states must also test students in science. Students in grades 10 through 12 are to be tested once during that grade span. No Child Left Behind includes sanctions for schools whose students do not make what the law terms "adequate yearly progress" toward meeting the standards. The law also requires that teachers be "highly qualified" to teach the subjects they teach; it includes a timeline for teachers not currently considered "highly qualified" under the law to become highly qualified.

2004 IDEA is amended (P.L. 108–446) to align with NCLB. The amendments address the IEP (Individual Education Plan) process as well as the content of the plans themselves, requiring that achievement standards for children in special education programs be aligned with state standards. P.L. 108–446 adds a number of provisions that relate to the discipline of special education students and to due process for them.

2005 The fifth National Educational Summit on High Schools takes place in Washington, D.C. Hosted by the National Governors Association and Achieve, Inc., with sponsorship from the Business Roundtable, the James B. Hunt Institute, and the Education Commission of the States, this summit specifically addresses the improvement of high schools in the United States. Participants discuss strategies for making high schools more rigorous, increasing the graduation rate, and ensuring that students are prepared for college or work when they graduate from high school.

2005 Jonathan Kozol, educational researcher, chronicler, and critic, publishes *The Shame of the Nation: The Restoration of Apartheid Schooling in America*. Kozol bases his book on his observations and conversations with children and adults during visits to 60 schools in 11 states. The book decries the segregation of black and Hispanic children in schools in the United States that Kozol claims is worse than it has been since 1968, the regimentation and the prison-like system of discipline that black and Hispanic children endure in many of these segregated schools, and the effects on the curriculum and the teaching because of high-stakes, standardized testing.

2006   The Rand Corporation publishes a study, "Evaluating Comprehensive School Reform Models at Scale." The study, an investigation of how schools have implemented four comprehensive school reform models, finds that very few schools that "adopt" comprehensive school reform models actually fully implement them, and that there were few practices observed in schools implementing the models that were different from practices observed in schools not implementing comprehensive school reform models. According to the authors of the study, "it is not surprising that research to date has found only modest effects of CSR [comprehensive school reform] models on student achievement" (Vernez, Karam, Mariano, and DeMartini 2006, 135).

2007   The United States Supreme Court, in a 5–4 ruling, decides that school districts may not use race as a factor in determining how children are assigned to schools. The two cases brought together before the Court were from Seattle, Washington, and Louisville, Kentucky, where race-based assignment was part of voluntary integration plans; plaintiffs in the cases had argued that their children were not assigned to schools of their choice in the two school districts because they were white. The decision of the Supreme Court overturns rulings of lower courts that had upheld the school districts' use of race in assigning children to schools to achieve racial integration. The decision has the potential to undo voluntary integration plans in school districts around the country and to erode further the school desegregation efforts of the past half-century.

2007   NCLB, the current authorization of the Elementary and Secondary Education Act, is scheduled for reauthorization, and a plan for reauthorization is put forward by Secretary of Education Margaret Spellings. But due to disagreement in Congress and across the country about what such a reauthorization should include, no reauthorization bill is introduced in Congress. It is likely that a reauthorization will not be debated until after the new administration takes office in 2009.

2008   In his State of the Union address, President Bush describes progress in student achievement that he attributes to NCLB. In particular, he asserts that test scores in mathematics of fourth- and eighth-graders and reading scores in general have increased. He challenges the nation to continue on the path of NCLB: "Now we must work together to increase accountability, add flexibility for states and districts, reduce the number of high school dropouts, provide extra help for struggling schools" (Bush 2008).

2008   Secretary of Education Margaret Spellings proposes a number of changes in NCLB regulations that she says will strengthen NCLB. The proposed regulations address how schools report their students' achievement publicly, the interventions that schools identified as needing restructuring have available to them, the creation of a National Technical Advisory Council, and ensuring that parents are notified in a timely manner about their public school choices and options for supplementary services. Most importantly, Spellings calls for a uniform method of gathering data about graduation rates. Because states gather data in different ways, it is difficult, if not impossible to calculate a national graduation rate. When a uniform method, such as the number of students entering ninth grade who complete high school in four years, is used, it will be possible to compare across states and to aggregate data nationally.

2008   The Forum for Education and Democracy publishes "Democracy at Risk: The Need for a New Federal Policy in Education." This report, authored by a group of distinguished educators headed by Linda Darling-Hammond and George Wood, is based on the premise that the implementation of NCLB has not resulted in the world-class education it promises. "Democracy at Risk" proposes a very different education policy at the federal government level that invests in equal educational opportunity, supports the development of a world-class cadre of skilled teachers, supports educational research and innovation, and educates local communities about and engages local communities in creating schools that ensure that all children have opportunities for world-class learning. The report, based on sound educational research, provides a strategic plan for implementing such a federal education policy.

2008 In response to concerns raised by a number of states, Secretary of Education Margaret Spellings announces a pilot program that will allow states some flexibility in identifying schools for improvement, corrective action, and restructuring. According to Spellings, this "differentiated accountability" allows states to allocate more resources to schools where the problems require more intensive interventions. States must apply to be part of the pilot program of this differentiated accountability.

References

Bush, G. W. 2008. State of the Union address. http://www.whitehouse.gov/news/releases/2008/01/20080128–13.html.

Clinton, W. J. 1997. State of the Union address. http://clinton2.nara.gov/WH/SOU97.

Currence, C. 1985. "Governors Study Toughest Issues Facing Schools." *Education Week,* August 21. http://www.edweek.org/ew/articles/1985/08/21/06180029.h04.html.

National Education Goals Panel. November 1993. "Promises to Keep: Creating High Standards for American Students." Washington, DC. http://www.ed.gov/legislation/GOALS2000/TheAct/sec102.html.

Vernez, G., R. Karam, L. T. Mariano, and C. DeMartini. 2006. *Evaluating Comprehensive School Reform Models at Scale: Focus on Implementation.* Santa Monica, CA: Rand Corporation.

Vinovskis, M. A. 1998. *Overseeing the National Report Card: The Creation and Evolution of the National Assessment Governing Board.* Washington, DC: The National Assessment Governing Board.

5

Biographical Sketches

Public education in the United States is just that, public, and many people have been influential in its reform. The list of educators, scholars, policy makers, politicians, and researchers who are and have been involved in some way in improving education in the United States is long, a testament to the historical commitment to public education as a vital part of our democratic way of life. Each of the people described in this chapter have made significant contributions to education reform in the United States. They are not only researchers and scholars, but also practitioners of their research and scholarship; they have rolled up their sleeves and involved themselves in the work of school reform at the school, school district, state, and national level.

James A. Banks (1941–)

James A. Banks has worked throughout his career toward social justice in education in general, and in particular in social studies education. As a child in the segregated South, Banks experienced firsthand the effects of discrimination and an educational system that denied the realities of the lives of African Americans under segregation. He began his career as an elementary teacher, and he earned his master's and doctoral degrees at Michigan State University. He joined the faculty of the University of Washington in 1969. At the University of Washington, Banks founded the Center for Multicultural Education in 1992, and since that time, he has held the post of director of the center. Currently, he is Kerry and Linda Killinger Professor of Diversity Studies at the university.

Banks has written extensively about multicultural education, including with his wife, Cherry A. McGee Banks, *The Handbook of Research on Multicultural Education* (1997; 2004). His other books address issues of multicultural curriculum and teaching strategies, citizenship education, and creating multicultural schools and classrooms. In the United States, Banks is often called the "father of multicultural education," and in 2004, the American Educational Research Association awarded him with its first Social Justice in Education Award for his research that has advanced social justice.

Banks has been president of the American Educational Research Association and the National Council for Social Studies (NCSS). As a member and officer of NCSS, Banks edited and authored the organization's publications on multicultural education. He has presented distinguished lectures throughout the United States about multicultural education and education in a diverse society. In 2000, Banks was elected to the National Academy of Education.

David Berliner (1938–)

David Berliner, Regents Professor in Educational Leadership and Policy Studies at Arizona State University, is an educational psychologist. With his fellow educational psychologist Bruce Biddle, Berliner challenged the popular notion that schools in the United States are failing. In their book, *The Manufactured Crisis: Myths, Fraud, and the Attack on America's Public Schools* (1995), Berliner and Biddle argue that the idea that U.S. schools are failing is rhetoric intended to support the undoing of the universal, free public education that has been the cornerstone of our democratic society. They acknowledge that there are many problems facing education in the United States and around the world. However, they aver, the solutions that have been proposed, including choice and privatization, cannot adequately address the problems, and instead, may serve to dismantle our system of public education. Berliner's book *Collateral Damage: The Effects of High-Stakes Testing on America's Schools* (2007), coauthored with Sharon L. Nichols, analyzes the effects of the high-stakes testing required in No Child Left Behind as harmful to children and schools.

Berliner has been president of the American Educational Research Association, as well as the Division of Educational

Psychology of the American Psychological Association. He has received many awards and honors for his work. Among them are the Friends of Education Award from the National Education Association, the Brock International Prize for distinguished contributions to education, the E. L. Thorndike award in educational psychology, and an award for distinguished contributions from the American Educational Research Association.

Berliner earned his PhD in educational psychology at Stanford University. His career has included teaching at the University of Massachusetts, the University of Oregon, and Stanford University. He also has taught in Australia, Israel, and Spain. He continues to advocate for public education in the United States, arguing that the onus for improving student achievement in schools should be not only on schools but also on society. Berliner argues that data that link educational outcomes with such factors as income and stability show that poverty is one of the biggest factors in children's learning.

Benjamin Bloom (1913–1999)

Benjamin Bloom (1913–1999), psychologist, was one of the founders of the International Association for the Evaluation of Educational Achievement (IEA). His work with the IEA set the stage for the evaluations that enable international comparisons of student achievement. From the beginning of the international evaluations, according to Elliot Eisner (2000), Bloom cautioned that test scores cannot be interpreted or compared without considering the students' educational environments and contexts.

Taxonomy of Educational Objectives: Handbook I, The Cognitive Domain (1956) is probably the work that most people associate with Benjamin Bloom. Bloom and a group of his colleagues developed the taxonomy to classify test questions; for him, initially, the value of the taxonomy was to develop questions for examinations at the University of Chicago, where he earned his PhD in 1942 and where he was the university examiner from 1943 until 1959. (He began working as a staff member of the University of Chicago Board of Examinations in 1940.) Teachers associate Bloom's name with the categories of the taxonomy: knowledge, comprehension, application, analysis, synthesis, and evaluation. When teachers talk about higher-level thinking skills, they typically refer to the higher levels of the taxonomy that has come to be known as Bloom's Taxonomy.

Bloom's work extended to areas beyond the taxonomy. He believed, for example, that all students could learn, and his work laid the foundation for mastery learning and, later, outcome-based education, where the design of teaching requires teachers to vary the time for learning and the teaching strategies but to expect all students to be able to learn well. Bloom was instrumental in the development of the Head Start program, testifying in Congress about the importance of the first four years of a child's life in cognitive development.

Besides his work at the University of Chicago, where he earned his doctorate and spent his academic career, Bloom served as president of the American Educational Research Association. He also served as adviser to a number of governments outside the United States, including India and Israel.

Jerome Bruner (1915–)

Jerome Bruner, an American psychologist, has greatly influenced the way educators and psychologists view how people learn and think. Bruner's research investigated how humans form concepts, and he argued that learning is a process of discovery, with meanings shaped by culture and the environment. In other words, humans learn through making sense of their experiences, by categorizing the experiences rather than by memorizing knowledge. Bruner proposed a three-level hierarchy of representing learning: enactive representation (in which the learner "acts out" the learning), iconic representation (in which the learner creates images of the learning), and symbolic representation (in which the learner uses language to represent the learning). He argued that symbolic representation is mediated by one's culture, making learning a cultural product.

Bruner earned a PhD in psychology from Harvard in 1941. After serving in World War II, he taught at Harvard, beginning in 1945. From 1960 to 1972, Bruner worked at the Center for Cognitive Studies at Harvard. He left Harvard in 1972 for Wolfson College at Oxford University, where he was appointed Watts Professor of Psychology and Fellow. Returning to the United States in 1980, he worked at Harvard until 1981, when he took a position at the New School for Social Research in New York and became director of the New York Institute for the Humanities. He is currently a senior research fellow at the School of Law at New York University.

Bruner was involved in the wave of school reform that was generated by the launch of Sputnik. In 1959, he was asked to head a reform group of scientists and educators charged with developing a new science curriculum that would help to make the United States competitive. He also helped to develop a social science curriculum, "Man: A Course of Study," that generated controversy and whose funding was dropped by the federal government.

Bruner's writings include many books, papers, and journal articles. Among them are *Acts of Meaning* (1991) and *The Culture of Education* (1996), books that have been most important in influencing how educators understand learning.

James P. Comer (1934–)

James P. Comer, MD, MPH, is the Maurice Falk Professor of Child Psychiatry at the Yale University School of Medicine Child Study Center. Comer has worked to improve schools for minority children for more than 40 years. His model of school reform, the School Development Program, is based on research about and an understanding of child development and a strong home-school-community connection. Comer has served on many national commissions and boards with the purpose of improving education. Among them are the Roundtable on Child and Adolescent Development Research and Teacher Education, organized by the National Association for the Accreditation of Teacher Education (NCATE) and the National Institute of Child Health and Human Development (NICHD).

Comer has written extensively about education for black children, and, in addition to many papers and articles, he has published nine books. These include *Beyond Black and White* (1972), *School Power: Implications of an Intervention Project* (1980), and *Leave No Child Behind: Preparing Today's Youth for Tomorrow's World* (2004).

Comer's work has influenced schools across the United States. Schools in many cities have used the School Development Program model as a basis for their reform efforts, empowering parents and building strong connections among families, schools, and communities. The Comer School Development Program at the Child Study Center at Yale University continues to provide professional development and support to schools that are implementing the program.

Linda Darling-Hammond (1951–)

Linda Darling-Hammond was named one of the 10 most influential people affecting education policy over the decade 1996–2006 by the Editorial Projects in Education Research Center. She earned her doctoral degree at Temple University, and she has been involved in education reform throughout her distinguished career, championing excellence and equity in public education and working to improve teacher education and public policy. Darling-Hammond is professor of education at Stanford University and co-executive director of the School Redesign Network and the Stanford Educational Leadership Institute. She is also one of the founders and conveners of the Forum for Education and Democracy.

Darling-Hammond was professor of education foundations at Teachers College, Columbia University before moving to Stanford. Her work in school reform at Teachers College included serving the National Center for Restructuring Education, Schools, and Teaching (NCREST) as codirector. Other school reform posts Darling-Hammond has held include senior social scientist and director of the Education and Human Resources Program at the RAND Corporation and director of the Excellence in Education Program of the National Urban Coalition.

Working to improve teacher preparation and teaching standards, Darling-Hammond has served as a member of the National Board for Professional Teaching Standards and as chair of the Model Standards Committee of the Interstate New Teacher Assessment and Support Consortium, a committee that developed licensing standards for new teachers. She is a member of the National Academy of Education, and she has served on many national advisory boards and panels. She is currently serving as a director of the National Commission on Teaching and America's Future.

Darling-Hammond's research focuses on education reform, and she has published many books, research reports, and journal articles. Darling-Hammond's vision for reforming schools can be found in her book *The Right to Learn: A Blueprint for Creating Schools that Work* (1997). Her current work focuses on teacher quality and the development and improvement of teacher education and preparation. Two of her books—*Preparing Teachers for a Changing World: What Teachers Should Learn and Be Able to Do* (2005) with John Bransford, Pamela LePage, Karen Hammerness, and Helen

Duffy, and *Powerful Learning: What We Know about Teaching for Understanding* (2008) with Brigid Barron, P. David Pearson, and Alan H. Schoenfeld—focus on what effective teachers do that results in high levels of learning and how teacher preparation programs can develop those effective teaching practices.

Lisa Delpit (1952–)

Lisa Delpit is the Knight Eminent Scholar and the director of the Center for Urban Education and Innovation at Florida International University. Delpit has devoted her career to understanding and helping teachers and prospective teachers to understand the importance of valuing and honoring children's culture in determining how and what to teach. She began her career as an urban elementary teacher, and during that time, Delpit began to question the effectiveness of the teaching methods she had learned in her teacher preparation program for urban children of color.

Delpit has conducted research on teaching in Alaska, New Guinea, Fiji, and urban and rural areas in the United States. She has written and spoken about how to teach children of color and particularly African American children. Delpit was awarded a MacArthur "genius" fellowship in 1990 for her work on school-community relations and cross-cultural communication. Her first book, *Other People's Children: Cultural Conflict in the Classroom* (1995), shows how teachers fail to understand that children come to school with cultural strengths that must be acknowledged, and that by valuing and honoring these cultural strengths, teachers can be more effective. Understanding the culture that children bring with them into the classroom is key to being able to communicate with and teach them. In the book, Delpit is critical of such teaching methods as whole language and process writing for African American children; instead, she believes, children should be taught specific skills and strategies for navigating the dominant society.

Formerly the Benjamin E. Mays Chair of Urban Educational Excellence at Georgia State University in Atlanta, Delpit was also director of the Center for Urban Educational Excellence at Georgia State. The work of the center focused on education and race. Delpit is the coeditor of two books that focus on issues of language and race in education. She coedited *The Real Ebonics Debate: Power,*

Language and the Education of African-American Children (1998) with Theresa Perry. This book deals with the issues surrounding the debate sparked by the Oakland, California, school board when it applied for funds to teach standard English as a second language for children whose first language was Ebonics. The essays in *The Skin That We Speak: Thoughts on Language and Culture in the Classroom* (2002), coedited with Joanne Kilgour Dowdy, explore the use of dialects in the classroom.

Delpit has received many accolades and awards, among them awards from her two alma maters. In 1993, the Harvard University Graduate School of Education, where Delpit earned both her master's and doctoral degrees, honored her with their Alumni Award for Outstanding Contribution to Education. Delpit earned her undergraduate degree at Antioch College, where she was given the Horace Mann Award for winning "some victory for humanity" in 2003.

Chester Finn (1944–)

Chester Finn recently published his autobiography, *Troublemaker: A Personal History of School Reform Since Sputnik* (2008), the account of his career-long involvement with school reform and improvement in the United States. His work, his voice, and his writing have focused on raising educational standards, offering high-quality choices for parents of school children, and improving the quality of public school teachers. Currently, he is the president of the Thomas B. Fordham Foundation, a senior fellow and chair of the Koret Task Force on K-12 Education at the Hoover Institution, an adjunct fellow at the Hudson Institute, and a Fellow of the International Academy of Education.

Finn earned his doctorate at Harvard University. He was a professor of education and public policy at Vanderbilt University from 1981 to 2002. He served as assistant secretary for research and improvement and counselor to the U.S. secretary of education from 1985 to 1988. In addition, he has held positions at a number of foundations and several advisory positions in government, among them staff assistant to the president of the United States, counsel to the U.S. ambassador to India, and legislative director for Senator Daniel Patrick Moynihan. From 1992 to 1994, Finn was one of the founding partners and a senior scholar of the Edison Project, which organizes and manages schools, including charter schools and schools operated under contract with school districts.

Paolo Freire (1921–1997)

Paolo Freire (1921–1997), Brazilian educator and educational philosopher, believed that people could be empowered through education. As director of the Department of Education and Culture of the Social Service of his state in Brazil (from 1946) and later as director of the Department of Cultural Extension of Recife University (1961–1963), Freire's work focused on teaching literacy to the poor.

At that time in Brazil, people had to be literate to be allowed to vote, and Freire's work was seen as upsetting the social order. After a coup d'état imposed military rule, Freire was imprisoned and eventually exiled from Brazil for nearly 16 years, which he spent in Chile, the United States (where he was invited to Harvard as a visiting professor), and Geneva, Switzerland. In Geneva, Freire worked for the World Council of Churches, promoting literacy in Third World countries. Freire returned to Brazil in 1980 and served as professor at the Catholic University of São Paulo and the State University of Campinas, and in 1988 he became municipal secretary of education in São Paolo, a position he held for two years. In 1990, he went back to full-time teaching and writing.

Among Paolo Freire's many publications are the books *Pedagogy of the Oppressed* (1970), *Pedagogy of Freedom: Ethics, Democracy, and Civic Courage* (1998), and *Teachers as Cultural Workers: Letters to those Who Dare Teach* (1998). All of these books challenge educators to learn with and from their students, to help students connect the curriculum with their lives and worlds outside their classrooms, and to model democracy in their classrooms.

Michael Fullan (1940–)

Michael Fullan is professor emeritus and former dean of the Ontario Institute for Studies in Education. His book *The New Meaning of Educational Change*, is in its fourth edition and is considered a classic text in education reform. Fullan believes that education reform is not about mandates and policy; instead, he argues that real change that has the potential to last is about building relationships and changing the culture of the school. This reculturing requires skills and habits of mind that include collaboration, reflective practice, and informed decision making.

Fullan believes that reform is systemic, and he has worked with schools and communities, school districts, and governments around the world to facilitate education reform. He has worked on large-scale reform efforts in Ontario, Canada; England; Wales; Australia; and the Netherlands, as well as in the United States. These reform efforts have all been focused on the improvement of learning for all students. He has been particularly interested in helping schools and school personnel form a deep commitment to closing the achievement gap and develop the knowledge and the skills to realize that commitment.

Fullan's many publications include *Breakthrough* (2006) with Peter Hill and Carmel Crévola, *Turnaround Leadership* (2006), *The Six Secrets of Change: What the Best Leaders Do to Help Their Organizations Survive and Thrive* (2008), and a second edition of *What's Worth Fighting for in the Principalship* (2008). All of Fullan's books are based on his work with schools and organizations around the world; they are both theoretical and practical, and they represent Fullan's stance as both consultant and learner.

Since his retirement, Fullan has served as special adviser in education to the premier of Canada and the Canadian minister of education. He has developed a course, Learning to Lead Change, through Microsoft's Partners in Learning global initiative to build and support effective school leadership in countries in Latin America, Asia, and Europe.

Mary Hatwood Futrell (1940–)

Mary Hatwood Futrell is dean of the Graduate School of Education and Human Development at George Washington University in Washington, D.C. In 1983, when Futrell was elected president of the National Education Association, *People* magazine called her "one of the most powerful black women in America." Prior to that election, she worked as a teacher and officer of the Virginia Education Association, an affiliate of the National Education Association. Futrell has dedicated her career to advocating for teachers, for improving their working conditions, and for raising public awareness of the difficulties of their work, and at the same time, helping to improve the quality of teacher preparation.

Futrell led the National Education Association in its response to "A Nation at Risk," when many blamed teachers for what the report described as the "rising tide of mediocrity" in the public schools in the United States. She defended teachers, arguing that teachers were not responsible for the economic and social problems that made teaching so difficult. When President Ronald Reagan tried to abolish the U.S. Department of Education, Futrell fought hard to maintain it as part of the president's cabinet.

Futrell was reelected twice to the presidency of the National Education Association. A strong advocate for teachers, Futrell was invited to join the Carnegie Forum on Education and the Economy. The Forum issued a report in 1986 that called for higher teacher salaries; it also recommended significant changes to teacher certification in the United States. As president of the National Education Association, Futrell also was instrumental in joining with the American Federation of Teachers, the second-largest teachers' union in the United States, to form the National Board for Professional Teaching Standards, the organization that now awards national teaching certification to master teachers.

In 1989, Futrell stepped down from the presidency of the National Education Association to become associate director of the Center for the Study of Education and National Development at George Washington University until 1992, and then director of the Center for Curriculum Studies and Technology, a post that she held until accepting the position of dean in 1995. In this position, she has continued to advocate for teachers even as she has helped to redesign the teacher preparation curriculum at George Washington University. That teacher preparation curriculum has become a model for other colleges and universities.

Howard Gardner (1943–)

Howard Gardner is a Harvard psychologist and educator whose theory of multiple intelligences challenges traditional theories of how intelligence is defined, evaluated, and supported. Gardner's notion of multiple intelligences differs from the traditional theory in that it proposes that intelligence is developed rather than inherited, and that there are many different ways of being intelligent. Instead of asking how smart someone is, the question for those espousing Gardner's theory is how someone is smart.

Gardner worked with Jerome Bruner on his "Man: A Course of Study" project and began his work with Project Zero at Harvard even before he completed his doctorate there. He has worked with Project Zero since that time, now serving as codirector. His work at Project Zero allowed him to study how people learn, which led him to the theory of multiple intelligences. Gardner originally identified seven intelligences and later, three more. The original seven intelligences include linguistic, logical-mathematical, spatial, bodily-kinesthetic, musical, interpersonal, intrapersonal. The additional three are naturalistic, existential, and moral intelligences.

Not only does Gardner's theory challenge definitions of intelligence, it also challenges teaching strategies. According to Gardner, if there are multiple intelligences, then there must be multiple corresponding ways to teach. His publications explore his theory in depth, as well as document how the theory has developed. *Frames of Mind: The Theory of Multiple Intelligences* (1983; 1993), *The Unschooled Mind: How Children Think and How Schools Should Teach* (1991), *Intelligence Reframed: Multiple Intelligences for the 21st Century* (1999), and *The Disciplined Mind: Beyond Facts and Standardized Tests* (1999) progress from Gardner's initial theory of seven intelligences to the identification of the eighth intelligence and the proposal for the ninth, and how the theory can be applied in schools so that children have opportunities to develop the whole range of intelligences.

A number of schools across the United States have used multiple intelligence theory to guide their curriculums and their teaching. The Key School in Indianapolis is one that uses multiple intelligence theory as the basis of all of their work with children.

John Goodlad (1920–)

John Goodlad is professor emeritus of education at the University of Washington and president of the Center for Educational Renewal, which he founded at the University of Washington in 1985 with Kenneth Sirotnik and Roger Soder. Goodlad's and the center's work has focused on teaching and learning in a democracy, the moral and political issues involved in teaching and learning, and the quality of and important role of teachers in schools and school renewal. Goodlad is considered one of the most influential educators and educational theorists of the last half of the 20th century.

Goodlad was born in Canada, and he taught in a one-room rural school there before coming to the United States and earning his doctoral degree at the University of Chicago. His 1984 book, *A Place Called School*, is considered a landmark study of education and schools in the United States. Since that time, Goodlad has conducted numerous studies on educational change and published many other books and articles about U.S. schooling. He held university posts in teacher education at a number of colleges and universities, among them Emory University, Agnes Scott College, and the University of California, Los Angeles (UCLA).

At UCLA, Goodlad was the director of the Laboratory School and dean of the Graduate School of Education. One of the factors that distinguished Goodlad's work is the strong connection between theory and practice that it represents, and Goodlad's appointment at UCLA represented his commitment to grounding theory in practice and also provided him with the laboratory needed to build that connection.

Ken Goodman (1927–)

Ken Goodman is an educational researcher whose work forms the basis of the psycholinguistic and sociolinguistic theory of reading called whole language. For Goodman and other proponents of whole language, reading is a process of "actively but tentatively constructing meaning, making predictions and inferences that were used in sampling the text to get meaning" that parallels the development of language (Goodman 2000). Goodman's theory and his work are controversial, and they have fueled a continuing debate about the nature of reading and language and about how teachers should teach reading.

Goodman earned his doctorate at UCLA as the first doctoral student of John Goodlad. He began his research on the reading process as an assistant professor at Wayne State University in Detroit, and his first book, *The Psycholinguistic Nature of the Reading Process* (1968), was the result of a conference by the same name that brought together a group of researchers to discuss using linguistics in the research of reading. From his continuing research, Goodman developed the notion that readers' mistakes, or as he calls them, "miscues," give insight into the strategies that readers use to make sense of the text. Yetta Goodman, Ken's wife and a researcher in her own right, developed the Reading Miscue

Inventory with Carolyn Burke and Dorothy Watson, based on the notion that analysis of learners' miscues can provide insight to teachers about what parts of the reading process the learners are controlling and what they are ready to learn.

Goodman's research led him to develop an increasingly sophisticated theory of reading as a linguistic process, and although his work has been controversial in the United States, it has been accepted in other places around the world, including Canada, Australia, New Zealand, and England. His book, *What's Whole in Whole Language* (1986), was published first in Canada. It has been translated into French, Spanish, Portuguese, Japanese, and Chinese. In 1993, as a response to a push in the United States to teach phonics, Goodman published his book *Phonics Phacts* about the relationship between sound systems and written language, based on his observation of miscues over years of research.

Goodman has been active professionally in the National Council of Teachers of English, and he has served as president of the International Reading Association, the National Conference on Research in Language and Literacy, and the Center for the Expansion of Language and Thinking. His articles have been published in many professional journals, and he has presented at literally hundreds of professional conferences and meetings. Goodman retired in 1998 from the University of Arizona, but he continues to write and speak about and work toward "freedom to learn, freedom to teach, and social justice" (Goodman 2000).

E. D. Hirsch, Jr. (1928–)

E. D. Hirsch, Jr., PhD, Yale University, is an educator retired from his position as professor of education and humanities and the Linden Kent Memorial Professor of English Emeritus at the University of Virginia. In the education arena, Hirsch is best known for promoting cultural literacy as the basis for curriculum and teaching.

Hirsch's own research led him to discover that students' background knowledge or lack of it affects how they understand what they read, and he founded the Core Knowledge Foundation in 1986 to promote the idea of cultural literacy as the basis of reading. The Core Knowledge Foundation has developed a school reform movement around a curriculum that identifies "core knowledge" to be learned at each grade level, pre-kindergarten through grade eight. According to the Core Knowledge Foundation, core knowledge is "solid"; that is, it is knowledge that doesn't change, like essential concepts in mathematics or "stories passed down from generation to generation." Core knowledge is sequenced, building carefully from one grade to the next. Core knowledge is specific, defining explicitly what children should learn at each grade level. And core knowledge is shared—it is the knowledge that is generally assumed in our culture. Hirsch himself published a series of books about what a child should know at each grade level.

Hirsch's ideas are controversial, but the Core Knowledge Foundation Web site includes a link to publications that report on the success of "core knowledge" in improving student learning and closing the achievement gap. In 2006, Hirsch published his book *The Knowledge Deficit*, again promoting the idea that background knowledge is critical to reading comprehension.

Madeline Cheek Hunter (1916–1994)

Madeline Cheek Hunter (1916–1994) was a teacher, school psychologist, school administrator, and UCLA lecturer. Her work focused on translating educational research and theory into teaching practice. Hunter viewed teaching as a process of making decisions, and she categorized those decisions in three ways—what should be taught (content), how it should be taught (instruction), and what students should know and be able to do (learning).

Hunter developed several models of instruction. Her lesson design for teaching knowledge and skills was adopted by 16 states and used in many more as the official model of lesson planning. It was also often used to evaluate teaching. Sadly, that model was used out of context; some states and school districts required that every lesson plan match each of the steps in that model, ignoring the fact that Hunter proposed and promoted more than one model of teaching. The instructional component of mastery learning, one of the pillars of outcome-based education, was based on Madeline Hunter's models of teaching.

Among Hunter's many publications was a series of books that translated "psychological principles into the language of the classroom." Some of the books in the series were *Reinforcement Theory for Teachers* (1967), *Motivation Theory for Teachers* (1969), *Teach More—Faster* (1969), *Teach for Transfer* (1971), and *Mastery Teaching* (1982).

Jonathan Kozol (1936–)

Jonathan Kozol is an activist for social justice in public schools. He has devoted his life to bringing to the public eye the plight of poor and minority children and their families in the United States. He has fought against the inequality that he identified early on, and he continues to fight, most recently even going on a fast to protest the effects of No Child Left Behind.

Kozol began his career in education as a fourth grade teacher in an inner city school in the Boston Public Schools; during his first year at the school, he was fired for teaching Langston Hughes's poetry to his students. His first book, *Death at an Early Age: The Destruction of the Hearts and Minds of Negro Children in the Boston Public Schools* (1967), documents that year of teaching, and it won a National Book Award. Kozol's experience teaching in the inner city led him to the civil rights movement. He taught several more years in Newton, Massachusetts, before devoting his life full time to social activism and writing.

Kozol's book *Savage Inequalities: Children in America's Schools* (1991) analyzed and described the huge disparities he observed between schools that serve poor, minority children and schools that serve children from more affluent families. *Amazing Grace: The Lives of Children and the Conscience of a Nation* (1995) takes a closer look at how the disparities in society and in education affect children. Based on his observations of and interactions with children in the South Bronx in New York City, the book tells about the lives of real children living in poverty and attending schools that serve poor and minority children. Kozol's books *Ordinary Resurrections: Children in the Years of Hope* (1992) and *The Shame of the Nation: The Restoration of Apartheid Schooling in America* (2005) describe the resegregation of schools in the United States.

Gloria Ladson-Billings (1947–)

Gloria Ladson-Billings, PhD, Stanford University, is the Kellner Family Professor of Urban Education in the Department of Curriculum and Instruction at the University of Wisconsin–Madison. Ladson-Billings's work has focused on developing and promoting culturally relevant classrooms and schools as a way to ensure high-quality learning for minority children. Her critique of public education in the United States is based on her social justice perspective, and she calls for educational systems to address the societal, historical, moral, political, and ethical issues that have served to hinder the academic success of minority children.

Ladson-Billings has carried her social justice perspective into her writing. Her book *The Dreamkeepers: Successful Teachers of African American Children* (1997) describes how these teachers interact with African American children, how they teach, and how they communicate expectations for the children to be successful. In *Beyond the Big House: African American Educators on Teacher Education* (2005), Ladson-Billings describes the experiences of African American teacher educators as they work to foreground race and racial issues in teacher education and to prepare new teachers to create classrooms that are racially and culturally relevant. (Culturally relevant classrooms are those where children's cultural knowledge and background are included in the curriculum, where teachers actively communicate that the children's backgrounds and knowledge are valued, and where multicultural literature provides a variety of perspectives. All of this is so that children see themselves in the curriculum and work of the classroom.) Ladson-Billings has also worked to change the face of educational research. She has developed critical race theory into a research perspective and methodology, and she has conducted studies of schools, teachers, and classrooms from that perspective.

Ladson-Billings is a past president of the American Educational Research Association, and she has won several awards for her work. Among them are an honorary doctorate from Umea University in Sweden, the Palmer O. Johnson Outstanding Research Award, and the George and Louise Spindler Award for her work in educational anthropology.

Deborah Meier (1931–)

Deborah Meier, MA, University of Chicago, knows and understands education reform firsthand. She has not only taught in public schools, but she has also founded and directed both elementary and high schools that were innovative and extraordinarily successful. She began her career as a kindergarten and Head Start classroom teacher in the urban schools of Chicago, Philadelphia, and New York. After founding a network of successful elementary schools in East Harlem, she founded Central

Park East Secondary School, a New York public high school, where more than 90 percent of the entering students went on to graduate and attend college. Later, Meier founded the Mission Hill School in the Roxbury community in the Boston Public Schools.

The schools Meier founded were "coalition" schools, member schools of the Coalition for Essential Schools, and she founded a local center for the Coalition for Essential Schools while she was working at Central Park East Secondary School. From 1992 to 1996, Deborah Meier served as the director of the Coalition Campus Project, which successfully redesigned two formerly failing New York City high schools; the project also started a number of new Coalition schools. And from 1995 to 1997, Meier worked as an adviser to the Annenberg Challenge in New York City, as well as senior fellow at the Annenberg Institute for School Reform at Brown University.

Meier documented her work in her book *The Power of Their Ideas: Lessons to America from a Small School in Harlem* (1995). She has also written several other books and numerous journal articles about education reform. Currently, Meier is a faculty member at New York University; she is the director and adviser to the Forum for Democracy and Education, and she serves on the board of the Coalition for Essential Schools.

Sonia Nieto (1943–)

Sonia Nieto is professor emerita of language, literacy, and culture in the School of Education at the University of Massachusetts, Amherst, where she earned her PhD. During Nieto's career she has taught at every level, from elementary through graduate school, and she has worked toward helping teachers understand how to create multicultural classrooms that affirm and celebrate the diversity of the students in them.

Nieto's work, focusing on improving the education of Latinos and other linguistically diverse students, has informed her teaching and writing. Her text, *Affirming Diversity: The Sociopolitical Context of Multicultural Education* with co-author Patty Bode (fifth edition, 2008), is considered a seminal text in the field of multicultural education and is used in teacher preparation programs and teacher professional development programs across the United States and in other countries. Nieto has written and edited several other books as well as chapters in other books and articles in professional journals, all focused on equity and social justice.

An activist for equity and social justice in education, Nieto's advocacy has been recognized at the local, state, and national level. She has served on boards and panels whose work mirrors her own, including the Center for Applied Linguistics, Facing Ourselves and History, and Educators for Social Responsibility. Nieto has won many awards for her advocacy and her scholarship, including the Human and Civil Rights Award from the Massachusetts Teachers Association, the Multicultural Educator of the Year Award from the National Association for Multicultural Education, and the Criticas Journal Hall of Fame Spanish Language Community Advocate of the Year Award. She has won numerous awards from the American Educational Research Association, including the 2008 Social Justice in Education Award.

Although Nieto is retired from the University of Massachusetts, she continues to write, to speak, and to advocate for social justice and equity and for the development of classrooms that honor and value the cultural, ethnic, and linguistic backgrounds of all of the children in them.

Nel Noddings (1929–)

Nel Noddings is a feminist educator and philosopher; she has also worked in the area of mathematics education. Her contributions to the education reform conversation have been many, but she is best known for her work about the ethics of care. Noddings earned her PhD in education at Stanford University. Prior to Noddings's retirement, she held academic positions at Stanford University, Columbia University, and Colgate University. Since her retirement in 1998, she has been the Lee L. Jacks Professor of Education, Emerita, at Stanford University.

Noddings applied her ideas of caring to education in a number of journal articles and books on the topic. Among her many publications, the books *The Challenge to Care in Schools: An Alternative Approach to Education* (1992), *Educating Moral People* (2002), and *Happiness and Education* (2003) challenge educators to create nurturing schools where children are cared about and cared for, so that they learn to care for and about others. In 2007, Noddings published *When School Reform Goes Wrong*, a critique of No Child

Left Behind that calls for society and schools to address children's physical and social needs, as well as nurturing and caring for children, as prerequisites for learning.

Rod Paige (1933–)

Rod Paige was confirmed as the seventh United States Secretary of Education in 2001. As secretary of education for four years, Paige worked first to pass No Child Left Behind and then was responsible for partnering with states, school districts, and schools to implement the reforms the No Child Left Behind legislation called for.

Paige came to the office of U.S. secretary of education as the first school superintendent to be appointed to that position. Before his appointment, Paige was superintendent of the Houston (Texas) Independent School District (ISD), where he had overseen reforms that included incentive pay for teachers and increased accountability. His tenure in the Houston Independent School District also included the development of a system of charter schools and "the Houston miracle"—claims of vastly improved student achievement and increased high school graduation, claims which have been challenged by subsequent research and analysis of the Houston data.

Paige brought with him to the superintendency of the Houston ISD and the U.S. Department of Education experience as a college teacher and coach. He served as dean of the College of Education at Texas Southern University for 10 years, and in that position, he established the Center for Excellence in Urban Education at Texas Southern. From 1989 to 1994, Paige served as a trustee of the Houston Independent School District Board of Education before becoming superintendent in 1994.

Paige grew up in segregated Mississippi with parents who were both educators. He earned his undergraduate degree from Jackson State University and master's and doctoral degrees from Indiana University. He has won several awards for his service, including the Richard R. Green Award as outstanding urban educator from the Council of Great City Schools, the National Alliance of Black School Educators' Superintendent of the Year award, and the National Superintendent of the Year award by the American Association of School Administrators. Currently Paige is the chairman of Chartwell Education Group.

Diane Ravitch (1938–)

Diane Ravitch led the U.S. Department of Education's effort to develop national and state curriculum standards when she served as assistant secretary of education for educational research and improvement and counselor to Secretary of Education Lamar Alexander from 1991 to 1993.

Ravitch, who earned a PhD from Columbia University, is currently a research professor at Steinhardt School of Education at New York University. She is a historian of education, a policy analyst, and a senior fellow at the Brookings Institution and the Hoover Institution, where she also serves as a member of the Koret Task Force on K-12 Education.

Ravitch has held several positions that involved her directly in education reform or that provided her the opportunity to critique education reform efforts. She was appointed by then secretary of education Richard Riley to the National Assessment Governing Board, a post she held from 1997 to 2004. She edited Brookings Papers on Education and held the Brown Chair in Education Studies at the Brookings Institution from 1995 to 2005.

She has received many awards for her work throughout her career, among them the John Dewey Award from the New York City United Federation of Teachers in 2005, the Gaudium Award from the Breukelein Institute in 2005, and the Leadership Award of the New York City Council of Supervisors and Administrators in 2004. Her many publications include *Left Back: A Century of Battles Over School Reform* (2000) and *The Language Police: How Pressure Groups Restrict What Students Learn* (2003).

Lauren B. Resnick (1936–)

Lauren B. Resnick has been a leader of the standards movement since its beginning in the United States. Resnick's research in the cognitive science of learning and teaching has informed her work with teachers, schools, and school districts; her work with panels and boards on the national level; and her work in the development of the Institute for Learning, which she directs at the University of Pittsburgh. Professor of psychology at the University of Pittsburgh with a doctoral degree from Harvard University, Resnick also directs the Learning Research and Development Center there.

Resnick was cofounder and codirector with Marc Tucker of the New Standards Project, whose work is described in more detail in earlier chapters. The New Standards Project involved educators across the country in the development of standards and assessments; that work continues to influence the education reform of states, school districts, and schools. She also served as adviser to the first chair of the National Goals Panel, and she was a member of the National Council on Education Standards and Testing; her work with the panel and the council helped to initiate the standards movement in the United States. As part of the standards movement, Resnick also served on the national Commission on the Skills of the American Workforce, as chair of the assessment committee of the SCANS Commission, as chair of the Resource Group on Student Achievement of the National Education Goals Panel, on the Commission on Behavioral and Social Sciences and Education, and on the Mathematical Sciences Education Board of the National Research Council.

Based on her research and that of many others, Resnick and her colleagues at the University of Pittsburgh developed a set of nine Principles of Learning, principles that describe the kinds of school and classroom conditions, teacher behaviors and attitudes, and student behaviors that lead to high levels of learning for all students. Resnick and her colleagues have used the Principles of Learning in their support of and work with urban school districts across the country in the process of reform. The Principles of Learning are (1) organizing for effort; (2) clear expectations; (3) fair and credible evaluations; (4) recognition of accomplishment; (5) academic rigor in a thinking curriculum; (6) accountable talk; (7) socializing intelligence; (8) self-management of learning; and (9) learning as apprentice (Principles of Learning 2007).

Resnick is the editor of "Research Points," a policy brief published by the American Educational Research Association that connects research with policy, and she has had numerous publications about the learning and thinking processes. Resnick's work has been recognized in the United States by the American Psychological Association's E. L. Thorndike Award and in Europe with the Oeuvre Award of the European Association for Research on Learning and Instruction.

Theodore Sizer (1932–)

Theodore Sizer has been a leader in the reform of schools in the United States throughout his career. Retired in 1996 from Brown University, where he was a professor of education, Sizer's career included several teaching positions in addition to his position at Brown. Among them are dean of the Harvard Graduate School of Education (where he had earlier earned a PhD), headmaster of Philips Academy in Andover, Massachusetts, and coprincipal with his wife, Nancy Sizer, of the Frances W. Parker Charter Essential School, a school that serves students in grades 7 through 12 in Devens, Massachusetts.

Sizer's area of research and the focus of his school reform efforts has been the design of American education, and in particular, the American high school. Based on his work with high schools since the late 1970s and a large-scale study of the American high school that he conducted with several other researchers, Sizer published three books that focused on the state of the American high school and the possibilities that he sees for redesigning the high school. His book *Horace's Compromise: The Dilemma of the American High School* (1984) described the state of the high school, while two of his later books, *Horace's School: Redesigning the American High School* (1992) and *Horace's Hope: What Works for the American High School* (1997), describe how the high school can be redesigned to improve student engagement, achievement, and ultimately, high school completion.

Sizer founded the Coalition of Essential Schools at Brown University in 1984 around a set of 10 common principles critical to a high performing school. Initially, 11 schools were part of the coalition; today it has grown to include hundreds of schools and several affiliate centers around the country. Sizer was also the founding director of the Annenberg Institute for School Reform, begun in 1993.

Mark Tucker (?–)

Marc Tucker has been a major force in the development of the standards movement in education in the United States. He created the National Center on Education and the Economy (NCEE) in 1988, and he is currently its president and CEO. The mission of

NCEE from its inception has been to develop and adopt world-class standards for education in the United States so that students would leave school with the skills and knowledge to compete in a global economy.

Tucker initiated the Commission on the Skills of the American Workforce in 1989, and he was the author of *America's Choice: High Skills or Low Wages*, released in 1990, that was based on research in Europe and Asia conducted by the commission. This report, according to the NCEE, "made the case for standards-driven reform in American Education" and influenced the Goals 2000 legislation, the National Skills Standards Act, the School to Work Act, and the Workforce Investment Act, as well as school reform legislation in a number of states (NCEE 2005). President Bill Clinton appointed Tucker to the National Skills Standards Board, and Tucker collaborated with Lauren Resnick to design and chair the New Standards Project. Tucker is also one of the creators of America's Choice, a comprehensive school reform model that is aimed at helping school districts implement standards-based reform.

Tucker was a professor of education in the graduate school at the University of Rochester and a senior staff member at Carnegie Corporation, where he wrote the report "A Nation Prepared: Teacher for the 21st Century," which proposed the creation of the National Board for Professional Teaching Standards. Tucker served as the first president of that board.

Grant Wiggins (1950–)

Grant Wiggins is a leader in educational reform, particularly in the areas of curriculum change and authentic assessment. He is the president of Grant Wiggins & Associates and Authentic Education, a New Jersey-based firm that provides consulting, professional development, workshops, and training throughout the United States on the redesign of education. Wiggins earned his doctoral degree in education at Harvard University.

Wiggins works with schools, school districts, and state education agencies on school reform, and he has worked with some of the biggest and most important assessment projects in the country. He was a teacher of English and philosophy at a boarding school for a number of years. According to Wiggins, living, working, and eating with his students, he came to know each student as talented and having individual interests. His work with teachers, schools, and school districts is grounded in that practical experience.

Wiggins was involved in the development of the Vermont portfolio system, the first large-scale portfolio assessment to be used statewide. He has established statewide consortia for assessment reform in the states of New Jersey and North Carolina, and he helped to design performance-based portfolio assessment systems in those states. He has worked with Ted Sizer and the Coalition for Essential Schools as the first director of research for the Coalition.

Understanding by Design and its accompanying *The Understanding by Design Handbook*, both of which Wiggins coauthored with Jay McTighe, are two of his best-known publications. Both of these books describe and lead readers through the process of backward design of curriculum that begins with determining learning goals and then developing learning activities and assessments that align with the goals. Wiggins promotes the design of assessments that are "educative," part of the learning process rather than separate from it, as well as key elements of an authentic curriculum. Wiggins has also published *Educative Assessment* and *Assessing Student Performance*, as well as many journal articles about curriculum and assessment design.

In addition to his work with K-12 education, Wiggins has worked with colleges and universities on educational design, and he was appointed scholar in residence at the College of New Jersey. Wiggins's work has been supported by the Pew Charitable Trust, the Geraldine R. Dodge Foundation, the National Science Foundation, and the Education Commission of the States.

References

Eisner, E. W. 2000. "Benjamin Bloom." *Prospects: The Quarterly Review of Comparative Education* 30 (30). Paris: UNESCO.

Goodman, K. S. 2000. "Ken Goodman on his Life in Reading." *History of Reading News* 23 (2). http://www.historyliteracy.org/scripts/search_display.php?Article_ID=173.

National Center on Education and the Economy. 2005. "Marc Tucker." http://www.ncee.org/ncee/leadership/marc_tucker.jsp?setProtocol=true.

Principles of Learning. 2007. Pittsburgh, PA: Learning Research and Development Center, University of Pittsburgh. http://ifl.lrdc.pitt.edu/ifl/index.php?section=pol.

6

Data and Documents

This chapter includes a set of primary documents pertinent to education reform and its direction in the United States, as well as some sets of data about students' academic achievement in the United States. These documents demonstrate reform efforts aimed at both achieving equity in education and improving the quality of education in our nation's public schools.

Brown v. Board of Education

The Supreme Court case, Brown v. Board of Education, *347 U.S. 483 (1954), barred states and school districts from segregating schools by race. This landmark case began the push for equity in public education at the national level in the United States. The text of the decision follows.*

SUPREME COURT OF THE UNITED STATES
Brown v. Board of Education, 347 U.S. 483 (1954) (USSC+)
347 U.S. 483
Argued December 9, 1952
Reargued December 8, 1953
Decided May 17, 1954
APPEAL FROM THE UNITED STATES DISTRICT COURT FOR THE DISTRICT OF KANSAS*
Syllabus
Segregation of white and Negro children in the public schools of a State solely on the basis of race, pursuant to state laws permitting or requiring such segregation, denies to Negro children the equal protection of the laws guaranteed by the Fourteenth Amendment—even

though the physical facilities and other "tangible" factors of white and Negro schools may be equal.

(a) The history of the Fourteenth Amendment is inconclusive as to its intended effect on public education.

(b) The question presented in these cases must be determined not on the basis of conditions existing when the Fourteenth Amendment was adopted, but in the light of the full development of public education and its present place in American life throughout the Nation.

(c) Where a State has undertaken to provide an opportunity for an education in its public schools, such an opportunity is a right which must be made available to all on equal terms.

(d) Segregation of children in public schools solely on the basis of race deprives children of the minority group of equal educational opportunities, even though the physical facilities and other "tangible" factors may be equal.

(e) The "separate but equal" doctrine adopted in **Plessy v. Ferguson, 163 U.S. 537**, has no place in the field of public education.

(f) The cases are restored to the docket for further argument on specified questions relating to the forms of the decrees.

Opinion
WARREN
MR. CHIEF JUSTICE WARREN delivered the opinion of the Court.

These cases come to us from the States of Kansas, South Carolina, Virginia, and Delaware. They are premised on different facts and different local conditions, but a common legal question justifies their consideration together in this consolidated opinion.

In each of the cases, minors of the Negro race, through their legal representatives, seek the aid of the courts in obtaining admission to the public schools of their community on a nonsegregated basis. In each instance, they had been denied admission to schools attended by white children under laws requiring or permitting segregation according to race. This segregation was alleged to deprive the plaintiffs of the equal protection of the laws under the Fourteenth Amendment. In each of the cases other than the Delaware case, a three-judge federal district court denied relief to the plaintiffs on the so-called "separate but equal" doctrine announced by this Court in **Plessy v. Fergson, 163 U.S. 537**. Under that doctrine, equality of treatment is accorded when the races are provided substantially equal facilities, even though these facilities be separate. In the Delaware case, the Supreme Court of Delaware adhered to that doctrine, but ordered that the plaintiffs be admitted to the white schools because of their superiority to the Negro schools.

The plaintiffs contend that segregated public schools are not "equal" and cannot be made "equal," and that hence they are deprived of the equal protection of the laws. Because of the obvious importance of the question presented, the Court took jurisdiction. Argument was heard in the 1952 Term, and reargument was heard this Term on certain questions propounded by the Court.

Reargument was largely devoted to the circumstances surrounding the adoption of the Fourteenth Amendment in 1868. It covered exhaustive consideration of the Amendment in Congress, ratification by the states, then-existing practices in racial segregation, and the views of proponents and opponents of the Amendment. This discussion and our own investigation convince us that, although these sources cast some light, it is not enough to resolve the problem with which we are faced. At best, they are inconclusive. The most avid proponents of the post-War Amendments undoubtedly intended them to remove all legal distinctions among "all persons born or naturalized in the United States." Their opponents, just as certainly, were antagonistic to both the letter and the spirit of the Amendments and wished them to have the most limited effect. What others in Congress and the state legislatures had in mind cannot be determined with any degree of certainty.

An additional reason for the inconclusive nature of the Amendment's history with respect to segregated schools is the status of public education at that time. In the South, the movement toward free common schools, supported by general taxation, had not yet taken hold. Education of white children was largely in the hands of private groups. Education of Negroes was almost nonexistent, and practically all of the race were illiterate. In fact, any education of Negroes was forbidden by law in some states. Today, in contrast, many Negroes have achieved outstanding success in the arts and sciences, as well as in the business and professional world. It is true that public school education at the time of the Amendment had advanced further in the North, but the effect of the Amendment on Northern States was generally ignored in the congressional debates. Even in the North, the conditions of public education did not approximate those existing today. The curriculum was usually rudimentary; ungraded schools were common in rural areas; the school term was but three months a year in many states, and compulsory school attendance was virtually unknown. As a consequence, it is not surprising that there should be so little in the history of the Fourteenth Amendment relating to its intended effect on public education.

In the first cases in this Court construing the Fourteenth Amendment, decided shortly after its adoption, the Court interpreted it as proscribing all state-imposed discriminations against the Negro race. The doctrine of "separate but equal" did not make its appearance in this Court until 1896 in the case of **Plessy v. Ferguson**, supra, involving not education but transportation. American courts have since labored with the doctrine for over half a century. In this Court, there have been six cases involving the "separate but equal" doctrine in the field of public education. In **Cumming v. County Board of Education, 175 U.S. 528**, and **Gong Lum v. Rice, 275 U.S. 78**, the validity of the doctrine itself was not challenged. In more recent cases, all on the graduate school level, inequality was found in that specific benefits enjoyed by white students were denied to Negro students of the same educational qualifications. **Missouri ex rel. Gaines v. Canada, 305 U.S. 337; Sipuel v. Oklahoma, 332 U.S. 631; Sweatt v. Painter, 339 U.S. 629; McLaurin v. Oklahoma State Regents, 339 U.S. 637.** In none of these cases was it necessary to reexamine the doctrine to grant relief to the Negro plaintiff. And in **Sweatt v. Painter**, supra, the Court expressly reserved decision on the question whether **Plessy v. Ferguson** should be held inapplicable to public education.

In the instant cases, that question is directly presented. Here, unlike **Sweatt v. Painter**, there are findings below that the Negro and white schools involved have been equalized, or are being equalized, with respect to buildings, curricula, qualifications and salaries of teachers, and other "tangible" factors. Our decision, therefore, cannot turn on merely a comparison of these tangible factors in the Negro and white schools involved in each of the cases. We must look instead to the effect of segregation itself on public education.

In approaching this problem, we cannot turn the clock back to 1868, when the Amendment was adopted, or even to 1896, when **Plessy v. Ferguson** was written. We must consider public education in the light of its full development and its present place in American life throughout the Nation. Only in this way can it be determined if segregation in public schools deprives these plaintiffs of the equal protection of the laws.

Today, education is perhaps the most important function of state and local governments. Compulsory school attendance laws and the great expenditures for education both demonstrate our recognition of the importance of education to our democratic society. It is required in the performance of our most basic public responsibilities, even service in the armed forces. It is the very foundation of good citizenship. Today it is a principal instrument in awakening the child to cultural values, in preparing him for later professional training, and in helping him to adjust normally to his environment. In these days, it is doubtful that any child may reasonably be expected to succeed in life if he is denied the opportunity of an education. Such an opportunity, where the state has undertaken to provide it, is a right which must be made available to all on equal terms.

We come then to the question presented: Does segregation of children in public schools solely on the basis of race, even though the physical facilities and other "tangible" factors may be equal, deprive the children of the minority group of equal educational opportunities? We believe that it does.

In **Sweatt v. Painter**, supra, in finding that a segregated law school for Negroes could not provide them equal educational opportunities, this Court relied in large part on "those qualities which are incapable of objective measurement but which make for greatness in a law school." In **McLaurin v. Oklahoma State Regents**, supra, the Court, in requiring that a Negro admitted to a white graduate school be treated like all other students, again resorted to intangible considerations: ". . . his ability to study, to engage in discussions and exchange views with other students, and, in general, to learn his profession." Such considerations apply with added force to children in grade and high schools. To separate them from others of similar age and qualifications solely because of their race generates a feeling of inferiority as to their status in the community that may affect their hearts and minds in a way unlikely ever to be undone. The effect of this separation on their educational opportunities was well stated by a finding in the Kansas case by a court which nevertheless felt compelled to rule against the Negro plaintiffs:

Segregation of white and colored children in public schools has a detrimental effect upon the colored children. The impact is greater when it has the sanction of the law, for the policy of separating the races is usually interpreted as denoting the inferiority of the negro group. A sense of inferiority affects the motivation of a child to learn. Segregation with the sanction of law, therefore, has a tendency to [retard] the educational and mental development of negro children and to deprive them of some of the benefits they would receive in a racial[ly] integrated school system.

Whatever may have been the extent of psychological knowledge at the time of **Plessy v. Ferguson**, this finding is amply supported by modern authority. Any language in **Plessy v. Ferguson** contrary to this finding is rejected.

We conclude that, in the field of public education, the doctrine of "separate but equal" has no place. Separate educational facilities are inherently unequal. Therefore, we hold that the plaintiffs and others similarly situated for whom the actions have been brought are, by reason of the segregation complained of, deprived of the equal protection of the laws guaranteed by the Fourteenth Amendment. This disposition makes unnecessary any discussion whether such segregation also violates the Due Process Clause of the Fourteenth Amendment.

Because these are class actions, because of the wide applicability of this decision, and because of the great variety of local conditions, the formulation of decrees in these cases presents problems of considerable complexity. On reargument, the consideration of appropriate relief was necessarily subordinated to the primary question—the constitutionality of segregation in public education. We have now announced that such segregation is a denial of the equal protection of the laws. In order that we may have the full assistance of the parties in formulating decrees, the cases will be restored to the docket, and the parties are requested to present further argument on Questions 4 and 5 previously propounded by the Court for the reargument this Term The Attorney General of the United States is again invited to participate. The Attorneys General of the states requiring or permitting segregation in public education will also be permitted to appear as amici curiae upon request to do so by September 15, 1954, and submission of briefs by October 1, 1954.

It is so ordered.

*Together with **No. 2, Briggs et al. v. Elliott et al.**, on appeal from the United States District Court for the Eastern District of South Carolina, argued December 9–10, 1952, reargued December 7–8, 1953; **No. 4, Davis et al. v. County School Board of Prince Edward County, Virginia, et al.**, on appeal from the United States District Court for the Eastern District of Virginia, argued December 10, 1952, reargued December 7–8, 1953, and **No. 10, Gebhart et al. v. Belton et al.**, on certiorari to the Supreme Court of Delaware, argued December 11, 1952, reargued December 9, 1953.

Brown v. Board of Education, 347 U.S. 483 (1954) (USSC+). The National Center for Public Policy Research. http://www.nationalcenter.org/brown.html.

Brown v. Board of Education II

The Brown v. Board of Education *case was returned to the U.S. Supreme Court in 1955 because there had been very little movement to dismantle segregation in schools.* The Brown II *decision of the U.S. Supreme Court underscored the court's original decree, and demanded that the school districts involved in the case act "with all deliberate speed." The entire text of the decision follows.*

SUPREME COURT OF THE UNITED STATES
Brown v. Board of Education, 349 U.S. 294 (1955) (USSC+)
349 U.S. 294
Reargued on the question of relief April 11–14, 1955
Opinion and judgments announced May 31, 1955
APPEAL FROM THE UNITED STATES DISTRICT COURT FOR THE DISTRICT OF KANSAS.
Syllabus
1. Racial discrimination in public education is unconstitutional, 347 U.S. 483, 497, and all provisions of federal, state or local law requiring or permitting such discrimination must yield to this principle.
2. The judgments below (except that in the Delaware case) are reversed and the cases are remanded to the District Courts to take such proceedings and enter such orders and decrees consistent with this opinion as are necessary and proper to admit the parties to these cases to public schools on a racially nondiscriminatory basis with all deliberate speed.
(a) School authorities have the primary responsibility for elucidating, assessing and solving the varied local school problems which may require solution in fully implementing the governing constitutional principles.
(b) Courts will have to consider whether the action of school authorities constitutes good faith implementation of the governing constitutional principles.
(c) Because of their proximity to local conditions and the possible need for further hearings, the courts which originally heard these cases can best perform this judicial appraisal.
(d) In fashioning and effectuating the decrees, the courts will be guided by equitable principles—characterized by a practical flexibility in shaping remedies and a facility for adjusting and reconciling public and private needs.

(e) At stake is the personal interest of the plaintiffs in admission to public schools as soon as practicable on a nondiscriminatory basis.

(f) Courts of equity may properly take into account the public interest in the elimination in a systematic and effective manner of a variety of obstacles in making the transition to school systems operated in accordance with the constitutional principles enunciated in 347 U.S. 483, 497; but the vitality of these constitutional principles cannot be allowed to yield simply because of disagreement with them.

(g) While giving weight to these public and private considerations, the courts will require that the defendants make a prompt and reasonable start toward full compliance with the ruling of this Court.

(h) Once such a start has been made, the courts may find that additional time is necessary to carry out the ruling in an effective manner.

(i) The burden rests on the defendants to establish that additional time is necessary in the public interest and is consistent with good faith compliance at the earliest practicable date.

(j) The courts may consider problems related to administration, arising from the physical condition of the school plant, the school transportation system, personnel, revision of school districts and attendance areas into compact units to achieve a system of determining admission to the public schools on a nonracial basis, and revision of local laws and regulations which may be necessary in solving the foregoing problems.

(k) The courts will also consider the adequacy of any plans the defendants may propose to meet these problems and to effectuate a transition to a racially nondiscriminatory school system.

(l) During the period of transition, the courts will retain jurisdiction of these cases.

3. The judgment in the Delaware case, ordering the immediate admission of the plaintiffs to schools previously attended only by white children, is affirmed on the basis of the principles stated by this Court in its opinion, 347 U.S. 483, but the case is remanded to the Supreme Court of Delaware for such further proceedings as that Court may deem necessary in the light of this opinion.

98 F.Supp. 797, 103 F.Supp. 920, 103 F.Supp. 337 and judgment in No. 4, reversed and remanded.

91 A.2d 137, affirmed and remanded.

Opinion

MR. CHIEF JUSTICE WARREN delivered the opinion of the Court.

These cases were decided on May 17, 1954. The opinions of that date, declaring the fundamental principle that racial discrimination in public education is unconstitutional, are incorporated herein by reference. All provisions of federal, state, or local law requiring or permitting such discrimination must yield to this principle. There remains for consideration the manner in which relief is to be accorded.

Because these cases arose under different local conditions and their disposition will involve a variety of local problems, we requested further argument on the question of relief. In view of the nationwide importance of the decision, we invited the Attorney General of the United States and the Attorneys General of all states requiring or permitting racial discrimination in public education to present their views on that question. The parties, the United States, and the States of Florida, North Carolina, Arkansas, Oklahoma, Maryland, and Texas filed briefs and participated in the oral argument.

These presentations were informative and helpful to the Court in its consideration of the complexities arising from the transition to a system of public education freed of racial discrimination. The presentations also demonstrated that substantial steps to eliminate racial discrimination in public schools have already been taken, not only in some of the communities in which these cases arose, but in some of the states appearing as amici curiae, and in other states as well. Substantial progress has been made in the District of Columbia and in the communities in Kansas and Delaware involved in this litigation. The defendants in the cases coming to us from South Carolina and Virginia are awaiting the decision of this Court concerning relief.

Full implementation of these constitutional principles may require solution of varied local school problems. School authorities have the primary responsibility for elucidating, assessing, and solving these problems; courts will have to consider whether the action of school authorities constitutes good faith implementation of the governing constitutional principles. Because of their proximity to local conditions and the possible need for further hearings, the courts which originally heard these cases can best perform this judicial appraisal. Accordingly, we believe it appropriate to remand the cases to those courts.

In fashioning and effectuating the decrees, the courts will be guided by equitable principles. Traditionally, equity has been characterized by a practical flexibility in shaping its remedies and by a facility for adjusting and reconciling public and private needs. These cases call for the exercise of these traditional attributes of equity power. At stake is the personal interest of the plaintiffs in admission to public schools as soon as practicable on a nondiscriminatory basis. To effectuate this interest may call for elimination of a variety of obstacles in making the transition to school systems operated in accordance with the constitutional principles set forth in our May 17, 1954, decision. Courts of equity may properly take into account the public interest in the elimination of such obstacles in a systematic and effective manner. But it should go without saying that the vitality of these constitutional principles cannot be allowed to yield simply because of disagreement with them.

While giving weight to these public and private considerations, the courts will require that the defendants make a prompt and reasonable start toward full compliance with our May 17, 1954, ruling. Once such a start has been made, the courts may find that additional time is necessary to carry out the ruling in an effective manner. The burden rests upon the defendants to establish that such time is necessary in the public interest and is consistent with good faith compliance at the earliest practicable date. To that end, the courts may consider problems related to administration, arising from the physical condition of the school plant, the school transportation system, personnel, revision of school districts and attendance areas into compact units to achieve a system of determining admission to the public schools on a nonracial basis, and revision of local laws and regulations which may be necessary in solving the foregoing problems. They will also consider the adequacy of any plans the defendants may propose to meet these problems and to effectuate a transition to a racially nondiscriminatory school system. During this period of transition, the courts will retain jurisdiction of these cases.

The judgments below, except that, in the Delaware case, are accordingly reversed, and the cases are remanded to the District Courts to take such proceedings and enter such orders and decrees consistent with this opinion as are necessary and proper to admit to public schools on a racially nondiscriminatory basis with all deliberate speed the parties to these cases. The judgment in the Delaware case—ordering the immediate admission of the plaintiffs to schools previously attended only by white children—is affirmed on the basis of the principles stated in our May 17, 1954, opinion, but the case is remanded to the Supreme Court of Delaware for such further proceedings as that Court may deem necessary in light of this opinion.

It is so ordered.

Brown v. Board of Education, 349 U.S. 294 (1955) (USSC+). The National
Center for Public Policy Research. http://www.nationalcenter.org/
cc0725.htm.

National Defense Education Act, P.L. 85–864

*The National Defense Education Act (NDEA), P.L. 85–864, was the
first federal legislation that provided support to reform public education.
NDEA was enacted in response to the fear that the Soviet Union's educational system was producing better outcomes than that of the United
States, particularly in the areas of mathematics and science. NDEA promoted the notion that education was a part of the national defense. The
introduction to Title I of the NDEA follows.*

TITLE I—GENERAL PROVISIONS
FINDINGS AND DECLARATION OF POLICY

SEC. 101. The Congress hereby finds and declares that the security
of the Nation requires the fullest development of the mental resources
and technical skills of its young men and women. The present emergency demands that additional and more adequate educational opportunities be made available. The defense of this Nation depends upon
the mastery of modern techniques developed from complex scientific
principles. It depends as well upon the discovery and development of
new principles, new techniques, and new knowledge. We must increase
our efforts to identify and educate more of the talent of our Nation. This
requires programs that will give assurance that no student of ability
will be denied an opportunity for higher education because of financial
need; will correct as rapidly as possible the existing imbalances in our
educational programs which have led to an insufficient proportion of
our population educated in science, mathematics, and modern foreign
languages and trained in technology. The Congress reaffirms the principle and declares that the States and local communities have and must
retain control over and primary responsibility for public education.
The national interest requires, however, that the Federal Government
give assistance to education for programs which are important to our
defense. To meet the present educational emergency requires additional
effort at all levels of government. It is therefore the purpose of this Act
to provide substantial assistance in various forms to individuals, and to
States and their subdivisions, in order to insure trained manpower of
sufficient quality and quantity to meet the national defense needs of the
United States.

National Defense Education Act, P.L. 85–864, September 2, 1958. *United States Statutes at Large 72*, 1580–1605.

A Nation at Risk: The Imperative for Educational Reform

In 1983, the Commission on Excellence and Education issued a report on the state of education in the United States. That report, "A Nation at Risk: The Imperative for Educational Reform," was both a serious indictment against the quality of public education in the United States, and a call for reform. The report, subtitled, "An Open Letter to the American People," was based on the notion that the quality of public education in the United States was responsible for the nation's "being overtaken by competitors throughout the world." The introduction to the report follows.

A Nation at Risk: The Imperative for Educational Reform
Introduction

All, regardless of race or class or economic status, are entitled to a fair chance and to the tools for developing their individual powers of mind and spirit to the utmost. This promise means that all children by virtue of their own efforts, competently guided, can hope to attain the mature and informed judgement needed to secure gainful employment, and to manage their own lives, thereby serving not only their own interests but also the progress of society itself.

Our Nation is at risk. Our once unchallenged preeminence in commerce, industry, science, and technological innovation is being overtaken by competitors throughout the world. This report is concerned with only one of the many causes and dimensions of the problem, but it is the one that undergirds American prosperity, security, and civility. We report to the American people that while we can take justifiable pride in what our schools and colleges have historically accomplished and contributed to the United States and the well-being of its people, the educational foundations of our society are presently being eroded by a rising tide of mediocrity that threatens our very future as a Nation and a people. What was unimaginable a generation ago has begun to occur—others are matching and surpassing our educational attainments.

If an unfriendly foreign power had attempted to impose on America the mediocre educational performance that exists today, we might well have viewed it as an act of war. As it stands, we have allowed this to happen to ourselves. We have even squandered the gains in student achievement made in the wake of the Sputnik challenge. Moreover, we have dismantled essential support systems which helped make those gains possible. We have, in effect, been committing an act of unthinking, unilateral educational disarmament.

Our society and its educational institutions seem to have lost sight of the basic purposes of schooling, and of the high expectations and disciplined effort needed to attain them. This report, the result of 18 months of study, seeks to generate reform of our educational system in fundamental ways and to renew the Nation's commitment to schools and colleges of high quality throughout the length and breadth of our land.

That we have compromised this commitment is, upon reflection, hardly surprising, given the multitude of often conflicting demands we have placed on our Nation's schools and colleges. They are routinely called on to provide solutions to personal, social, and political problems that the home and other institutions either will not or cannot resolve. We must understand that these demands on our schools and colleges often exact an educational cost as well as a financial one.

On the occasion of the Commission's first meeting, President Reagan noted the central importance of education in American life when he said: "Certainly there are few areas of American life as important to our society, to our people, and to our families as our schools and colleges." This report, therefore, is as much an open letter to the American people as it is a report to the Secretary of Education. We are confident that the American people, properly informed, will do what is right for their children and for the generations to come.

The Risk

History is not kind to idlers. The time is long past when American's destiny was assured simply by an abundance of natural resources and inexhaustible human enthusiasm, and by our relative isolation from the malignant problems of older civilizations. The world is indeed one global village. We live among determined, well-educated, and strongly motivated competitors. We compete with them for international standing and markets, not only with products but also with the ideas of our laboratories and neighborhood workshops. America's position in the world may once have been reasonably secure with only a few exceptionally well-trained men and women. It is no longer.

The risk is not only that the Japanese make automobiles more efficiently than Americans and have government subsidies for development and export. It is not just that the South Koreans recently built the world's most efficient steel mill, or that American machine tools, once the pride of the world, are being displaced by German products. It is also that these developments signify a redistribution of trained capability throughout the globe. Knowledge, learning, information, and skilled intelligence are the new raw materials of international commerce and are today spreading throughout the world as vigorously as miracle drugs, synthetic fertilizers, and blue jeans did earlier. If only to keep and improve on the slim competitive edge we still retain in world markets, we must dedicate ourselves to the reform of our educational system for the benefit of all—old and young alike, affluent and poor, majority and minority. Learning is the indispensable investment required for success in the "information age" we are entering.

Our concern, however, goes well beyond matters such as industry and commerce. It also includes the intellectual, moral, and spiritual strengths of our people which knit together the very fabric of our society. The people of the United States need to know that individuals in our society who do not possess the levels of skill, literacy, and training essential to this new era will be effectively disenfranchised, not simply from the material rewards that accompany competent performance, but also from the chance to participate fully in our national life. A high level of shared education is essential to a free, democratic society and to the fostering of a common culture, especially in a country that prides itself on pluralism and individual freedom.

For our country to function, citizens must be able to reach some common understandings on complex issues, often on short notice and on the basis of conflicting or incomplete evidence.

Education helps form these common understandings, a point Thomas Jefferson made long ago in his justly famous dictum:

I know no safe depository of the ultimate powers of the society but the people themselves; and if we think them not enlightened enough to exercise their control with a wholesome discretion, the remedy is not to take it from them but to inform their discretion.

Part of what is at risk is the promise first made on this continent: All, regardless of race or class or economic status, are entitled to a fair chance and to the tools for developing their individual powers of mind and spirit to the utmost. This promise means that all children by virtue of their own efforts, competently guided, can hope to attain the mature and informed judgment needed to secure gainful employment, and to manage their own lives, thereby serving not only their own interests but also the progress of society itself.

Indicators of the Risk

The educational dimensions of the risk before us have been amply documented in testimony received by the Commission. For example:

- International comparisons of student achievement, completed a decade ago, reveal that on 19 academic tests American students were never first or second and, in comparison with other industrialized nations, were last seven times.
- Some 23 million American adults are functionally illiterate by the simplest tests of everyday reading, writing, and comprehension.
- About 13 percent of all 17-year-olds in the United States can be considered functionally illiterate. Functional illiteracy among minority youth may run as high as 40 percent.
- Average achievement of high school students on most standardized tests is now lower than 26 years ago when Sputnik was launched.
- Over half the population of gifted students do not match their tested ability with comparable achievement in school.
- The College Board's Scholastic Aptitude Tests (SAT) demonstrate a virtually unbroken decline from 1963 to 1980. Average verbal scores fell over 50 points and average mathematics scores dropped nearly 40 points.
- College Board achievement tests also reveal consistent declines in recent years in such subjects as physics and English.
- Both the number and proportion of students demonstrating superior achievement on the SATs (i.e., those with scores of 650 or higher) have also dramatically declined.
- Many 17-year-olds do not possess the "higher order" intellectual skills we should expect of them. Nearly 40 percent cannot draw inferences from written material; only one-fifth can write a persuasive essay; and only one-third can solve a mathematics problem requiring several steps.
- There was a steady decline in science achievement scores of U.S. 17-year-olds as measured by national assessments of science in 1969, 1973, and 1977.

- Between 1975 and 1980, remedial mathematics courses in public 4-year colleges increased by 72 percent and now constitute one-quarter of all mathematics courses taught in those institutions.
- Average tested achievement of students graduating from college is also lower.
- Business and military leaders complain that they are required to spend millions of dollars on costly remedial education and training programs in such basic skills as reading, writing, spelling, and computation. The Department of the Navy, for example, reported to the Commission that one-quarter of its recent recruits cannot read at the ninth grade level, the minimum needed simply to understand written safety instructions. Without remedial work they cannot even begin, much less complete, the sophisticated training essential in much of the modern military.

These deficiencies come at a time when the demand for highly skilled workers in new fields is accelerating rapidly. For example:

- Computers and computer-controlled equipment are penetrating every aspect of our lives—homes, factories, and offices.
- One estimate indicates that by the turn of the century millions of jobs will involve laser technology and robotics.
- Technology is radically transforming a host of other occupations. They include health care, medical science, energy production, food processing, construction, and the building, repair, and maintenance of sophisticated scientific, educational, military, and industrial equipment.

Analysts examining these indicators of student performance and the demands for new skills have made some chilling observations. Educational researcher Paul Hurd concluded at the end of a thorough national survey of student achievement that within the context of the modern scientific revolution, "We are raising a new generation of Americans that is scientifically and technologically illiterate." In a similar vein, John Slaughter, a former Director of the National Science Foundation, warned of "a growing chasm between a small scientific and technological elite and a citizenry ill-informed, indeed uninformed, on issues with a science component."

But the problem does not stop there, nor do all observers see it the same way. Some worry that schools may emphasize such rudiments as reading and computation at the expense of other essential skills such as comprehension, analysis, solving problems, and drawing conclusions. Still others are concerned that an overemphasis on technical and occupational skills will leave little time for studying the arts and humanities that so enrich daily life, help maintain civility, and develop a sense of community. Knowledge of the humanities, they maintain, must be harnessed to science and technology if the latter are to remain creative and humane, just as the humanities need to be informed by science and technology if they are to remain relevant to the human condition. Another analyst, Paul Copperman, has drawn a sobering conclusion. Until now, he has noted:

Each generation of Americans has outstripped its parents in education, in literacy, and in economic attainment. For the first time in the history of our country, the educational skills of one generation will not surpass, will not equal, will not even approach, those of their parents.

It is important, of course, to recognize that *the average citizen* today is better educated and more knowledgeable than the average citizen of a generation ago—more literate, and exposed to more mathematics, literature, and science. The positive impact of this fact on the well-being of our country and the lives of our people cannot be overstated. Nevertheless, *the average graduate* of our schools and colleges today is not as well-educated as the average graduate of 25 or 35 years ago, when a much smaller proportion of our population completed high school and college. The negative impact of this fact likewise cannot be overstated.

Hope and Frustration

Statistics and their interpretation by experts show only the surface dimension of the difficulties we face. Beneath them lies a tension between hope and frustration that characterizes current attitudes about education at every level.

We have heard the voices of high school and college students, school board members, and teachers; of leaders of industry, minority groups, and higher education; of parents and State officials. We could hear the hope evident in their commitment to quality education and in their descriptions of outstanding programs and schools. We could also hear the intensity of their frustration, a growing impatience with shoddiness in many walks of American life, and the complaint that this shoddiness is too often reflected in our schools and colleges. Their frustration threatens to overwhelm their hope.

What lies behind this emerging national sense of frustration can be described as both a dimming of personal expectations and the fear of losing a shared vision for America.

On the personal level the student, the parent, and the caring teacher all perceive that a basic promise is not being kept. More and more young people emerge from high school ready neither for college nor for work. This predicament becomes more acute as the knowledge base continues its rapid expansion, the number of traditional jobs shrinks, and new jobs demand greater sophistication and preparation.

On a broader scale, we sense that this undertone of frustration has significant political implications, for it cuts across ages, generations, races, and political and economic groups. We have come to understand that the public will demand that educational and political leaders act forcefully and effectively on these issues. Indeed, such demands have already appeared and could well become a unifying national preoccupation. This unity, however, can be achieved only if we avoid the unproductive tendency of some to search for scapegoats among the victims, such as the beleaguered teachers.

On the positive side is the significant movement by political and educational leaders to search for solutions—so far centering largely on the nearly desperate need for increased support for the teaching of mathematics and science. This movement is but a start on what we believe is a larger and more educationally encompassing need to improve teaching and learning in fields such as English, history, geography, economics, and foreign languages. We believe this movement must be broadened and directed toward reform and excellence throughout education.

Excellence in Education

We define "excellence" to mean several related things. At the level of the *individual learner*, it means performing on the boundary of individual ability in ways that test and push back personal limits, in school and in the workplace. Excellence characterizes a *school or college* that sets high expectations and goals for all learners, then tries in every way possible to help students reach them. Excellence characterizes a *society* that has adopted these policies, for it will then be prepared through the education and skill of its people to respond to the challenges of a rapidly changing world. Our Nation's people and its schools and colleges must be committed to achieving excellence in all these senses.

We do not believe that a public commitment to excellence and educational reform must be made at the expense of a strong public commitment to the equitable treatment of our diverse population. The twin goals of equity and high-quality schooling have profound and practical meaning for our economy and society, and we cannot permit one to yield to the other either in principle or in practice. To do so would deny young people their chance to learn and live according to their aspirations and abilities. It also would lead to a generalized accommodation to mediocrity in our society on the one hand or the creation of an undemocratic elitism on the other.

Our goal must be to develop the talents of all to their fullest. Attaining that goal requires that we expect and assist all students to work to the limits of their capabilities. We should expect schools to have genuinely high standards rather than minimum ones, and parents to support and encourage their children to make the most of their talents and abilities.

The search for solutions to our educational problems must also include a commitment to life-long learning. The task of rebuilding our system of learning is enormous and must be properly understood and taken seriously. Although a million and a half new workers enter the economy each year from our schools and colleges, the adults working today will still make up about 75 percent of the workforce in the year 2000. These workers, and new entrants into the workforce, will need further education and retraining if they—and we as a Nation—are to thrive and prosper.

The Learning Society

In a world of ever-accelerating competition and change in the conditions of the workplace, of ever-greater danger, and of ever-larger opportunities for those prepared to meet them, educational reform should focus on the goal of creating a Learning Society. At the heart of such a society is the commitment to a set of values and to a system of education that affords all members the opportunity to stretch their minds to full capacity, from early childhood through adulthood, learning more as the world itself changes. Such a society has as a basic foundation the idea that education is important not only because of what it contributes to one's career goals but also because of the value it adds to the general quality of one's life. Also at the heart of the Learning Society are educational opportunities extending far beyond the traditional institutions of learning, our schools and colleges. They extend into homes and workplaces; into libraries, art galleries, museums, and science centers; indeed, into every place where the individual can develop and mature in work and life. In our view, formal schooling in youth is the essential foundation for learning throughout one's life. But without life-long learning, one's skills will become rapidly dated.

In contrast to the ideal of the Learning Society, however, we find that for too many people education means doing the minimum work necessary for the moment, then coasting through life on what may have been learned in its first quarter. But this should not surprise us because we tend to express our educational standards and expectations largely in terms of "minimum requirements." And where there should be a coherent continuum of learning, we have none, but instead an often incoherent, outdated patchwork quilt. Many individual, sometimes heroic, examples of schools and colleges of great merit do exist. Our findings and testimony confirm the vitality of a number of notable schools and programs, but their very distinction stands out against a vast mass shaped by tensions and pressures that inhibit systematic academic and vocational achievement for the majority of students. In some metropolitan areas basic literacy has become the goal rather than the starting point. In some colleges maintaining enrollments is of greater day-to-day concern than maintaining rigorous academic standards. And the ideal of academic excellence as the primary goal of schooling seems to be fading across the board in American education.

Thus, we issue this call to all who care about America and its future: to parents and students; to teachers, administrators, and school board members; to colleges and industry; to union members and military leaders; to governors and State legislators; to the President; to members of Congress and other public officials; to members of learned and scientific societies; to the print and electronic media; to concerned citizens everywhere. America is at risk.

We are confident that America can address this risk. If the tasks we set forth are initiated now and our recommendations are fully realized over the next several years, we can expect reform of our Nation's schools, colleges, and universities. This would also reverse the current declining trend—a trend that stems more from weakness of purpose, confusion of vision, underuse of talent, and lack of leadership, than from conditions beyond our control.

The Tools at Hand

It is our conviction that the essential raw materials needed to re-form our educational system are waiting to be mobilized through effective leadership:

- the natural abilities of the young that cry out to be developed and the undiminished concern of parents for the well-being of their children;
- the commitment of the Nation to high retention rates in schools and colleges and to full access to education for all;
- the persistent and authentic American dream that superior performance can raise one's state in life and shape one's own future;
- the dedication, against all odds, that keeps teachers serving in schools and colleges, even as the rewards diminish;
- our better understanding of learning and teaching and the implications of this knowledge for school practice, and the numerous examples of local success as a result of superior effort and effective dissemination;
- the ingenuity of our policymakers, scientists, State and local educators, and scholars in formulating solutions once problems are better understood;
- the traditional belief that paying for education is an investment in ever-renewable human resources that are more durable and flexible than capital plant and equipment, and the availability in this country of sufficient financial means to invest in education;

- the equally sound tradition, from the Northwest Ordinance of 1787 until today, that the Federal Government should supplement State, local, and other resources to foster key national educational goals; and
- the voluntary efforts of individuals, businesses, and parent and civic groups to cooperate in strengthening educational programs.

These raw materials, combined with the unparalleled array of educational organizations in America, offer us the possibility to create a Learning Society, in which public, private, and parochial schools; colleges and universities; vocational and technical schools and institutes; libraries; science centers, museums, and other cultural institutions; and corporate training and retraining programs offer opportunities and choices for all to learn throughout life.

The Public's Commitment

Of all the tools at hand, the public's support for education is the most powerful. In a message to a National Academy of Sciences meeting in May 1982, President Reagan commented on this fact when he said:

This public awareness—and I hope public action—is long overdue. . . . This country was built on American respect for education . . . Our challenge now is to create a resurgence of that thirst for education that typifies our Nation's history.

The most recent (1982) Gallup Poll of the *Public's Attitudes Toward the Public Schools* strongly supported a theme heard during our hearings: People are steadfast in their belief that education is the major foundation for the future strength of this country. They even considered education more important than developing the best industrial system or the strongest military force, perhaps because they understood education as the cornerstone of both. They also held that education is "extremely important" to one's future success, and that public education should be the top priority for additional Federal funds. Education occupied first place among 12 funding categories considered in the survey—above health care, welfare, and military defense, with 55 percent selecting public education as one of their first three choices. Very clearly, the public understands the primary importance of education as the foundation for a satisfying life, an enlightened and civil society, a strong economy, and a secure Nation.

At the same time, the public has no patience with undemanding and superfluous high school offerings. In another survey, more than 75 percent of all those questioned believed every student planning to go to college should take 4 years of mathematics, English, history/U.S. government, and science, with more than 50 percent adding 2 years each of a foreign language and economics or business. The public even supports requiring much of this curriculum for students who do not plan to go to college. These standards far exceed the strictest high school graduation requirements of any State today, and they also exceed the admission standards of all but a handful of our most selective colleges and universities.

Another dimension of the public's support offers the prospect of constructive reform. The best term to characterize it may simply be the honorable word "patriotism." Citizens know intuitively what some of the best economists have shown in their research, that education is one of the chief engines of a society's material well-being. They know, too, that education is the common bond of a pluralistic society and helps tie us to other cultures around the globe. Citizens also know in their bones that the safety of the United States depends principally on the wit, skill, and spirit of a self-confident people, today and tomorrow. It is, therefore, essential—especially in a period of long-term decline in educational achievement—for government at all levels to affirm its responsibility for nurturing the Nation's intellectual capital.

And perhaps most important, citizens know and believe that the meaning of America to the rest of the world must be something better than it seems to many today. Americans like to think of this Nation as the preeminent country for generating the great ideas and material benefits for all mankind. The citizen is dismayed at a steady 15-year decline in industrial productivity, as one great American industry after another falls to world competition. The citizen wants the country to act on the belief, expressed in our hearings and by the large majority in the Gallup Poll, that education should be at the top of the Nation's agenda.

April 1983

National Commission on Excellence in Education. 1983. "A Nation at Risk: The Imperative for Educational Reform. http://www.ed.gov/pubs/NatAtRisk/risk.html.

Effective Schools Correlates

Based on analysis of many years of research about what makes schools effective, Larry Lezotte and Ronald Edmonds formulated a set of correlates that describe schools that result in high levels of learning for all children. The Effective Schools movement has promoted the correlates as a basis for education reform for more than 30 years. The correlates, as well as a description of them enacted in schools, are listed below. The "second generation" of each correlate represents continued analysis of data from schools and refinement from those data. The text is drawn from a 1991 document by Larry Lezotte, director of Effective Schools.

Correlates of Effective Schools

1. Safe and Orderly Environment

The First Generation: In the effective school there is an orderly, purposeful, businesslike atmosphere which is free from the threat of physical harm. The school climate is not oppressive and is conducive to teaching and learning. The Second Generation: In the first generation, the safe and orderly environment correlate was defined in terms of the absence of undesirable student behavior (e.g., students fighting). In the second generation, the concept of a school environment conducive to *Learning for All* must move beyond the elimination of undesirable behavior. The second generation will place increased emphasis on the presence of certain desirable behaviors (e.g., cooperative team learning). These second generation schools will be places where students actually help one another. . . .

2. Climate of High Expectations for Success

The First Generation: In the effective school there is a climate of expectation in which the staff believe and demonstrate that all students can attain mastery of the essential school skills, and the staff also believe that they have the capability to help all students achieve that mastery. The Second Generation: In the second generation, the emphasis placed on high expectations for success will be broadened significantly. In the first generation, expectations were described in terms of attitudes and beliefs that suggested how the teacher should behave in the teaching-learning situation. Those descriptions sought to tell teachers how they should initially deliver the lesson. High expectations meant, for example, that the teacher should evenly distribute questions asked among all students and should provide each student with an equal opportunity to participate in the learning process. Unfortunately, this "equalization of opportunity," though beneficial, proved to be insufficient to assure mastery for many learners. Teachers found themselves in the difficult position of having had high expectations and having acted upon them—yet some students still did not learn. In the second generation, the teachers will anticipate this and they will develop a broader array of responses. . . . to assure that all students do achieve mastery. Implementing this expanded concept of high expectations will require the school as an organization to reflect high expectations. . . . High expectations for success will be judged, not only by the initial staff beliefs and behaviors, but also by the organization's response when some students do not learn.

3. Instructional Leadership

The First Generation: In the effective school the principal acts as an instructional leader and effectively and persistently communicates that mission to the staff, parents, and students. The principal understands and applies the characteristics of instructional effectiveness in the management of the instructional program. The Second Generation: In the first generation, the standards for instructional leadership focused primarily on the principal and the administrative staff of the school. In the second generation, instructional leadership will remain important; however, the concept will be broadened and leadership will be viewed as a dispersed concept that includes all adults, especially the teachers. This is in keeping with the teacher empowerment concept; it recognizes that a principal cannot be the only leader in a complex organization like a school. With the democratization of organizations, especially schools, the leadership function becomes one of creating a "community of shared values." The mission will remain critical because it will serve to give the community of shared values a shared sense of "magnetic north," an identification of what this school community cares most about. The role of the principal will be changed to that of "a leader of leaders," rather than a leader of followers. Specifically, the principal will have to develop his/her skills as coach, partner and cheerleader. The broader concept of leadership recognizes that leadership is always delegated from the followership in any organization. It also recognizes what teachers have known for a long time and what good schools have capitalized on since the beginning of time: namely, expertise is generally distributed among many, not concentrated in a single person.

4. Clear and Focused Mission

The First Generation: In the effective school there is a clearly articulated school mission through which the staff shares an understanding of and commitment to the instructional goals, priorities, assessment procedures and accountability. Staff accept responsibility for students' learning of the school's essential curricular goals. The Second Generation: In the first generation the effective school mission emphasized teaching for *Learning for All.* The two issues that surfaced were: Did this really mean all students or just those with whom the schools had a history of reasonable success? When it became clear that this mission was inclusive of all students especially the children of the poor (minority and non-minority), the second issue surfaced. It centered itself around the question: Learn what? Partially because of the accountability movement and partially because of the belief that disadvantaged students could not learn higher-level curricula, the focus was on mastery of mostly low-level skills. In the second generation, the focus will shift toward a more appropriate balance between higher-level learning and those more basic skills that are truly prerequisite to their mastery. Designing and delivering a curriculum that responds to the demands of accountability, and is responsive to the need for higher levels of learning, will require substantial staff development. Teachers will have to be better trained to develop curricula and lessons with the "end in mind." They will have to know and be comfortable with the concept of "backward mapping," and they will need to know "task analysis." These "tools of the trade" are essential for an efficient and effective "results-oriented" school that successfully serves all students. Finally, a subtle but significant change in the concept of school mission deserves notice. Throughout the first generation, effective schools proponents advocated the mission of teaching for *Learning for All.* In the second generation the advocated mission will be *Learning for All.* The rationale for this change is that the "teaching for" portion of the old statement created ambiguity (although this was unintended) and kept too much of the focus on "teaching" rather than "learning." This allowed people to discount school learnings that were not the result of direct teaching. Finally, the new formulation of *Learning for All* opens the door to the continued learning of the educators as well as the students.

5. Opportunity to Learn and Student Time on Task

The First Generation: In the effective school teachers allocate a significant amount of classroom time to instruction in the essential skills. For a high percentage of this time students are engaged in whole class or large group, teacher-directed, planned learning activities. The Second Generation: In the second generation, time will continue to be a difficult problem for the teacher. In all likelihood, the problems that arise from too much to teach and not enough time to teach it will intensify. In the past, when the teachers were oriented toward "covering curricular content" and more content was added, they knew their response should be to "speed-up." Now teachers are being asked to stress the mission that assures that the students master the content that is covered. How are they to respond? In the next generation, teachers will have to become more skilled at interdisciplinary curriculum and they will need to learn how to comfortably practice "organized abandonment." They will have to be able to ask the question, "What goes and what stays?" One of the reasons that many of the mandated approaches to school reform have failed is that, in every case, the local school was asked to do more! One of the characteristics of the most effective schools is their willingness to declare that some things are more important than others; they are willing to abandon some less important content so as to be able to have enough time dedicated to those areas that are valued the most. The only alternative to abandonment would be to adjust the available time that students spend in school, so that those who need more time to reach mastery would be given it. The necessary time must be provided in a quality program that is not perceived as punitive by those in it, or as excessive, by those who will have to fund it. These conditions will be a real challenge indeed! If the American dream and the democratic ideal of educating everyone is going to move forward, we must explore several important policies and practices from the past. Regarding the issue of time to learn, for example, if the children of the disadvantaged present a "larger educational task" to the teachers and if it can be demonstrated that this "larger task" will require more time, then our notions of limited compulsory schooling may need to be changed. The current system of compulsory schooling makes little allowance for the fact that some students need more time to achieve mastery. If we could get the system to be more mastery-based and more humane at the same time, our nation and its students would benefit immensely.

6. Frequent Monitoring of Student Progress

The First Generation: In the effective school student academic progress is measured frequently through a variety of assessment procedures. The results of these assessments are used to improve individual student performance and also to improve the instructional program. The Second Generation: In the first generation, the correlate was interpreted to mean that the teachers should frequently monitor their students' learning and, where necessary, the teacher should adjust his/her behavior. Several major changes can be anticipated in the second generation. First, the use of technology will permit teachers to do a better job of monitoring their students' progress. Second, this same technology will allow students to monitor their own learning and, where necessary, adjust their own behavior. The use of computerized practice tests, the ability to get immediate results on homework, and the ability to see correct solutions developed on the screen are a few of the available "tools for assuring student learning." A second major change that will become more apparent in the second generation is already under way. In the area of assessment the emphasis will continue to shift away from standardized norm-referenced paper-pencil tests and toward curricular-based, criterion-referenced measures of student mastery. In the second generation, the monitoring of student learning will emphasize "more authentic assessments" of curriculum mastery. This generally means that there will be less emphasis on the paper pencil, multiple-choice tests, and more emphasis on assessments of products of student work, including performances and portfolios. Teachers will pay much more attention to the alignment that must exist between the intended, taught, and tested curriculum. Two new questions are being stimulated by the reform movement and will dominate much of the professional educators' discourse in the second generation: "What's worth knowing?" and "How will we know when they know it?" In all likelihood, the answer to the first question will become clear relatively quickly, because we can reach agreement that we want our students to be self-disciplined, socially responsible, and just. The problem comes with the second question, "How will we know when they know it?" Educators and citizens are going to have to come to terms with that question. The bad news is that it demands our best thinking and will require patience if we are going to reach consensus. The good news is that once we begin to reach consensus, the schools will be able to deliver significant progress toward these agreed-upon outcomes.

7. Home-School Relations

The First Generation: In the effective school parents understand and support the school's basic mission and are given the opportunity to play an important role in helping the school to achieve this mission. The Second Generation: During the first generation, the role of parents in the education of their children was always somewhat unclear. Schools often gave "lip service" to having parents more actively involved in the schooling of their children. Unfortunately, when pressed, many educators were willing to admit that they really did not know how to deal effectively with increased levels of parent involvement in the schools. In the second generation, the relationship between parents and the school must be an authentic partnership between the school and home. In the past when teachers said they wanted more parent involvement, more often than not they were looking for unqualified support from parents. Many teachers believed that parents, if they truly valued education, knew how to get their children to behave in the ways that the school desired. It is now clear to both teachers and parents that the parent involvement issue is not that simple. Parents are often as perplexed as the teachers about the best way to inspire students to learn what the school teaches. The best hope for effectively confronting the problem—and not each other—is to build enough trust and enough communication to realize that both teachers and parents have the same goal—an effective school and home for all children!

Excerpt from Lezotte, Lawrence W. 1991. *Correlates of Effective Schools: The First and Second Generation*. Okemos, MI: Effective Schools Products, Ltd.

National Education Goals

By 2002, when No Child Left Behind was enacted, the United States had its third set of national goals for education. The first list of six national goals for education were set by the nation's governors and President George Herbert Walker Bush. He announced them in 1990. The second set of national goals were the centerpiece of Goals 2000: Educate America Act. *In Goals 2000, Congress added two goals to the original six in the first list. No Child Left Behind is driven by five goals. Each of these sets of goals is listed below.*

National Goals for Education (1990)

Goal 1—Readiness for School: By the year 2000, all children in America will start school ready to learn.

Goal 2—High School Completion: By the year 2000, the high school graduation rate will increase to at least 90 percent.

Goal 3—Student Achievement and Citizenship: By the year 2000, American students will leave grades four, eight, and twelve having demonstrated competency in challenging subject matter including English, mathematics, science, history, and geography; and every school in America will ensure that all students learn to use their minds well, so they may be prepared for responsible citizenship, further learning, and productive employment in our modern economy.

Goal 4—Science and Mathematics: By the year 2000, U.S. students will be first in the world in science and mathematics achievement.

Goal 5—Adult Literacy and Lifelong Learning: By the year 2000, every adult American will be literate and will possess the knowledge and skills necessary to compete in a global economy and exercise the rights and responsibilities of citizenship.

Goal 6—Safe, Disciplined, and Drug-Free Schools: By the year 2000, every school in America will be free of drugs and violence and will offer a disciplined environment conducive to learning. Schools, families, and communities must work together to counteract negative social influences and create safe and orderly schools.

Excerpt from Swenson, B. B. 1991. "The National Education Goals: Questions and Answers." *ERIC Digest*. ERIC Document Number ED334715.

National Education Goals from *Goals 2000: Educate America Act* (1996)

SEC. 102. NATIONAL EDUCATION GOALS.

The Congress declares that the National Education Goals are the following:

(1) SCHOOL READINESS.

    (A) By the year 2000, all children in America will start school ready to learn.

    (B) The objectives for this goal are that—

        (i) all children will have access to high-quality and developmentally appropriate preschool programs that help prepare children for school;

        (ii) every parent in the United States will be a child's first teacher and devote time each day to helping such parent's preschool child learn, and parents will have access to the training and support parents need; and

        (iii) children will receive the nutrition, physical activity experiences, and health care needed to arrive at school with healthy minds and bodies, and to maintain the mental alertness necessary to be prepared to learn, and the number of low-birthweight babies will be significantly reduced through enhanced prenatal health systems.

(2) SCHOOL COMPLETION.

    (A) By the year 2000, the high school graduation rate will increase to at least 90 percent.

    (B) The objectives for this goal are that—

        (i) the Nation must dramatically reduce its school dropout rate, and 75 percent of the students who do drop out will successfully complete a high school degree or its equivalent; and

        (ii) the gap in high school graduation rates between American students from minority backgrounds and their non-minority counterparts will be eliminated.

(3) STUDENT ACHIEVEMENT AND CITIZENSHIP.

    (A) By the year 2000, all students will leave grades 4, 8, and 12 having demonstrated competency over challenging subject matter including English, mathematics, science, foreign languages, civics and government, economics, arts, history, and geography, and every school in America will ensure that all students learn to use their minds well, so they may be prepared for responsible citizenship, further learning, and productive employment in our Nation's modern economy.

(B) The objectives for this goal are that—

(i) the academic performance of all students at the elementary and secondary level will increase significantly in every quartile, and the distribution of minority students in each quartile will more closely reflect the student population as a whole;

(ii) the percentage of all students who demonstrate the ability to reason, solve problems, apply knowledge, and write and communicate effectively will increase substantially;

(iii) all students will be involved in activities that promote and demonstrate good citizenship, good health, community service, and personal responsibility;

(iv) all students will have access to physical education and health education to ensure they are healthy and fit;

(v) the percentage of all students who are competent in more than one language will substantially increase; and

(vi) all students will be knowledgeable about the diverse cultural heritage of this Nation and about the world community.

(4) TEACHER EDUCATION AND PROFESSIONAL DEVELOPMENT.

(A) By the year 2000, the Nation's teaching force will have access to programs for the continued improvement of their professional skills and the opportunity to acquire the knowledge and skills needed to instruct and prepare all American students for the next century.

(B) The objectives for this goal are that—

(i) all teachers will have access to preservice teacher education and continuing professional development activities that will provide such teachers with the knowledge and skills needed to teach to an increasingly diverse student population with a variety of educational, social, and health needs;

(ii) all teachers will have continuing opportunities to acquire additional knowledge and skills needed to teach challenging subject matter and to use emerging new methods, forms of assessment, and technologies;

(iii) States and school districts will create integrated strategies to attract, recruit, prepare, retrain, and support the continued professional development of teachers, administrators, and other educators, so that there is a highly talented work force of professional educators to teach challenging subject matter; and

(iv) partnerships will be established, whenever possible, among local educational agencies, institutions of higher education, parents, and local labor, business, and professional associations to provide and support programs for the professional development of educators.

(5) MATHEMATICS AND SCIENCE.
　(A) By the year 2000, United States students will be first in the world in mathematics and science achievement.
　(B) The objectives for this goal are that—
　　(i) mathematics and science education, including the metric system of measurement, will be strengthened throughout the system, especially in the early grades;
　　(ii) the number of teachers with a substantive background in mathematics and science, including the metric system of measurement, will increase by 50 percent; and
　　(iii) the number of United States undergraduate and graduate students, especially women and minorities, who complete degrees in mathematics, science, and engineering will increase significantly.

(6) ADULT LITERACY AND LIFELONG LEARNING.
　(A) By the year 2000, every adult American will be literate and will possess the knowledge and skills necessary to compete in a global economy and exercise the rights and responsibilities of citizenship.
　(B) The objectives for this goal are that—
　　(i) every major American business will be involved in strengthening the connection between education and work;
　　(ii) all workers will have the opportunity to acquire the knowledge and skills, from basic to highly technical, needed to adapt to emerging new technologies, work methods, and markets through public and private educational, vocational, technical, workplace, or other programs;
　　(iii) the number of quality programs, including those at libraries, that are designed to serve more effectively the needs of the growing number of part-time and midcareer students will increase substantially;
　　(iv) the proportion of the qualified students, especially minorities, who enter college, who complete at least two years, and who complete their degree programs will increase substantially;
　　(v) the proportion of college graduates who demonstrate an advanced ability to think critically, communicate effectively, and solve problems will increase substantially; and

(vi) schools, in implementing comprehensive parent involvement programs, will offer more adult literacy, parent training and life-long learning opportunities to improve the ties between home and school, and enhance parents' work and home lives.

(7) SAFE, DISCIPLINED, AND ALCOHOL- AND DRUG-FREE SCHOOLS.

(A) By the year 2000, every school in the United States will be free of drugs, violence, and the unauthorized presence of firearms and alcohol and will offer a disciplined environment conducive to learning.

(B) The objectives for this goal are that—

(i) every school will implement a firm and fair policy on use, possession, and distribution of drugs and alcohol;

(ii) parents, businesses, governmental and community organizations will work together to ensure the rights of students to study in a safe and secure environment that is free of drugs and crime, and that schools provide a healthy environment and are a safe haven for all children;

(iii) every local educational agency will develop and implement a policy to ensure that all schools are free of violence and the unauthorized presence of weapons;

(iv) every local educational agency will develop a sequential, comprehensive kindergarten through twelfth grade drug and alcohol prevention education program;

(v) drug and alcohol curriculum should be taught as an integral part of sequential, comprehensive health education;

(vi) community-based teams should be organized to provide students and teachers with needed support; and

(vii) every school should work to eliminate sexual harassment.

(8) PARENTAL PARTICIPATION.

(A) By the year 2000, every school will promote partnerships that will increase parental involvement and participation in promoting the social, emotional, and academic growth of children.

(B) The objectives for this Goal are that—

(i) every State will develop policies to assist local schools and local educational agencies to establish programs for increasing partnerships that respond to the varying needs of parents and the home, including parents of children who are disadvantaged or bilingual, or parents of children with disabilities;

(ii) every school will actively engage parents and families in a partnership which supports the academic work of children at home and shared educational decisionmaking at school; and

(iii) parents and families will help to ensure that schools are adequately supported and will hold schools and teachers to high standards of accountability.

Goals 2000: Educate America Act. 1994. P.L. 103–227. http://www.ed.gov/legislation/GOALS2000/TheAct/sec102.html.

Goals in "No Child Left Behind" (2002)

1. By 2013–2014, all students will reach high standards, at a minimum attaining proficiency or better in reading/language arts and mathematics.

2. All limited English proficient students will become proficient in English and reach high academic standards, at a minimum attaining proficiency or better in reading/language arts and mathematics.

3. By 2005–2006, all students will be taught by highly qualified teachers.

4. All students will be educated in learning environments that are safe, drug-free, and conducive to learning.

5. All students will graduate from high school.

No Child Left Behind: Reauthorization of the Elementary and Secondary Education Act

In 2002, President George W. Bush signed into law the latest reauthorization of the Elementary and Secondary Education Act (ESEA), named No Child Left Behind (NCLB). NCLB put into place the largest federal intervention in public education in the history of the United States, affecting nearly every program in every school. Interestingly, the provisions of NCLB mirror the correlates of effective schools listed above. The purpose (Sec. 1001) of Title I of NCLB is included here.

Title I—Improving The Academic Achievement Of The Disadvantaged

SEC. 101. IMPROVING THE ACADEMIC ACHIEVEMENT OF THE DISADVANTAGED.

Title I of the Elementary and Secondary Education Act of 1965 (20 U.S.C. 6301 et seq.) is amended to read as follows:

TITLE I—IMPROVING THE ACADEMIC ACHIEVEMENT OF THE DISADVANTAGED

SEC. 1001. STATEMENT OF PURPOSE.

The purpose of this title is to ensure that all children have a fair, equal, and significant opportunity to obtain a high-quality education and reach, at a minimum, proficiency on challenging State academic achievement standards and state academic assessments. This purpose can be accomplished by—

(1) ensuring that high-quality academic assessments, accountability systems, teacher preparation and training, curriculum, and instructional materials are aligned with challenging State academic standards so that students, teachers, parents, and administrators can measure progress against common expectations for student academic achievement;

(2) meeting the educational needs of low-achieving children in our Nation's highest-poverty schools, limited English proficient children, migratory children, children with disabilities, Indian children, neglected or delinquent children, and young children in need of reading assistance;

(3) closing the achievement gap between high- and low-performing children, especially the achievement gaps between minority and non-minority students, and between disadvantaged children and their more advantaged peers;

(4) holding schools, local educational agencies, and States accountable for improving the academic achievement of all students, and identifying and turning around low-performing schools that have failed to provide a high-quality education to their students, while providing alternatives to students in such schools to enable the students to receive a high-quality education;

(5) distributing and targeting resources sufficiently to make a difference to local educational agencies and schools where needs are greatest;

(6) improving and strengthening accountability, teaching, and learning by using State assessment systems designed to ensure that students are meeting challenging State academic achievement and content standards and increasing achievement overall, but especially for the disadvantaged;

(7) providing greater decision making authority and flexibility to schools and teachers in exchange for greater responsibility for student performance;

(8) providing children an enriched and accelerated educational program, including the use of schoolwide programs or additional services that increase the amount and quality of instructional time;

(9) promoting schoolwide reform and ensuring the access of children to effective, scientifically based instructional strategies and challenging academic content;

(10) significantly elevating the quality of instruction by providing staff in participating schools with substantial opportunities for professional development;

(11) coordinating services under all parts of this title with each other, with other educational services, and, to the extent feasible, with other agencies providing services to youth, children, and families; and

(12) affording parents substantial and meaningful opportunities to participate in the education of their children.

The Elementary and Secondary Education Act (The No Child Left Behind Act of 2001), P.L. 107–110. 2002. http://www.ed.gov/policy/elsec/leg/esea02/index.html.

The Dangerous Consequences of High-Stakes Standardized Testing

One of the provisions of No Child Left Behind is a protocol of standardized testing on a scale that greatly expanded standardized testing and at the same time, elevated the results of the testing to what many educators call "high stakes." Tests become "high stakes" when decisions based on scores from them affect the lives of children, their teachers, or their schools in serious ways. Under NCLB, schools can be labeled failing, and even closed, based on standardized test scores of the children they serve. FairTest, a watchdog organization for testing in education, has issued a statement that warns against such use of standardized testing.

The Dangerous Consequences of High-Stakes Standardized Testing

Tests are called "high-stakes" when they are used to make major decisions about a student, such as high school graduation or grade promotion. To be high stakes, a test has to be very important in the decision process or be able to override other information (for example, a student does not graduate if s/he does not pass the test regardless of how well s/he did in school). Currently, 17 states require students to pass a test to graduate, and 7 more are planning such tests.

Tests are called "standardized" when all students answer the same questions under similar conditions and their responses are scored in the same way. This includes commercial norm-referenced tests as well as state criterion-referenced or standards-based exams. They can include multiple-choice or open-ended (constructed) responses.

Research has shown that high-stakes testing causes damage to individual students and education. It is not a reasonable method for improving schools. Here are a few of the many reasons why:

1) High-stakes tests are unfair to many students.

Some students simply do not test well. Many students are affected by test anxiety or do not show their learning well on a standardized test, resulting in inaccurately lower scores.

Many students do not have a fair opportunity to learn the material on the test because they attend poorly-funded schools with large class sizes, too many teachers without subject area certification, and inadequate books, libraries, laboratories, computers and other facilities. These students are usually from low-income families, and many also suffer problems with housing, nutrition or health care. High-stakes tests punish them for things they cannot control.

Students with learning disabilities, whose first language is not English, or who attend vocational schools fail high-stakes tests far more frequently than do mainstream students.

Some people say that it is unfair to students to graduate them if they have not been adequately educated. But if students do not have access to an adequate and equitable education, they end up being held accountable while the system is not. States must take responsibility and be held accountable for providing a strong educational opportunity for all.

2) High-stakes testing leads to increased grade retention and dropping out.

Grade retention has repeatedly been proven to be counterproductive: students who are retained do not improve academically, are emotionally damaged by retention, suffer a loss of interest in school and self-esteem, and are more likely to drop out of school.

The most comprehensive national study finds that graduation tests lead to a higher dropout rate for students who are relatively low-achievers in school, while they do not produce improved learning for those who stay in school.

3) High-stakes testing produces teaching to the test.

The higher the stakes, the more schools focus instruction on the tests. As a result, what is not tested often is not taught. Whole subjects may be dropped; e.g., science, social studies, art or physical education may be eliminated if only language arts and math are tested. Important topics or skills that cannot be tested with paper-and-pencil tests—such as writing research papers or conducting laboratory experiments—are not taught.

Instruction starts to look like the tests. For example, reading is reduced to short passages followed by multiple-choice questions, a kind of "reading" that does not exist in the real world. Writing becomes the "five-paragraph essay" that is useless except on standardized tests.

Narrowing of curriculum and instruction happens most to low-income students. In schools serving wealthier areas, teachers and parents make sure most students gain the skills and knowledge they need to succeed in college and life. Too often, poor kids in under-funded schools get little more than test coaching that does not adequately prepare them for further learning. In some schools, the library budget is spent on test prep materials, and professional development is reduced to training teachers to be better test coaches. All this further limits educational opportunities for low-income children.

Some people say that teaching to the test is fine if test content is important. However:

- Most tests include many topics that are not important, while many important areas are not included on standardized tests because they cannot be measured by such tests.

- Teaching to the test produces a classroom climate and style of teaching that is ineffective and turns many students off to learning.

- Teaching to the test does not produce real and sustained gains on independent learning measures. Teaching to the test does not work if the goal is high-quality learning.

4) High-stakes testing drives out good teachers.

As learning largely depends on teacher quality, real improvements in schools can only come through teachers. Good teachers are often discouraged, even disgusted, by the overemphasis on testing. Many excellent teachers leave. It is absurd to believe that the "best and brightest" will want to become teachers when teaching is reduced to test prep and when schools are continually attacked by politicians, business leaders and the media. When narrow tests are used to hold schools accountable, teachers also leave low-performing schools where they are needed most.

5) High-stakes testing misinforms the public.

People have a right to know how well schools are doing. However, tests fail to provide sufficient information. The new federal requirement that only assessment scores be used to determine whether schools are improving will make the situation worse.

Teaching to the test causes score inflation (score gains that don't represent actual improvements in learning) which misleads the public into thinking schools are improving, when they may not be better—and due to teaching to the test, may even be worse.

Most tests are secret, so the public cannot know what students are expected to know. State academic content standards typically are too long, often too obscure, and much of what is in them is not tested.

Tests are a narrow slice of what parents and the public need to know about schools. They don't include non-academic areas and they are weak measures of academics.

Test results don't take into account non-school factors that affect learning, such as poverty, hunger, student mobility, lack of medical care, safety, community resources, parents' education—all of which must be addressed if "no children are to be left behind."

Conclusion: High-stakes testing does not improve education.

Test standards and major research groups such as the National Academy of Sciences clearly state that major educational decisions should not be based solely on a test score. High-stakes testing punishes students, and often teachers, for things they cannot control. It drives students and teachers away from learning, and at times from school. It narrows, distorts, weakens and impoverishes the curriculum while fostering forms of instruction that fail to engage students or support high-quality learning. In a high-stakes testing environment, the limit to educational improvement is largely dictated by the tests—but the tests are a poor measure of high-quality curriculum and learning. In particular, the emphasis on testing hurts low-income students and students from minority groups. Testing cannot provide adequate information about school quality or progress. High-stakes testing actively hurts, rather than helps, genuine educational improvement.

FairTest: The National Center for Fair and Open Testing. 2007. "The Dangerous Consequences of High-stakes Standardized Testing." http://www.fairtest.org/dangerous-consequences-highstakes-standardized-tes.

Trends in International Mathematics and Science Study

The Trends in International Mathematics and Science Study (TIMSS) gathers data periodically to compare the achievement of U.S. students with that of their peers in other countries. Students in the countries that participate are sampled; that is, not all students take the tests. The tests are translated, both literally and culturally, so that items are comparable in all the languages in which the test is administered.

The data in Tables 6.1 and 6.2 below represent scale scores, scores that have been converted from raw scores to allow for comparison between versions of the test and across test years. They are presented here to show how the performance of students in the United States ranks with students in the other countries that participated in the 2003 TIMSS.

Scores of fourth grade students in the United States ranked 12th of the 25 countries participating in the 2003 TIMSS. Eighth grade students' scores ranked 15th of the 44 countries whose eighth graders participated in the study.

The scores in Tables 6.1 and 6.2 are drawn from tables in Gonzales, P., J. C. Guzman, L. Partelow, E. Pahlke, L. Jocelyn, D. Kastberg, and T. Williams. *Highlights from the Trends in International Mathematics and Science Study (TIMSS) 2003* (NCES 2005–005). U.S. Department of Education, National Center for Education Statistics. Washington, DC: U.S. Government Printing Office, 2004.

TABLE 6.1

Average 2003 TIMSS Mathematics Scores of Fourth Grade Students, by Country

Country	Average Fourth Grade Score
Singapore	594
Hong Kong SAR	575
Japan	565
Chinese Taipei	564
Belgium–Flemish	551
Netherlands	540
Latvia	536
Lithuania	534
Russian Federation	532
England	531
Hungary	529
United States	518
Cyprus	510
Republic of Moldova	504
Italy	503
Australia	499
New Zealand	493
Scotland	490
Slovenia	479
Armenia	456
Norway	451
Iran	389
Philippines	358
Morocco	347
Tunisia	339

Source: Gonzales et al., 2004, 4.

TABLE 6. 2
Average 2003 TIMSS Mathematics Scores of Eighth Grade Students, by Country

Country	2003
Singapore	605
Republic of Korea	589
Hong Kong SAR	586
Chinese Taipei	585
Japan	570
Belgium—Flemish	537
Netherlands	536
Estonia	531
Hungary	529
Malaysia	508
Latvia	508
Russian Federation	508
Slovak Republic	508
Australia	508
United States	504
Lithuania	502
Sweden	499
Scotland	498
Israel	496
New Zealand	494
Slovenia	493
Italy	484
Armenia	478
Serbia	477
Bulgaria	476
Romania	475
Norway	461
Republic of Moldova	460
Cyprus	459
Republic of Macedonia	435
Lebanon	433
Jordan	424
Iran	411
Indonesia	411
Tunisia	410
Egypt	406
Palestinian National Authority	401
Chile	390
Morocco	387
Philippines	378
Botswana	366
Saudi Arabia	332
Ghana	276
South Africa	264

Source: Gonzales et al., 2004, 5.

The Progress in International Reading Literacy Study

The Progress in International Reading Literacy Study (PIRLS) is an international study that compares the reading literacy of fourth grade students in the United States with their fourth grade peers from other countries. The PIRLS was first administered in 2001, with the most recent administration in 2006. The data reported in Table 6.3 below are scale scores that come from a report that compares the outcomes of the 2001 PIRLS with those of the 2006 PIRLS. Note that scores missing from 2001 indicates that those

TABLE 6.3

Average PIRLS Reading Scores of Fourth Grade Students by Country, 2001 and 2006, in Order of their 2006 Rankings (from highest to lowest)

Country	2001 Scores	2006 Scores
Russian Federation	528	565
Hong Kong SAR	528	564
Canada, Alberta		560
Singapore	528	558
Canada, British Columbia		558
Luxembourg		557
Canada, Ontario	548	555
Italy	541	551
Hungary	543	551
Sweden	561	549
Germany	539	548
Netherlands	554	547
Belgium–Flemish		547
Bulgaria	550	547
Denmark		546
Canada, Nova Scotia		542
Latvia	545	541
United States	542	540
England	553	539
Austria		538
Lithuania	543	537
Chinese Taipei		535
Canada, Quebec	537	533
New Zealand	529	532
Slovak Republic	518	531
Scotland	528	527
France	535	522

TABLE 6.3
Average PIRLS Reading Scores of Fourth Grade Students by Country, 2001 and 2006, in Order of their 2006 Rankings (from highest to lowest) (*Continued*)

Country	2001 Scores	2006 Scores
Slovenia	502	522
Poland		519
Spain		513
Israel	509	512
Iceland	512	511
Republic of Moldova	492	500
Belgium—French		500
Norway		498
Romania		489
Georgia		471
Macedonia		442
Trinidad and Tobago		436
Iran		421
Indonesia		405
Qatar		353
Kuwait		330
Morocco		323
South Africa		302

Source: Baer, J., S. Baldi, K. Ayotte, and P. Green. 2007. *The Reading Literacy of U.S. Fourth-Grade Students in an International Context: Results From the 2001 and 2006 Progress in International Reading Literacy Study (PIRLS)* (NCES 2008–017). National Center for Education Statistics, Institute of Education Sciences, U.S. Department of Education. Washington, DC: U.S. Government Printing Office.

countries did not participant in the 2001 PIRLS. The scores are listed from highest to lowest of the 2006 scores.

On the 2001 administration of the PIRLS, U.S. fourth grade students' scores ranked eighth of the 23 countries whose students participated. In 2006, U.S. fourth graders' scores ranked 18th of the 45 participating countries.

The Programme for International Student Assessment (PISA)

The Programme for International Student Assessment (PISA) is a survey that is conducted every three years of 15-year-olds' knowledge and skills. The survey is conducted through the Organization for Economic Co-operation and Development (OECD). In 2006, students from 57 countries participated in the survey that gathered data about science, mathematics, and reading achievement. Table 6.4 below shows the average (mean) scale score for each country, as well as that country's ranking for science, mathematics, and reading. There are no reading data available for the United States. The data in the table are from

TABLE 6.4
Program in International Student Assessment (PISA) Scores, 2006

Country	Mean Score Science	Country Rank in Science	Mean Score Math	Country Rank in Math	Mean Score Reading	Country Rank in Reading
Finland	563	1	548	1	547	2
Canada	534	2	527	5	527	3
Japan	531	3	523	6	498	12
New Zealand	530	4	522	7	521	4
Australia	527	5	520	9	513	6
Netherlands	525	5	531	3	507	9
Korea	522	7	547	2	556	1
Germany	516	8	504	14	495	13
United Kingdom	515	9	495	18	495	13
Czech Republic	513	10	510	11	483	20
Switzerland	512	11	530	4	499	11
Austria	511	12	505	13	490	16
Belgium	510	13	520	8	510	7
Ireland	508	14	501	16	517	5
Hungary	504	15	491	21	482	21
Sweden	503	16	502	15	507	9
OECD average	500	—	498	—	500	—
Poland	498	17	495	19	508	8
Denmark	496	18	513	10	494	15
France	495	19	496	17	488	17
Iceland	491	20	506	12	484	18
United States	489	21	474	25	*	*
Slovak Republic	488	22	492	20	466	25
Spain	488	23	480	24	461	26
Norway	487	24	490	22	484	18
Luxembourg	486	25	490	23	479	22
Italy	475	26	462	27	469	24
Portugal	474	27	466	26	472	23
Greece	473	28	459	28	460	27
Turkey	424	29	424	29	447	28
Mexico	410	30	406	30	410	29

*Reading data for the United States were withdrawn.

OECD. 2007. "Executive Summary." *PISA 2006: Science Competencies for Tomorrow's World*. Paris: Author.

Data in this table are drawn from the OECD. Executive Summary of the 2007 PISA report. *PISA 2006: Science Competencies for Tomorrow's World*. Paris: Author, 2007, pp. 22, 47, 53.

Data from the National Assessment of Educational Progress (NAEP)

The National Assessment of Education Progress (NAEP) is administered periodically to students in fourth, eighth, and 12th grades across the country. The tables below (Tables 6.5, 6.6, 6.7, 6.8, 6.9, and 6.10) summarize average scores from the various administrations (1992–2007) of the test. Data in the tables are scale scores drawn from reports issued by the U.S. Department of Education, Institute of Education Sciences, National Center for Education Statistics, National Assessment of Education Progress. Scale scores allow for comparison across years and across tests. In other words, the use of scale scores allows for a representation of real growth that is not corrupted by differences in raw scores or different tests. Additional data, as well as more in-depth analysis of the data in a series of publications titled "The Nation's Report Card" can be found at http://nces.ed.gov/nationsreportcard/.

Data in Table 6.5 show average reading scores for students in fourth and eighth grades for each of the administrations of NAEP

TABLE 6.5
Average Reading Scores for Fourth and Eighth Grades

Year	Average Fourth Grade Score	Average Eighth Grade Score
1992	217	260
1994	214	260
1998	217/215*	264/263*
2000	213	
2002	219	264
2003	218	263
2005	219	262
2007	221	263

*The first score represents testing without accommodations, the second with accommodations.

Source: National Center for Education Statistics. 2008. *The Nation's Report Card: Reading 2007*. Washington, DC: U.S. Department of Education.

between 1992 and 2007. During that time period, those scores have risen only slightly.

Table 6.6 shows the average fourth and eighth grade scores in mathematics from 1990 to 2007. Scores at both the fourth and eighth grade levels have increased significantly and consistently during that time period.

TABLE 6.6
Average Mathematics Scores for Fourth and Eighth Grades

Year	Average Fourth Grade Score	Average Eighth Grade Score
1990	213	263
1992	220	268
1996	224/224*	272/270*
2000	226	273
2003	235	278
2005	238	279
2007	240	281

Source: National Center for Education Statistics. 2008. *The Nation's Report Card: Mathematics 2007*. Washington, DC: U.S. Department of Education.

Table 6.7 presents average scores for fourth, eighth, and 12th grade students in science over the three years science has been tested by the NAEP. The average scores of fourth grade students have risen slightly, while those of eighth grade students have remained the same, and 12th grade students' scores have decreased slightly.

TABLE 6.7
Average Science Scores for Fourth, Eighth, and Twelfth Grades

Year	Average Fourth Grade Scores	Average Eighth Grade Scores	Average Twelfth Grade Scores
1996	147	149	150
2000	147	149	146
2005	151	149	147

Source: National Center for Education Statistics. 2006. *The Nation's Report Card: Mathematics 2005*. Washington, DC: U.S. Department of Education.

Civics scores for fourth, eighth, and 12th grade students on the NAEP are presented in Table 6.8. The scores show that between the two years that civics was included on the test, fourth grade students' scores increased, eighth grade students' scores remained the same, and 12th grade students' scores increased slightly.

TABLE 6.8
Average Civics Scores for Fourth, Eighth, and Twelfth Grades

Year	Average Fourth Grade Scores	Average Eighth Grade Scores	Average Twelfth Grade Scores
1998	150	150	150
2006	154	150	151

Source: National Center for Education Statistics. 2007. *The Nation's Report Card: Civics 2006.* Washington, DC: U.S. Department of Education.

The NAEP has measured students' U.S. history knowledge three times—1994, 2001, and 2006. Data for those three years are presented in Table 6.9. They show that the scores of all three grade levels tested, fourth, eighth, and 12th, have risen consistently.

TABLE 6.9
Average U.S. History Scores for Fourth, Eighth, and Twelfth Grades

Year	Average Fourth Grade Scores	Average Eighth Grade Scores	Average Twelfth Grade Scores
1994	205	259	286
2001	208/209*	260/262*	287/287*
2006	211	263	290

*The first score represents testing without accommodations, the second with accommodations.

Source: National Center for Education Statistics. 2007. *The Nation's Report Card: Civics 2006.* Washington, DC: U.S. Department of Education.

Fourth, eighth, and 12th grade students' knowledge of geography has been assessed on the NAEP twice, in 1994 and in 2001. Table 6.10 shows the average scores of fourth, eighth, and 12th grade students during those years. Fourth and eighth grade students' scores rose slightly between the two administrations of the test; 12th grade students' scores remained the same.

TABLE 6.10
Average Geography Scores for Fourth, Eighth, and Twelfth Grades

Year	Average Fourth Grade Score	Average Eighth Grade Score	Average Twelfth Grade Score
1994	206	260	285
2001	209	262	285

Source: National Center for Education Statistics. 2002. *The Nation's Report Card: Geography 2001.* Washington, DC: U.S. Department of Education.

7

Directory of Organizations

There are many, many organizations involved in the reform of education in the United States. The organizations listed in this chapter are intended to represent the types of organizations working toward school reform. Each of the organizations listed here has a mission that involves education reform or school improvement, and each has a perspective or philosophical base that can be seen throughout the organization's work and publications.

This list is not intended to be exclusive or exhaustive. The organizations listed below are representative of the myriad groups working toward education reform.

The directory begins with governmental agencies. These include the U.S. Department of Education, as well as the networks of support agencies created by and funded through the No Child Left Behind legislation. Included in the governmental agencies are some of the state education agencies' school improvement or education reform support Web sites. Next, there are agencies whose primary focus is conducting and disseminating research about education reform. The organizations in the third category are those that are issue-focused; they provide information and professional development about a clearly defined issue related to education reform. The last category includes membership organizations that provide information, publications, and other services in support of education reform.

Governmental Agencies

U.S. Department of Education
www.ed.gov

The U.S. Department of Education provides a wealth of information and support for students, parents, teachers, administrators, schools, school districts, and states about the reform of education, including a wide range of data and statistics that describe the state of education in the United States. The Web site links to myriad online resources that include lesson plans and activities, information about grants, and information about how to comply with No Child Left Behind. In addition, under No Child Left Behind, the U.S. Department of Education funds a network of 10 regional educational laboratories, a network of 16 comprehensive regional and 5 content centers, and 62 parent information and resource centers, all of which provide information, guidance, and technical assistance to support education reform.

Regional Educational Laboratories

REL
555 New Jersey Ave, NW
Washington, DC 20208
800-USA-LEARN
http://ies.ed.gov/ncee/edlabs/

The Regional Educational Laboratory (REL) program is a network of 10 laboratories that provide research-based technical assistance to schools, school districts, and states in their regions. Each of the laboratories conducts and disseminates research and works with schools, school districts, and states to apply the research in their education reform efforts. In addition, REL has a number of publications available on the Web that are intended to support education reform.

The 10 laboratories, the states they serve, and their contact information are listed below. Each of the laboratories has a number of partner agencies that provide more targeted assistance. That information is available on the individual REL Web sites.

REL Appalachia at CNA
4825 Mark Center Drive
Alexandria, VA 22311

703-824-2828 or 800-344-0007 ext. 2828
RELAppalachia@cna.org
http://www.RELAppalachia.org/

REL Appalachia serves the states of Kentucky, Tennessee, Virginia, and West Virginia.

REL Mid-Atlantic
Pennsylvania State University
277 Chambers Building
University Park, PA 16802
866-RELMAFYI
info@relmid-atlantic.org

REL Mid-Atlantic serves Delaware, Maryland, New Jersey, Pennsylvania, and Washington, D.C.

REL Mid-Continent Research for Education and Learning
4601 DTC Boulevard, Suite 500
Denver, CO 80237
303-337-0990
relcentral@mcrel.org
http://mcrel.org/

REL Central serves Colorado, Kansas, Missouri, Nebraska, North Dakota, South Dakota, and Wyoming.

REL Midwest at Learning Point Associates
1120 East Diehl Road
Naperville, IL 60563
866-730-6735
relmidwest@learningpt.org
http://www.learningpt.org

REL Midwest serves Illinois, Indiana, Iowa, Michigan, Minnesota, Ohio, and Wisconsin.

REL Northeast & Islands at Education Development Center, Inc.
55 Chapel Street
Newton, MA 02458
617-618-2747
jweber@edc.org
http://www.edc.org

REL Northeast and Islands serves Connecticut, Maine, Massachusetts, New Hampshire, New York, Puerto Rico, Rhode Island, Vermont, and the Virgin Islands.

REL Northwest at Northwest Regional Educational Laboratory
101 SW Main, Suite 500
Portland, OR 97204
800-547-6339 ext. 486 or 454
info@NWREL.org
http://www.nwrel.org

REL Northwest serves Alaska, Idaho, Montana, Oregon, and Washington.

REL Pacific at Pacific Resources for Education and Learning
900 Fort Street Mall, Suite 1300
Honolulu, HI 96813
800-377-4773
burniskj@prel.org
http://www.prel.org

REL Pacific serves the state of Hawaii and the territories of American Samoa, the Federated States of Micronesia, Guam, the Northern Mariana Islands, the Republic of the Marshall Islands, and the Republic of Palau.

REL Southeast at SERVE Center
University of North Carolina at Greensboro
Gateway University Research Park
5900 Summit Ave.
Browns Summit, NC 27214
800-755-3277
RELSoutheast@serve.org
http://www.serve.org/

REL Southeast serves Alabama, Florida, Georgia, Mississippi, North Carolina, and South Carolina.

REL Southwest at Edvance Research, Inc.
9901 1H-10 West, Suite 700
San Antonio, TX 78230
877-EDVANCE (338-2623)

RELinfo@edvanceresearch.com
http://www.edvanceresearch.com

REL Southwest serves Arkansas, Louisiana, New Mexico, Oklahoma, and Texas.

REL West at WestEd
730 Harrison Street
San Francisco, CA 94107
866-853-1831
relwest@wested.org
http://www.wested.org/

REL West serves Arizona, California, Nevada, and Utah.

Comprehensive Centers

Each of the 16 regional comprehensive centers provides research-based technical assistance to assist in implementing No Child Left Behind and reforming and improving educational programs and schools. The comprehensive centers provide information, publications, and professional development to schools in the states they serve. Many of them also provide such tools as school improvement planning guides, podcasts, and webinars for the clients in their states. The 16 centers, the states they serve, and their contact information are listed below.

The Alaska Comprehensive Center serves Alaska.
1016 W. 6th Avenue, Suite 401
Anchorage, AK 99501
907-349-0651
210 Ferry Way
Juneau, AK 99801
907-586-6806
http://www.alaskacc.org/contact

The Appalachia Regional Comprehensive Center serves Kentucky, North Carolina, Tennessee, Virginia, and West Virginia.
P.O. Box 1348
Charleston, WV 25325-1348
800-624-9120
304-347-0461

304-347-1847 (fax)
http://www.arcc.edvantia.org/

The California Comprehensive Center serves California.
1107 9th Street–4th Floor
Sacramento, CA 95814-3607
916-492-4053
http://www.cacompcenter.org/cs/cacc/print/htdocs/cacc/
home.htm

The Florida and the Islands Regional Comprehensive Center serves Florida, Puerto Rico, and the U.S. Virgin Islands.
1000 North Ashley Drive, Suite 312
Tampa, FL 33602
800-756-9003
813-228-0632
http://www.ets.org/flicc/

The Great Lakes East Regional Comprehensive Center serves Indiana, Michigan, and Ohio.
Learning Point Associates
1120 East Diehl Road, Suite 200
Naperville, IL 60563-1486
800-356-2735
630-649-6700 (fax)
http://www.learningpt.org/greatlakeseast/

The Great Lakes West Regional Comprehensive Center serves Illinois and Wisconsin.
Learning Point Associates
1120 East Diehl Road, Suite 200
Naperville, IL 60563-1486
800-356-2735
630-649-6700 (fax)
http://www.learningpt.org/greatlakeswest/

The Mid-Atlantic Region Comprehensive Center serves Delaware, Maryland, New Jersey, and Pennsylvania, and the District of Columbia.
George Washington University
Center for Equity and Excellence in Education (GW-CEEE)
1555 Wilson Blvd., Suite 515

Arlington, Virginia 22209-2004
703-528-3588 or 800-925-3223
703-528-5973 (fax)
maccinfo@ceee.gwu.edu
http://www.macc.ceee.gwu.edu/

The Mid-Continent Comprehensive Center serves Arkansas,
Kansas, Missouri, and Oklahoma.
555 E. Constitution
Norman, OK 73072
405-325-1729 or 800-228-1766
405-325-1824 (fax)
http://www.mc3edsupport.org/

The New England Region Comprehensive Center serves
Connecticut, Maine, Massachusetts, New Hampshire, Rhode
Island, and Vermont.
RMC Research Corporation
1000 Market Street
Portsmouth, NH 03801
603-422-8888
800-258-0802
http://www.necomprehensivecenter.org/

The New York Comprehensive Center serves New York.
RMC Research Corporation
60 East 42nd Street, Suite 1345
New York, NY 10165-1345
212-972-4762
212-972-4763 (fax)
http://www.nycomprehensivecenter.org/

The North Central Region Comprehensive Center serves
Iowa, Minnesota, Nebraska, North Dakota, and South
Dakota.
North Central Comprehensive Center
Hamline University
1536 Hewitt Avenue, MS C-1924
St. Paul, MN 55104
651-523-2079
http://www.mcrel.org/nccc/

The Northwest Region Comprehensive Center serves Idaho, Montana, Oregon, Washington, and Wyoming.
Northwest Regional Educational Laboratory
101 SW Main Street, Suite 500
Portland, OR 97204-3297
503-275-9500
http://www.nwrel.org/nwrcc/

The Pacific Region Comprehensive Center serves Hawaii, American Samoa, Commonwealth of the Northern Mariana Islands, Federated States of Micronesia (Chuuk, Kosrae, Pohnpei, and Yap), Guam, Republic of the Marshall Islands, and the Republic of Palau.
http://www.pacificcompcenter.org/

The Southeast Region Comprehensive Center serves Alabama, Georgia, Louisiana, Mississippi, and South Carolina.
3501 N. Causeway Blvd., Suite 700
Metairie, LA 70002
800-644-8671
http://secc.sedl.org/

The Texas Comprehensive Center serves Texas.
SEDL
4700 Mueller Blvd.
Austin, TX 78723
512-476-6861
http://txcc.sedl.org/

The West/Southwest Region Comprehensive Center serves Arizona, Colorado, Nevada, New Mexico, and Utah.
Southwest Comprehensive Center
2020 N. Central Avenue, Suite 660
Phoenix, AZ 85004-4598
866-979-7322
info@swcompcenter.org
http://www.swcompcenter.org/cs/swcc/print/htdocs/swcc/home.htm

National Content Centers

Five national content centers provide assistance targeted at specific content needs for educational reform. They address assessment and accountability, high schools, innovation and improvement, instruction, and teacher quality. The centers, the focus of their work, and their contact information are listed below.

Assessment and Accountability Comprehensive Center
http://www.aacompcenter.org/cs/aacc/print/htdocs/aacc/home.htm

No Child Left Behind has rigorous requirements for assessment of students and programs and for accountability for student learning. The **Assessment and Accountability Comprehensive Center** is a collaboration between WestEd and the National Center for Research on Evaluation, Standards, and Student Testing (CRESST) that provides support, research, and technical assistance to states, school districts, and comprehensive centers in meeting the responsibilities for assessment and accountability under No Child Left Behind.

National High School Center
http://www.betterhighschools.org/

The National High School Center, housed at the American Institutes of Research, serves as a central source of information and research on high school improvement for the regional comprehensive centers and states, and center staff collaborate with regional comprehensive center staff to offer technical assistance to state and school districts. The Web site of the National High School Center offers a wealth of online resources for improvement and reform of high schools and high school programs, including links to a wide range of research and reports.

Center on Improvement and Innovation
http://www.centerii.org/

The **Center on Improvement and Innovation** provides support and technical assistance to comprehensive centers on school restructuring, innovation, and outreach to parents. Like the other content centers, staff members collaborate with comprehensive center staff to provide assistance to states and school districts. On its Web site, the Center on Improvement and Innovation has several tools for developing plans for school improvement and sustaining school improvement that are available online. With the Council of Chief State School Officers, the center publishes a "support for school improvement" e-newsletter that describes successful efforts for school reform and improvement, innovation, and outreach to parents, also available through the center's Web site.

Center on Instruction
http://www.centeroninstruction.org/

The **Center on Instruction** serves as a conduit for research on, information about, and descriptions of best practices in K-12 instruction in the areas of mathematics, science, reading, English language learning, and special education, aimed primarily at supporting the work of the comprehensive centers; the resources, however, are publicly available and may be accessed by teachers, school administrators, and others interested in the improvement of instruction. The center's Web site has links to research briefs about instruction in each of the areas, and a center newsletter disseminates additional information, research briefs, and research news on instruction.

National Comprehensive Center on Teacher Quality
http://www.tqsource.org/

The **National Comprehensive Center on Teacher Quality** is a clearinghouse of information about highly qualified teachers— identifying, recruiting, evaluating, and keeping them. While the information at this site would be most valuable for school administrators, there is also information about the progress of states in ensuring that all students have highly qualified teachers.

Parent Information and Resource Centers

Funded also under No Child Left Behind, the network of 62 Parent Information and Resource Centers (PIRCs) provides technical assistance and support for designing and developing parental involvement programs that lead to improved student achievement and strengthened partnerships between parents and families on the one hand and schools, teachers, school administrators, and other school personnel on the other. The PIRCs are funded through grants from the United States Department of Education. Each of the PIRCs has a local board of directors, a mission statement, and specific objectives for their work. The PIRCs provide a wide variety of services to parents and school and school district personnel; those services are described on their individual Web sites. The PIRCs and their contact information are listed below.

Alabama State PIRC
10520 U.S. Highway 231
Wetumpka, AL 36092
334-567-2252
http://www.alabamaparentcenter.com/

Alaska State PIRC
AKPIRC
210 Ferry Way
Juneau, AK 99801
http://www.akpirc.org

American Samoa PIRC
5770 Fagatogo
Pago Pago, AS 96799
684-633-6094
http://www.aspirc.org

Arizona State PIRC
2600 W. Knox Road
Chandler, AZ 85224
480-224-2060
http://www.azpirc.com

Arkansas State PIRC
Jones Family Resource Center, Suite 113
614 E. Emma
Springdale, AR 72764
501-364-7580
http://www.parenting-ed.org

California PIRC
16033 E. San Bernardino Road
Covina, CA 91722
626-814-4441 ext. 103
http://www.bilingualeducation.org

California PIRC
4300 Sisk Road, Suite D

Modesto, CA 95356
209-545-9766
http://www.calpirc.org

Colorado PIRC
3607 Martin Luther King Blvd.
Denver, CO 80205
303-355-5387 ext. 327
http://www.cpirc.org

Colorado PIRC
7150 Hooker Street, Suite B
Westminster, CO 80030
720-890-0123
http://www.ctpirc.org

Connecticut State PIRC
SERC 25 Industrial Park Road
Middletown, CT 06457
860-632-1485
http://www.coparentcoalition.org

Delaware PIRC
5570 Kirkwood Highway
Orchard Commons Business Center
Wilmington, DE 19808
302-999-7394
http://www.DEPIRC.org

District of Columbia PIRC
Multicultural Community Service at the Josephine Butler Parks
Center
2437 15th Street NW
Washington, DC 20009
202-238-9385
http://www.mcsdc.org

Federated States of Micronesia (FSM) PIRC
900 Fort St. Mall, Suite 1300
Honolulu, HI 96813
808-441-1316
http://www.prel.org/programs/clt/pirc-fsm.aspx

Florida PIRC
2735 Whitney Road
Clearwater, FL 33760
727-523-1130
http://www.floridapirc.org

Florida PIRC
3500 East Fletcher Avenue, Suite 301
Tampa, FL 33613
813-974-2673
http://www.floridapirc.usf.edu

Georgia State PIRC
600 West Peachtree Street, Suite 1200
Atlanta, GA 30308
404-881-3292
http://www.cisga.org

Guam PIRC
Suite 101-C, J & G Commercial Center
138 E. Marine Corps Drive
Hagatna, GU 96910
671-477-7472
http://www.guampirc.org

Hawaii State PIRC
1485 Linapuni Street, Suite 105
Honolulu, HI 96819
808-841-6177
http://www.hawaiipirc.org

Idaho State PIRC
3010 W. State, Suite 104
Boise, ID 83703
208-345-3344 ext. 1005
http://www.idahopirc.org

Illinois State PIRC
600 S. Michigan Avenue
Chicago, IL 60605
312-369-8824
http://www.colum.edu/CCAP/Programs/Illinois_PIRC.php

Indiana State PIRC
921 E. 86th Street, Suite 108
Indianapolis, IN 46240
317-205-2595
http://www.fscp.org

Iowa State PIRC
12199 Stratford Drive
Clive, IA 50325
641-751-4010
http://www.iowaparents.org

Kansas State PIRC
3500 SW 10th Avenue
Topeka, KS 66604
866-711-6711
http://www.kpirc.org

Kentucky State PIRC
100 Alpine Drive
P.O. Box 1249
Shelbyville, KY 40066
502-647-3533 ext. 210 or 800-251-4676 ext. 210
http://www.kypirc.org

Louisiana State PIRC
520 Olive Street, Suite C04
Shreveport, LA 71104
318-429-6958
http://www.LPIRC.org

Maine State PIRC
12 Shuman Avenue
P.O. Box 2067
Augusta, ME 04330
207-623-2145
http://www.mpf.org

Maryland State PIRC
5272 River Road, Suite 340
Mid-Atlantic Equity Consortium, Inc.
Bethesda, MD 20816

301-657-7741 ext. 118
http://www.mdpirc.org/

Massachusetts State PIRC
1135 Tremont Street, Suite 420
Boston, MA 02120
617-399-8344
http://www.pplace.org

Michigan State PIRC
11172 Adams Street
Holland, MI 49423
616-396-7566 ext. 116
http://www.lifeservicessystem.org

Minnesota State PIRC
8161 Normandale Blvd.
Bloomington, MN 55437
952-838-9000
http://www.pacer.org/mpc/

Mississippi State PIRC
333 Yazoo Street
Lexington, MS 39095
662-834-0905
http://www.mississippipirc.org

Missouri PIRC
1300 E. Bradford Parkway
Springfield, MO 65804
417-269-7245

Missouri PIRC
815 Olive Street, Suite 22
St. Louis, MO 63101
816-926-4278
http://www.missouri-pirc.org

Montana State PIRC
2525 Palmer Street, Suite 1
Missoula, MT 59808
406-543-3550
http://www.montanapirc.com

Nebraska State PIRC
215 Centennial Mall South, Suite 200
Lincoln, NE 68508
877-843-6651
http://www.nebraskapirc.org

Nevada State PIRC
380 Edison Way
Reno, NV 89502
775-353-5533
http://www.nevadapirc.org

New Hampshire State PIRC
P.O. Box 2405
Concord, NH 03302
603-224-7005
http://www.parentinformationcenter.org

New Jersey State PIRC
103 Church Street, Suite 210
New Brunswick, NJ 08901
732-246-8060 ext. 110
http://www.njpirc.org

New Mexico State PIRC
1920B Columbia Drive SE
Albuquerque, NM 87106
505-247-0192
http://www.parentsreachingout.org

New York PIRC
1000 Main Street
Buffalo, NY 14202
716-332-4140
http://Epicforchildren.org

New York PIRC
203 N. Hamilton Street
Watertown, NY 13601
315-788-8450
http://www.nyspirc.org/

North Carolina State PIRC
907 Barra Row, Suite 102/103

Davidson, NC 28036
800-962-6817
http://www.ecac-parentcenter.org

North Dakota State PIRC
North Dakota Parent Assistance & Supportive Schools (NDPASS)
1600 2nd Avenue SW, Suite #29
Minot, ND 58701
701-837-7511
http://www.ndstatepirc.org

Ohio State PIRC
2400 Reading Road
Cincinnati, OH 45202
888-OHPIRC9 or 513-762-7118

Oklahoma State PIRC
Eagle Ridge Institute
4801 North Classen Blvd., Suite 212
Oklahoma City, OK 73118
405-478-4078
http://www.okpirc.org

Oregon State PIRC
101 SW Main, Suite 500
Portland, OR 97204
503-275-9500 ext. 552
http://www.nwrel.org/pirc/index.php

Pennsylvania State PIRC
275 Grandview Avenue, Suite 200
Camp Hill, PA 17011
717-763-1661
http://www.center-school.org/pa-pirc/

Puerto Rico PIRC
13 Jose Fernandez St.
San Juan, PR 00928
787-763-4665
http://www.apnipr.org

Republic of Marshall Islands (RMI) PIRC
900 Fort St. Mall, Suite 1300

Honolulu, HI 96813
692-625-2343
http://www.prel.org/centers/clt.asp

Rhode Island State PIRC
175 Main Street
Pawtucket, RI 02860
401-724-0867 ext. 156
http://www.ristatepirc.org

South Carolina State PIRC
1634 Main St. Suite 100
Columbia, SC 29201
803-744-4029
http://www.scparentwise.org

South Dakota State PIRC
P.O. Box 218
Sturgis, SD 57785
605-347-6260
http://www.sdpirc.org

Tennessee State PIRC
701 Bradford Ave.
Nashville, TN 37204
615-269-7751 ext. 212
http://www.tnvoices.org

Texas State PIRC
5835 Callaghan, Suite 350
San Antonio, TX 78228
210-444-1710
http://www.idra.org

Utah State PIRC
2500 S. State Street, RM D120
Salt Lake City, UT 84115
801-646-4608
http://www.ufpn.org

Vermont State PIRC
600 Blair Park, Suite 301

Williston, VT 05495
802-876-5315
http://www.pircvermont.org

Virgin Islands PIRC
51 Golden Grove, Box 913
Kingshill, St. Croix, VI 00821
340-643-9888

Virginia State PIRC
100 N. Washington St., Suite 234
Falls Church, VA 22046
800-869-6782
http://www.peatc.org

Washington State PIRC
ESD-123, 3918 West Court Street
Pasco, WA 99301
509-544-5770

West Virginia State PIRC
P.O. Box 1348
Charleston, WV 25325
304-347-0478
http://wvpc.edvantia.org

Wisconsin State PIRC
660 E. Mason Street, Suite 100
Milwaukee, WI 53202
414-755-8702
http://www.parentspluswi.org

Wyoming State PIRC
5 N. Lobban Avenue
Buffalo, WY 82834
307-684-7441
http://www.wpen.net

In addition to federal and federally funded agencies and organizations that support education reform, many states also have their own offices of education reform and school improvement. Information about these offices can be found at the individual states' education Web sites.

Research Organizations and Institutes

In the United States, there are many research organizations and institutes that conduct and disseminate research about education in general, and about education reform. Public funding supports some of them, but many others are privately funded or funded through foundations and other granting agencies. Some of the research organizations represent partisan positions. They work to conduct research from a particular perspective or to support a particular point of view, while others are nonpartisan. The research organizations and institutes listed below are representative of the many such organizations in the United States.

Brown Center on Education Policy
Brookings Institution
1775 Massachusetts Ave., NW
Washington, DC 20036
202-797-6000
www.brookings.edu/brown.aspx

The Brown Center on Education Policy at the Brookings Institution has as its goal to improve the quality of education in the United States. The center's research is focused on understanding the problems of the education system in the United States and proposing practical solutions to those problems. The research reports produced by the center are intended, not only for use by researchers and academics, but also for informing policy makers and the public. The Web site includes many papers and research that are available to download.

Institute of Education Sciences
555 New Jersey Ave., NW
Washington, DC 20208
800-USA-LEARN
http://ies.ed.gov

The Institute of Education Sciences (IES) was established by Congress in the Education Sciences Reform Act of 2002, P.L. 107–179, as part of the U.S. Department of Education. IES reports present data, statistics, and evaluations about education in the United States. In IES, there are four research centers: the National Center for Education Research (http://ies.ed.gov/ncer/) supports rigorous, scientifically based research to improve educational outcomes and educational quality; the National Center for Education Statistics (http://nces.ed.gov/) provides statistics on education in the United States, including data that compare U.S. education with that of other countries; the National Center for Education Evaluation and Regional Assistance (http://ies.ed.gov/ncee/) conducts evaluations of federal education programs and disseminates the analyses and the results of those evaluations; and the National Center for Special Education Research (http://ies.ed.gov/ncser/) sponsors a program of research that seeks to expand knowledge and understanding of children with disabilities.

SRI International
333 Ravenswood Avenue
Menlo Park, CA 94025-3493
650-859-2000
http://sri.com

SRI International is an independent, nonprofit, client-sponsored research institute. SRI is the parent organization of many smaller research institutes that include the Center for Education and Human Services, whose topics of research and reports include community services, disability policy, early childhood education, and school partnerships (http://policyweb.sri.com/cehs/publications/publications.jsp); the Center for Science, Technology, and Economic Development, whose topics of research and reports include economic development, science and technology policy analysis, research and training program evaluations, centers of excellence program evaluations, and Fulbright program outcome assessments (http://www.sri.com/policy/csted/reports/); the Center for Technology in Learning, whose research topics and reports include program assessments, learning environments, teacher learning, and technology development (http://ctl.sri.com/publications/publications.jsp); and the Center for Education Policy, whose research topics and reports include school reform, teaching and learning, and transitions to college and beyond (http://policyweb.sri.com/cep/publications/publications.jsp).

What Works Clearinghouse
P.O. Box 2393
Princeton, NJ 08543-2393
866-503-6114
http://ies.ed.gov/ncee/wwc/

The What Works Clearinghouse is, according to its Web site, "a central and trusted source of scientific evidence for what works in education." The research presented on the Web site addresses early childhood education, reading instruction, mathematics instruction, character education, English language learning, and dropout prevention. In each of these areas, there is a searchable database of research about interventions, programs, and products appropriate to that area.

Issues-Focused Education Reform Organizations

The organizations listed below are focused on specific issues in or areas of education reform. While there are many more such organizations, the ones included here are intended to be representative of the wide array of such organizations.

Academic Achievement

Achieve, Inc.
1775 Eye Street NW, Suite 410
Washington, DC 20006
202-419-1540
http://www.achieve.org

Achieve, Inc., was established in 1995 by governors and business leaders to help states raise academic standards and student achievement, with the goal of preparing all students to graduate and be ready for college, careers, and citizenship. Among the action initiatives of Achieve, Inc., is the American Diploma Project Network, a project to align high school assessments and graduation requirements with the expectations of higher education and of prospective employers. Achieve, Inc., provides a number of "outreach tools," including a toolkit that provides examples, planning materials, fact sheets, and other information to assist states in school reform.

Education Trust
1250 H St. NW, Suite 700
Washington, DC 20005
202-293-1217
202-293-2605 (fax)

Education Trust-West
155 Grand Avenue, Suite 1025
Oakland, CA 94612
510-465-6444
510-465-0859 (fax)
http://www2.edtrust.org/edtrust/

The Education Trust is an organization committed to high academic achievement for all students at all levels of education. The trust works toward this commitment through advocacy and support of schools and communities in their own advocacy, through testimony before Congress and other policy-making bodies, through research and dissemination of research, and through assistance to school districts, colleges, and community-based organizations, all with a focus on raising academic achievement of all students, and particularly of minority students and students in poverty. The Education Trust provides professional development for teachers and school leaders through a model—Standards in Practice—that has been developed by Education Trust staff members. The Education Trust produces a series of "actorvist productions," theater for the education reform movement. Information about all of these activities is found on the Education Trust Web site.

Bill and Melinda Gates Foundation
P.O. Box 23350
Seattle, WA 98102
206-709-3100 (Reception)
206-709-3140 (Grant Inquiries)
http://gatesfoundation.org/unitedstates/education
info@gatesfoundation.org

The Bill and Melinda Gates Foundation has a vision of all students graduating from high school ready to go to college, for a career, and for life. The foundation supports education reform efforts in the areas of early childhood education and high school graduation and college readiness through the development of model schools and initiatives at the school district and state levels. The foundation also provides scholarships through a variety of scholarship programs for capable students with limited finances, as well as sponsoring research designed to identify practices that lead to the realization of the foundation's vision.

Standards Work
1001 Connecticut Ave. NW, Suite 640
Washington, DC 20036
202-835-2000
http://www.standardswork.org
info@standardswork.org

Standards Work is a consulting agency that works with parents, communities, businesses and civic organizations, schools, school districts, and states to improve student achievement through the development of higher standards. Standards Work offers a number of publications about educational standards and designing educational programs to align with standards, as well as publications designed specifically for parents. These are available through the Standards Work Web site.

Inclusion

Inclusive Schools Network
Education Development Center, Inc.
55 Chapel Street
Newton, MA 02458-1060
877-332-2870
617-964-5448 (TTY)
617-969-3440 (Fax)
http://www.inclusiveschools.org/

The Inclusive Schools Network is an organization that provides information about developing schools and programs that include all children, organizes meetings and conferences about various aspects of inclusion, and serves as a connecting point for students, parents, teachers, and school administrators who are committed to inclusive schools. The Web site describes tips for inclusion, differentiating instruction, and transition for children with disabilities.

National Institute for Urban School Improvement
NCCRESt, NUISI AND NUISI-LeadScape
Mary Lou Fulton College of Education
P.O. Box 872011
Farmer Bldg #316
Tempe, AZ 85287-2011
480-965-0391 or 480-965-8378

480-727-7012 (fax)
http://www.urbanschools.org/

The National Institute for Urban School Improvement (NIUSI) has as its mission to work with urban schools, communities, and families to "develop powerful networks of urban districts and schools that embrace and implement a data-based, continuous improvement approach for inclusive practices" that are culturally relevant for students who have disabilities. NIUSI provides networking for such urban schools and school districts, as well as professional development and a wide range of online resources for school personnel, families, and communities involved in education reform, not only of special education, but also of regular education programs.

Gender Issues in Education

American Association of University Women
1111 Sixteenth Street NW
Washington, DC 20036
800-326-AAUW
http://www.aauw.org/

The American Association of University Women (AAUW) has worked since 1881, when it was founded, for education and equity for women and girls. AAUW has funded numerous studies of equity in education, among them the landmark study by Myra Sadker and David Sadker, *How Schools Shortchange Girls* (1995), and *Beyond the Gender Wars: A Conversation about Girls, Boys, and Education* (2001). AAUW is a membership organization, and it supports students, researchers, and organizations whose work aligns with the AAUW mission through fellowship and grant programs.

National Association for Single Sex Public Education (NASSPE)
19710 Fisher Avenue, Suite J
P. O. Box 108
Poolesville, MD 20837
301-461-5065
http://www.singlesexschools.org/

The National Association for Single Sex Public Education (NASSPE) was founded to provide information about the advantages, the legality, and the implementation of single sex education. The Web site includes research reports, transcripts and explanations of federal legislation and regulations that govern or relate to single sex education, and links to information from other sources. NASSPE provides professional development for school districts and schools interested in or involved in implementing single-sex education, and the organization also sponsors an online forum and an annual conference about single-sex education.

Comprehensive Education Reform Models

Center for Comprehensive School Reform and Improvement (CSRI)
1100 17th St. NW, Suite 500
Washington, DC 20036
202-223-6690
http://www.centerforcsri.org/

The Center for Comprehensive School Reform and Improvement (CSRI) is funded by the U.S. Department of Education to help schools organize, plan for, and implement school reform and improvement. CSRI promotes research-based strategies for school reform by providing technical assistance and support to schools planning or implementing school reform. CSRI publishes a newsletter, policy and research briefs, and other publications that address such issues as No Child Left Behind. The Web site of CSRI also includes a number of Webcasts and podcasts of training and professional development for parents, teachers, and school administrators, as well as an opportunity to "ask an expert" by e-mailing questions to center personnel.

Coalition of Essential Schools (CES) National
1330 Broadway, Suite 600
Oakland, CA 94612
510-433-1451
http://www.essentialschools.org/

The Coalition of Essential Schools (CES) promotes an education reform model that is based on "five common beliefs" about the purposes and practices of education. The Coalition sponsors a network of schools that subscribe to its principles and have either redesigned their schools to align with the five principles or are in the process of doing so. The Coalition provides support, professional development, and feedback for schools both through its national Center and through its Affiliate Centers. Ted Sizer, a leader in school reform, particularly at the high-school level, was the founder of the Coalition for Essential Schools and remains its chair emeritus.

Comer School Development Program
55 College Street
New Haven, CT 06510
203-737-1020
http://www.med.yale.edu/comer/

The Comer School Development Program (SDP) claims to be unique in promoting the idea that development of the whole child is the key to school improvement, and in their work, SDP program staff assist schools in making decisions based on the six areas of development identified through James Comer's research. SDP offers training, professional development, and ongoing support to educators, parents, and community members, as well as a variety of materials for schools that affiliate with the SDP.

Effective Schools
Dept. AO
2199 Jolly Road, Suite 160
Okemos, MI 48864
800-827-8041
http://www.effectiveschools.com

Effective Schools is an organization that is committed to providing support to educators, schools, and school districts in their efforts to implement the principles of effective schools, principles that were identified through research more than 30 years ago by such researchers as Ronald Edmonds and Larry Lezotte. Through publications, training, and consultations, Effective Schools works with urban, suburban, and rural schools and school districts and state departments of education throughout the United States. Effective Schools publishes and maintains an extensive "library" of research and research briefs about education reform and the implementation of the effective schools principles.

Institute for Research and Reform in Education
303 Glendale Drive
Toms River, NJ 08753

732-557-0200
http://www.irre.org

The Institute for Research and Reform in Education (IRRE) is the developer of an education reform initiative, First Things First, that works with middle schools and high schools in school districts in the process of systemic school reform. First Things First is research based, and IRRE works with schools and school districts to gather, analyze, and use data about teaching and learning in their schools as the basis of their school reform efforts. IRRE provides technical assistance through consultations and publications termed as "tools" for implementation of First Things First. A longitudinal study released in 2006 of First Things First in the Kansas City, Kansas, school district showed "district-wide reduction of ethnic and economic achievement gaps in reading" (http://www.irre.org/about/). IRRE also works with state departments of education, foundations that support education, and education professionals.

Just for the Kids
National Center for Educational Achievement
4030–2 West Braker Lane
Austin, TX 78759
800-762-4645
jftk@just4kids.org
http://www.just4kids.org/en/jftk/

Just for the Kids is an organization sponsored by the National Center for Educational Achievement. Just for the Kids promotes a school reform process that consists of three steps: inform (analyzing school achievement potential); inspire (learning from practices of consistently high performers); and improve (intentional and targeted improvement planning). Just for the Kids supports the process with training and professional development at the school district and school levels, as well as "tools" and materials for school improvement based on the National Center for Educational Achievement's framework for best practice. Just for the Kids provides services through affiliates in state departments of education, universities, and businesses in the 18 states that are its members.

Modern Red SchoolHouse Institute
1901 21st Ave., S.
Nashville, TN 37212

888-275-6774 ext. 10
http://www.mrsh.org/

The Modern Red SchoolHouse Institute is an organization that works toward reforming schools to improve children's academic achievement through professional development and other technical assistance focused on the particular needs of a school or school district. The Modern Red SchoolHouse practices, according to its Web site, are research based and results of their work have been evaluated, both internally and externally. Reports of the evaluations and case studies of schools that have been or are part of the Modern Red SchoolHouse Initiative are included on the Web site.

Small Schools Workshop
1608 North Milwaukee Avenue, Suite 912
Chicago, IL 60647
773-384-1030
http://www.smallschoolsworkshop.org/

The Small Schools Workshop is an organization that promotes and supports the development of small learning communities in public schools, based on research that shows that small schools offer opportunities for more intimate and personal learning environments that more closely meet the needs of the children and teachers in them. The members of the Workshop provide professional development and technical assistance in all aspects of school restructuring and comprehensive school reform at the elementary, middle, and high-school levels. In addition, consultants from the Workshop work with clients to develop grant applications, gather and analyze data about the feasibility of change, and offer conferences and workshops on small schools.

Curriculum and Assessment Reform

AIMS Education Foundation
P.O. Box 8120
Fresno, CA 93747-8120
888-733-2467 or 559-255-4094
559-255-6396 (fax)
http://www.aimsedu.org/

The AIMS Education Foundation is a nonprofit organization dedicated to the improvement of the teaching and learning of mathematics and science. Their work, which is research based and built on best practice, as well as brain research, is focused on helping children build a solid understanding of mathematics and science. The AIMS Education Foundation Web site provides information about teaching mathematics and science, a searchable database of lesson plans and activities for teaching mathematics and science, and many curriculum materials. The AIMS Education Foundation has several publications, including a monthly e-newsletter that is available free of charge.

Authentic Education
P.O. Box 148
Hopewell, NJ 08525-0148
609-466-8080
http://www.grantwiggins.org

Authentic Education, whose motto is "exploring the essential questions of education," is an organization that works directly with schools and school districts on issues of curriculum design, teaching for understanding, designing assessments that support understanding, and "thoughtful school change." The work that Authentic Education consultants do with schools is based on the belief that education and schools should be designed locally; they plan professional development and other support services for each school they work with around a framework called Understanding by Design, that is aimed at improving student learning. Authentic Education publishes a newsletter, *Big Ideas*, and a database titled *good ideas*, both available through its Web site. Authentic Education also sponsors workshops and conferences for educators.

FairTest: The National Center for Fair & Open Testing
342 Broadway
Cambridge, MA 02139
617-864-4810
http://www.fairtest.org

The work of FairTest: The National Center for Fair & Open Testing is aimed at improving education through the use of tests and assessments that are fair, open, valid, and educationally beneficial to students, teachers, and schools, as well as promoting the appropriate use of tests and pointing out inappropriate use or misuse. FairTest also works to uncover bias in standardized tests or in the way that they are administered. The organization provides research and other information for students, educators, parents, and policy makers about appropriate and fair testing and evaluation in the form of publications that include a set of "fact sheets" and a newsletter, *The Examiner*, that are available through the Web site.

The National Forum to Accelerate Middle-Grades Reform
P.O. Box 11346
Champaign, IL 61826-1346
http://www.mgforum.org/

The National Forum to Accelerate Middle-Grades Reform has as its mission to support the development of middle schools that are academically excellent, developmentally responsive, and socially equitable. The National Forum has developed a set of criteria that describe exemplary middle schools, and each year it identifies a number of "Schools to Watch" that meet those criteria. In 2008, 47 middle schools in 16 states were identified as "Schools to Watch." The Forum has developed a curriculum for developing leaders for middle grades education, as well as a resource directory of publications about middle grades education that are linked to the Web site.

Teacher Quality

Center for Teaching Quality
500 Millstone Drive, Suite 102
Hillsborough, NC 27278
919-241-1575
ContactUS@teachingquality.org
http://www.teachingquality.org/

The Center for Teaching Quality focuses its work on how teachers can be key to educational reform. Its mission is to improve "student learning through developing teacher leadership, conducting practical research, and engaging various communities." The center sponsors a virtual network, the Teacher Leaders Network, that links teacher leaders, as well as an initiative called TeacherSolutions that brings together teachers from around the country to design solutions to problems with public education. The center publishes an electronic journal, *Teaching Quality: Best Practices & Policies*, that is available free of charge at the center's Web site.

National Commission on Teaching and America's Future
2100 M Street NW, Suite 660
Washington, DC 20037
202-429-2570
dkincaid@nctaf.org
http://www.nctaf.org

The National Commission on Teaching and America's Future is a nonprofit organization dedicated to ensuring that all children learn with competent, caring, and qualified teachers. To enact their mission, the commission's work centers on three strategies: (1) creating strong learning communities in schools; (2) assuring quality teacher preparation programs; and (3) supporting professionally rewarding teaching careers. The organization supports research, demonstration projects, and a state coalition network to further its mission and strategies. The National Commission on Teaching and America's Future also sponsors roundtable discussions, forums, symposia, and conferences for policy makers and educators.

School Choice

Center for Education Reform
910 17th Street NW, Suite 1120
Washington, DC 20006
800-521-2118
cer@edreform.com
http://www.edreform.com

The Center for Education Reform was founded in 1993, and according to its Web site, "creates opportunities for and challenges obstacles to better education for America's communities." The focus of the center is educational choice; the center serves as a clearinghouse for information about school choice in general, and more specifically, about charter schools. The Center for Education Reform Web site includes information about laws and regulations that govern charter schools across the country.

Center for Civic Innovation
The Manhattan Institute
52 Vanderbilt Avenue
New York, NY 10017
212-599-7000
http://www.manhattan-institute.org/html/cci.htm#02

The Center for Civic Innovation, part of the Manhattan Institute, works to reform education mainly in the areas of school choice and accountability. The center promotes school choice to improve the options, such as charter schools and vouchers, available to parents of children in public schools. The center's work on accountability focuses on improving educational achievement by making all stakeholders—students, teachers, and administrators—accountable for students' and schools' success or failure. The center provides scholars and experts to assist policy makers and schools and school districts in their education reform efforts.

Urban Education

Annenberg Institute for School Reform
Brown University
Box 1985
Providence, RI 02919
401-863-7990
http://www.annenberginstitute.org/

The work of the Annenberg Institute for School Reform is guided by a vision of transforming school systems into "smart education systems" that link schools with community organizations and services to provide "high quality learning opportunities in all areas of students' lives." The institute works particularly with urban school systems and schools that serve disadvantaged children. The institute conducts research, works through partners with school districts and communities, and develops publications that document reform efforts. Publications of the Annenberg Institute include a series of "tools" for planning for school improvement; these are available at http://www.annenberginstitute.org/tools/index.php.

Council of the Great City Schools
1301 Pennsylvania Avenue NW, Suite 702
Washington, DC 20004
202-393-2427
http://www.cgcs.org/

The Council of the Great City Schools is a coalition of the public school districts of 66 of the largest cities in the United States. The mission of the council is to advocate for and to help children in urban public schools to achieve high standards, to improve the public perception of urban school districts, and to foster relationships between urban parents and the schools that serve their children. The council has conducted research on a variety of topics related to urban education and publishes reports and briefs about that research. The council also publishes a monthly journal, *Urban Educator*, that presents news about its member districts, upcoming urban education meetings and conferences, and issues of interest to urban educators. All of these publications are available through the council Web site.

National Center for Urban School Transformation
4238 El Cajon Blvd., Suite 100
San Diego, CA 92105
619-592-7905
ncust@mail.sdsul.edu
http://ncust.org

The National Center for Urban School Transformation, located at San Diego (CA) State University, works to help urban schools transform themselves into places where children learn well, where they love learning, and where they graduate prepared to succeed in post-secondary education, in a career, and in their communities. The National Center's work is funded by an endowment begun by QUALCOMM, which allows them to work directly with urban schools in need of improvement. Besides providing professional development for planning and implementing reform, the National Center also evaluates schools and conducts research on effective urban schools.

Equity and Civil Rights

Center for Law and Education
1875 Connecticut Avenue NW, Suite 510
Washington, DC 20009
202-986-3000
pweckstein@cleweb.org
http://www.cleweb.org/

The Center for Law and Education aims to ensure that all children have access to the quality education to which they are entitled. They do this through organizing parents, community members, teachers, and other school personnel to maximize the benefits of federal legislation, including Title I of the Elementary and

Secondary Education Act (No Child Left Behind), special education, vocational education, and schools-to-work programs. The center addresses standards-based reform, high school restructuring, implementation and enforcement of the rights of students with disabilities, and parent and community involvement in education. They provide consulting, advocacy, capacity building, and publications about education reform. Besides serving schools and school personnel directly, the center also provides consulting and assistance to attorneys advocating for the educational rights of children, assistance in the development of educational policy, and access to networks of resources throughout the country.

Citizens' Commission on Civil Rights
2000 M St. NW, Suite 400
Washington, DC 20036
202-659-5565
202-223-5302 (fax)
http://www.cccr.org/

Achievement Alliance
1250 H Street NW, Suite 700
Washington, DC 20005
202-293-1217 ext. 402
http://www.achievementalliance.org/contact/

The Citizens' Commission on Civil Rights is a bipartisan organization that monitors civil rights policies and practices of the federal government. The commission is committed to a progressive civil rights agenda, and it has worked to ensure equity in the reform of education at the national level. The commission has conducted numerous studies about education and equity; the reports can be downloaded from the Web site. The Citizens' Commission on Civil Rights also sponsors the Achievement Alliance, an organization that is committed to the success of No Child Left Behind. The Achievement Alliance has published a number of reports that seek to dispel myths and to provide accurate information about NCLB.

Forum for Democracy and Education
P.O. Box 216
Amesville, OH 45711
740-662-0503
1307 New York Avenue NW, Suite 300

Washington, DC 20005-4701
202-478-4572
http://www.forumforeducation.org/

The Forum for Democracy and Education was convened by a group of prominent educators and school reformers to advocate for and promote public schooling in the United States. Based on their belief in the role of education as a critical factor in a strong democratic society, the Forum stands for public education that is both high quality and equitable, and that is controlled democratically. The Web site of the Forum describes its work primarily as organizing and advocacy. The report "Democracy at Work: The Need for a New Federal Policy in Education" is available at the Forum's Web site. It summarizes the positions of the Forum and proposes new ways for the federal government to support education reform when the Elementary and Secondary Education Act is reauthorized.

Education Policy

Center on Education Policy (CEP)
1001 Connecticut Avenue NW, Suite 522
Washington, DC 20036
202-822-8065
www.cep-dc.org

The Center on Education Policy (CEP) is a private, nonprofit organization committed to the improvement of public education in the United States and to helping people understand the role of public education in our democracy. The center publishes reports, holds meetings and conferences, and makes presentations at the national, state, and local level. Rather than representing a particular political point of view of special interest, the center's work is focused on presenting information that helps to make sense of conflicting opinions and positions about the improvement of education. The center's Web site includes links to many papers and research reports about public education and its improvement.

Education Commission of the States
700 Broadway, #810
Denver, CO 80203-3442
303-299-3600
http://www.ecs.org/

The Education Commission of the States was organized in 1965 as an organization that would help state policy makers and education leaders "build partnerships, share information, and promote the development of policy based on available research and strategies" (http://www.ecs.org/ecsmain.asp?page=/html/aboutECS/home_aboutECS.htm). Each of the 49 member states, three territories, and the District of Columbia is represented by a set of commissioners that include the governor and six legislators or education leaders. The Education Commission of the States disseminates information about current educational policy and research, organizes workshops and conferences for its member commissioners and educators to exchange information and collaborate, and provides customized technical assistance to support states' development of educational policy and other initiatives. The Commission publishes a quarterly report, "The Progress of Education Reform." Recent reports address such topics as same sex schooling, dropout prevention, and science and mathematics education.

Parent and Community Partnerships

Home and School Institute
1500 Massachusetts Ave. NW
Washington, DC 20005
202-292-2400 (fax)
edstaff@megaskills.org
http://www.megaskillshsi.org/

The Home and School Institute is an organization that was founded in 1964 to promote improved student achievement through its online MegaSkills Education Center. MegaSkills is a program that develops motivation, effort, and responsibility throughout the academic curriculum. The Home and School Institute offers training for teachers and community members, as well as print and online materials. President and founder of the Home and School Institute Dorothy Rich is well known for her work that connects schools and families.

Partnership for 21st Century Skills
177 N. Church Avenue, Suite 305
Tucson, AZ 85701
520-623-2466
http://www.21stcenturyskills.org/

The Partnership for 21st Century Skills has among its founding partners the U.S. Department of Education, the National Education Association, Apple Computer, Inc., AOL Time Warner, Dell Computer, Cable in the Classroom, and a number of other organizations. The Partnership's mission is to "position 21st century skills at the center of K-12 education" through partnerships with education, community, business, and government leaders. The Partnership provides support for states, school districts, and schools in developing such partnerships, and it hosts Route 21, an online "shop" for resources for school improvement.

Project Appleseed
520 Melville
St. Louis, MO 63130
615-686-2195
headquarters@projectappleseed.org
http://www.projectappleseed.org

Project Appleseed, the National Campaign for School Improvement, works through parent and community involvement, to raise student achievement, improve children's nutrition and physical fitness, and create "green" learning environments through involving alumni and communities in fundraising to improve the environmental impact of schools. The Web site provides information for parents and parent organizers about organizing, finding information about the quality of schools, and selecting schools. Project Appleseed has a "toolbox" for improving parental involvement in schools, as well as training both for parents and for schools interested in building stronger relationships with parents and including them in education reform efforts.

Membership Organizations

The organizations listed below are but a few of the myriad professional education organizations whose missions address issues of education reform. These organizations all provide materials and services to their members; most of the materials and services are also available to nonmembers at a nominal cost.

Association for Supervision and Curriculum Development (ASCD)
1703 N. Beauregard St.

Alexandria, VA 22311-1714
800-933-2723
http://www.ascd.org

The Association for Supervision and Curriculum Development (ASCD) is a membership organization of more than 175,000 educators from around the United States and around the world. The mission of ASCD is to facilitate a community of educators committed to advocacy and best practice with the goal of the success of every learner. ASCD publishes a journal, *Educational Leadership*, and a newsletter, *Education Update*, as well as many books and videos, all focused on improving education. A blog for the ASCD community, *inservice*, provides for conversation and resources for educators. ASCD advocates for the development of policy that supports high quality teaching and learning. The organization also provides professional development and training, as well as national and regional conferences and meetings for educators.

Center for School Improvement
American Federation of Teachers
555 New Jersey Ave. NW
Washington, DC 20001
http://www.aft.org/topics/csi/index.htm

The Center for School Improvement, sponsored by the American Federation of Teachers, provides technical assistance, professional development, and information about education reform for educators and parents. The Web site includes information about the school improvement process, profiles of school districts that have been successful in reforming their schools, strategies for inclusive school improvement processes, and links to other organizations and resources for reform.

International Reading Association (IRA)
800 Barksdale Road
P.O. Box 8139
Newark, DE 19714-8139
800-336-READ (800-336-7323), U.S. and Canada
302-731-1600, elsewhere
302-731-1057 (fax)
http://www.reading.org

The International Reading Association (IRA) has been committed to the improvement of the teaching of reading since its beginning in 1956. IRA also works to conduct and disseminate research about reading and to encourage reading as a lifelong habit. IRA advocates for the reform of education in general and more particularly reading education, for policy, and for curriculum in the United States and around the world; it has numerous affiliate organizations and councils, as well as a network of special interest groups that study particular aspects of reading and reading instruction. IRA provides grants for professional development and research, and recognizes exemplary teaching, service, authorship of children's books, and media coverage of reading with annual awards. The IRA Web site includes information about the numerous publications of the organization, and it provides a wealth of online resources for teachers, including lesson plans, booklists, and resources for working with parents. IRA also sponsors online discussion groups that allow group members to ask and respond to questions and discuss issues and problems related to teaching reading.

National Council for the Social Studies (NCSS)
8555 Sixteenth Street, Suite 500
Silver Spring, MD 20910
301-588-1800
301-588-2049 (fax)
http://www.socialstudies.org/

The National Council for the Social Studies (NCSS) is a membership organization that, along with its 110 affiliate organizations, focuses its work on the teaching of social studies—history, geography, economics, political science, sociology, psychology, anthropology, and law-related education. NCSS has published curriculum standards for social studies K-12, continuously revising them to reflect research and new understandings of both what to teach and how to teach in the social studies. NCSS provides support and advocacy for the improvement of social studies teaching through its presence at national meetings and forums, its journals and other publications, professional development, and teaching resources that include lesson plans and learning activities.

National Council of Teachers of English (NCTE)
1111 W. Kenyon Road
Urbana, IL 61801-1096

217-328-3870 or 877-369-6283
http://www.ncte.org/

The National Council of Teachers of English (NCTE) works to improve the teaching of literacy and English language arts for all children through professional development and research. NCTE publishes 12 journals and periodicals that address issues specific to teaching reading and English language arts; NCTE also developed and publishes standards for English language arts K-12. Through its research foundation, NCTE supports research and awards grants for research. NCTE has many affiliate organizations, some national and some regional, as well as such curriculum-specific organizations as the Whole Language Umbrella. The Web site of NCTE includes resources for teachers, for parents, and for students; it also provides information for policy makers about literacy and English language arts.

National Council of Teachers of Mathematics (NCTM)
906 Association Drive
Reston, VA 20191-1502
703-620-9840
703-476-2970 (fax)
http://www.nctm.org/

The National Council of Teachers of Mathematics (NCTM) brings together teachers, administrators, and other school personnel around a mission of high-quality and equitable mathematics education for all children. NCTM has been involved in the standards movement from its beginning, having developed standards for K-12 mathematics as one of the first comprehensive sets of curriculum standards. NCTM provides many resources for the improvement of mathematics education—journals and books, workshops, and lesson plans. NCTM also advocates for high-quality mathematics education on a national level.

National Science Teachers Association (NSTA)
1840 Wilson Blvd.
Arlington, VA 22201
703-243-7100
703-243-7177 (fax)
http://www.nsta.org/

The National Science Teachers Association (NSTA) is a membership organization that works to help science teachers throughout the country network to improve the teaching and learning of science for all students. NSTA publishes journals about teaching science and supports research about science education; the organization also has developed standards for quality science teaching that are available through the NSTA Web site. NSTA has an online mentoring program, e-mentoring, that is available to science teachers; the organization also provides grants for teachers for developing exemplary teaching tools and projects.

Phi Delta Kappa International (PDK)
408 N. Union Street
Bloomington, IN 47405-3800
800-766-1156
812-339-0018
http://www.pdkintl.org/

Phi Delta Kappa International (PDK) is one of the oldest professional organizations for educators in the United States; it celebrated its 100th anniversary in 2006. It has a network of chapters throughout the United States, Canada, Europe, and Asia. The mission of PDK is to promote high-quality public education as a critical part of a democratic way of life. PDK supports practicing educators and helps to prepare new teachers through research, the development of strong leadership, and service to the teaching profession. PDK hosts an annual Summit on Education as part of its advocacy for public education, and it publishes books, journals, and newsletters that are research based and responsive to the needs of practicing educators. The Web site includes an archive of publications, many of which are available through the Web site, as well as teaching tips and information about current trends and issues in education.

8

Resources

Print Resources

History of Education Reform
Books
The Editors of Black Issues in Higher Education. 2004. *The Unfinished Agenda of Brown v. Board of Education (Landmarks in Civil Rights History)*. Hoboken, NJ: Wiley.

This collection of essays explores the legacy of *Brown v. Board of Education*, how far we have come, and how far we have to go to realize the promise of *Brown*.

Finn, C. E., Jr. 2008. *Troublemaker: A Personal History of School Reform Since Sputnik*. Princeton, NJ: Princeton University Press.

As Finn tells his personal story of his involvement in education reform, he tells the story of education reform in the United States. He has been involved in education reform from the perspective of a teacher, a professor, an aide to politicians, an undersecretary of the Department of Education, a writer, a foundation president, and more. Besides telling the story of education reform, Finn shares what he has learned along the way about reforming education.

Frankenberg, E., and G. Orfield, eds. 2007. *Lessons in Integration: Realizing the Promise of Racial Diversity in American Schools*. Charlottesville: University of Virginia Press.

This book contains a series of essays about school integration and the lessons that can be learned, from both successful and not-so-successful integration efforts of schools and school districts in the United States. The essays are based on the premise that integration benefits both minority and majority children, and that the lessons are valuable for all schools and school communities as communities in the United States become increasingly diverse.

The Jossey-Bass Reader on School Reform. 2001. San Francisco: Jossey-Bass.

The Jossey-Bass Reader on School Reform brings together a wide variety of perspectives and voices on school reform. The chapters describe and discuss models of school reform and issues that have been addressed, or, in the opinions of the authors should be addressed, by school reform. There is also a chapter that includes primary documents related to school reform.

Kozol, J. 2005. *The Shame of the Nation: The Restoration of Apartheid Schooling in America.* New York: Crown.

In this book, Jonathan Kozol describes the resegregation of inner city schools in the United States. Poor African American and Hispanic children attend schools that are as segregated as they were, according to Kozol, in 1968. It is not only the racial segregation that Kozol finds disturbing; it is also the demeaning and militaristic discipline that characterizes the schools and the effects of standardized testing that have narrowed the curriculum and reduced instruction to rote memorization and meaningless drill. Kozol challenges the United States to do better for our children.

Ravitch, D., and M. Vinovskis, eds. 1995. *Learning from the Past: What History Teaches Us about School Reform.* Baltimore, MD: Johns Hopkins University Press.

Based on the premise that everything that happens has a basis in history, the authors of the 14 essays in this book trace the historical backgrounds of issues that have been raised in the conversation about the reform of education in the United States.

Spring, J. 2004. *Deculturalization and the Struggle for Equity: A Brief History of the Education of Dominated Cultures in the United States.* Boston: McGraw Hill.

Spring shows how the dominant culture in the United States has exercised power and control in schools to marginalize, segregate, and dominate other cultures. That domination is evident in the history of education in the United States, and Spring tells about how practices in U.S. schools have served to continue the domination.

Street, P. 2005. *Segregated Schools: Educational Apartheid in Post-Civil Rights America.* **New York: Routledge.**

Street describes the state of education in the United States as educational apartheid and the disparities of the schools that he attributes to that apartheid—school funding, teacher quality, class size, curriculum, opportunities for learning, and more. He argues that the United States is not committed to equity or to the full implementation of the *Brown v. Board of Education* U.S. Supreme Court decision, and he analyzes public policy that allows segregation and inequity to continue.

Thernstrom, A., and S. Thernstrom. 2003. *No Excuses: Closing the Racial Gap in Learning.* **New York: Simon and Schuster.**

Manhattan Institute for Policy Research Senior Fellows Abigail Thernstrom and Stephan Thernstrom describe the racial gap in student achievement in the United States and analyze and critique school reform efforts that have been aimed at closing the achievement gap. The Thernstroms call for radical change to education to address the achievement gap, focusing on choice and the development of independent schools as a means to closing it, based on their assumption that the politics of public school systems impede real reform.

Journals and Journal Articles
Education Commission of the States. *The Progress of Education Reform.* **http://www.ecs.org/html/educationIssues/ProgressofRe form.asp**

The Progress of Education Reform is a bimonthly publication available in pdf. Each issue addresses one aspect of education reform, with recent issues having addressed college counseling, developmental education, early care and education, and school improvement. The issues document progress made relative to the aspects of reform addressed, and they include review and analysis of research pertinent to the topic of the issue, policy implications of the issues, and links to other resources related to the issue.

Hanna, J. 2005. "The Elementary and Secondary Education Act: 40 Years Later." News Features & Releases. Harvard Graduate School of Education. http://www.gse.harvard.edu/news_events/features/2005/08/esea0819.html

In this article, Julie Hanna describes the history of the Elementary and Secondary Education Act from its conception in the 1960s through all of its reauthorizations. Hanna's article provides insight into the debates and issues that have shaped ESEA into the law we have today, No Child Left Behind.

Hunt, T. C. 2005. "Education Reforms—Lessons from History." Phi Delta Kappan 87 (1): 84–89.

T. C. Hunt describes the education reform process in the United States as a search for a panacea. Educators and policy makers alike propose "sure-fire remedies" and pursue them with total confidence, only to be disappointed when they don't prove to be *the* answer. Hunt views this as a cycle, and he argues that until we are willing to analyze and learn from these experiences, the cycle will continue.

Lowe, R. 2004. "The Strange History of School Desegregation." Rethinking Schools 18 (3). http://www.rethinkingschools.org/archive/18_03/stra183.shtml

Robert Lowe traces the history of school desegregation beginning with *Brown v. Board of Education*, and he argues that not only has the promise of Brown not been realized but also the real beneficiaries of desegregation have been middle-class whites, not African Americans.

Mace-Matluck, B. 1987. The Effective Schools Movement: Its History and Context. Austin, TX: Southwest Educational Development Lab. (ERIC Document Reproduction Service No. ED304781).

It is important to understand the Effective Schools movement because its correlates undergird nearly every education reform effort and initiative in the United States. Betty Mace-Matluck provides insight into how the correlates were developed and the research behind them.

Valentin, I. 1997. "Title IX: A Brief History." *25 Years of Title IX Digest.* **Newton, MA: Women's Educational Equity Act (WEEA) Resource Center at EDC. http://www2.edc.org/GDI/ publications_SR/t9digest.pdf**

This article describes how Title IX came about, the context of the original legislation, and the original intent of the legislation. It also describes the process of developing regulations for Title IX and how Title IX shaped the women's movement in the United States.

Reports

Center for Public Education. 2007. "At-a-Glance: Changing Demographics." *Practical Information and Analysis about Public Education.* **http://www.centerforpubliceducation.org/site/c. kjJXJ5MPIwE/b.3633965/Demographics**

Center for Public Education. 2007. "School Context: What is the Racial and Ethnic Make-up of our Schools?" *Practical Information and Analysis about Public Education.* **http://www.center forpubliceducation.org/site/c.kjJXJ5MPIwE/b.3523701/k.5B61/ School_context_What_is_the_racial_and_ethnic_make_up_of_ our_schools.htm#national**

These two reports and others available at the Web site of the Center for Public Education provide extensive demographic and background information about education in the United States.

Loveless, T. 2007. *The 2007 Brown Center Report on American Education: How Well are American Students Learning?* **Washington, DC: Brookings Institution.**

This report, the seventh in the Brown Center series of such reports, analyzes and discusses data from the 2007 National Assessment of Educational Progress (NAEP), looks at enrollment patterns in public and private schools in the United States, and analyzes international mathematics test data to see if there is a relationship between the amount of time students spend learning mathematics in different countries and how well they learn mathematics. The report can be ordered or downloaded from the Web site of the Brookings Institution.

U.S. Department of Education. 2008. *A Nation Accountable: Twenty-five Years After A Nation at Risk.* Washington, DC. http://www.ed.gov/rschstat/research/pubs/accountable/

This report takes a critical look at the outcomes of public education in the United States, comparing them to outcomes described in the landmark report, "A Nation at Risk," that called for reforming U.S. education in 1983. The new report argues that we remain "a nation at risk," with schools not keeping up with the demands of the global economy, and with most of the same risk factors still not resolved.

Modern Issues in Education Reform
Books
Brouillette, L. 2002. *Charter Schools: Lessons in School Reform.* Mahwah, NJ: Lawrence Erlbaum Associates.

Brouillette uses case studies of seven charter schools in three states to explain the ins and outs of charter schools—what they are and how they differ from other public schools, how charter schools are initiated and operated, and the lessons that can be learned from these seven schools about charter schools.

Carr, J. F., and D. E. Harris. 2001. *Succeeding with Standards: Linking Curriculum, Assessment, and Action Planning.* Alexandria, VA: Association for Supervision and Curriculum Development.

Teachers often struggle with implementing standards in their schools and classrooms. In this book Carr and Harris share their experience with the standards-linking process. They provide strategies for teachers in schools or school districts to determine who is to teach and assess each standard, to create a curriculum and assessment plan, to define effective practice, to create a comprehensive assessment system, and to map out a path to success through action planning. The book includes a "Learning Opportunities Survey" for teachers that could be used as a needs assessment for professional development and a glossary of terms related to the implementation of standards.

Chenoweth, K. 2007. *"It's Being Done": Academic Success in Unexpected Schools.* Cambridge, MA: Harvard Education Press.

In *"It's Being Done,"* Chenoweth describes examples of schools and classrooms where teaching and learning have been transformed and where children excel despite their difficult social and economic circumstances. The models in this book show that despite the odds, teachers who hold high expectations for their students, who understand their students and their learning needs, and who teach in ways that meet those learning needs are being effective. There is much that teachers, schools, and communities can learn from the schools and classrooms described in the book.

Clewell, B. C., P. B. Campbell, and L. Perlman. 2007. *Good Schools in Poor Neighborhoods: Defying Demographics, Achieving Success.* **Washington, DC: Urban Institute Press.**

This book describes how two urban schools, one serving predominantly African American children and the other serving predominantly Latino children, are "beating the odds" and providing a high-quality education that results in academic success for the children. The two schools can serve as models for how urban schools can be good schools, in spite of their demographics that might suggest otherwise.

Darling-Hammond, L., B. Barron, P. D. Pearson, A. H. Schoenfeld, E. K. Stage, T. D. Zimmerman, G. N. Cervetti, and J. L. Tilson. 2008. *Powerful Learning: What We Know about Teaching for Understanding.* **San Francisco: Jossey-Bass.**

Powerful Learning: What We Know about Teaching for Understanding is a compendium of effective K-12 teaching practices that include project-based learning, cooperative learning, performance-based assessment, and teaching strategies for literacy, mathematics, and science. The authors of the book use rich classroom stories to explain how these practices lead to deep understanding, critical thinking, and effective problem solving. The book is accompanied by a series of videos of effective and innovative teaching; they can be found on the Edutopia Web site (www.edutopia.org).

David, J. L., and L. Cuban. 2006. *Cutting Through the Hype: A Taxpayer's Guide to School Reforms.* **Bethesda, MD: Education Week Press.**

In this book, Jane David and Larry Cuban ask, "What does it take to make school reforms actually work?" Their answer is a review of 20 of the most popular education reforms. The authors explain each of the reforms, describing them in plain language and taking a critical look at their claims for success. This guide offers common-sense information to help educators, policy makers, parents, and community members cut through the jargon that is often used to describe the reforms and make informed decisions about reform efforts.

Dingerson, L., B. Miner, B. Peterson, and S. Walters, eds., 2008. *Keeping the Promise? The Debate Over Charter Schools.* **Milwaukee, WI: Rethinking Schools.**

The essays in this book, including those written by such well-known education reformers as Ted Sizer and Linda Darling-Hammond, analyze the charter school movement from the perspective of commitment to public education as part of the democratic process in the United States.

Fullan, M. 2007. *The New Meaning of Educational Change,* **4th ed. New York: Teachers College Press.**

Since the first edition of this book in 1982, Michael Fullan has chronicled the processes and the progress of education reform. The fourth edition takes a comprehensive look at education reform, drawing on current research about school reform, leadership, organization, and teaching, and describing how education, school districts, and schools must change to improve education. Fullan asserts, as he has in earlier editions, that the process of educational change must be meaningful, and educators must find meaning in it for the changes to become institutionalized and to result in improvement.

Fullan, M. 2007. *Turnaround Leadership.* **San Francisco: Jossey-Bass.**

In this book, Michael Fullan looks at the critical role of leadership in general, and in particular, how a leader can use even the most difficult and seemingly negative circumstances as opportunities to "turn around" a school. Fullan approaches leadership from a systems perspective as he explains how a "turnaround" leader can motivate a school staff to transform the entire system—the school—using the strategies described and illustrated in the book.

Gill, B. P., P. M. Timpane, and D. J. Brewer. 2007. *Rhetoric Versus Reality: What We Know and What We Need to Know About Vouchers and Charter Schools.* **Santa Monica, CA: RAND Corporation.**

This book is a critical examination of the improvement of education through parental choice in the forms of charter schools and vouchers. The authors argue and provide evidence to support their argument for the effectiveness of charter schools and vouchers. They also offer guidance for the development of charter schools and voucher policies.

Glass, G. V. 2008. *Fertilizers, Pills, and Magnetic Strips: The Fate of Public Education in America.* **Charlotte, NC: Information Age Publishing.**

Gene Glass, an educational psychologist and analyst, argues in this book that the American public's obsession with competition and accountability have worked not to bring about school reform, but against it. He describes problems with test design and statistical sampling, with how the data have been analyzed and reported, and with how those problems have been "glossed over" in reporting the results of national and international comparisons of student achievement. While he believes that accountability is important, he also argues that test scores do not represent, in and of themselves, the state of education or the state of education reform.

Goodman, K., P. Shannon, Y. Goodman, and R. Rapoport, eds. 2004. *Saving Our Schools: The Case for Public Education: Saying No to "No Child Left Behind."* **Berkeley, CA: RDR Books.**

In *Saving Our Schools*, the authors, all leading educators and researchers, decry the effects of No Child Left Behind on children, teachers, schools, and the system of public education in the United States. The essays in the book address the marginalization of effective teaching practices, curriculum, professional development, and teacher education programs inherent in No Child Left Behind, as well as the inordinate amount of money NCLB spends on testing rather than on instruction. The authors call for action to save public education.

Hargreaves, A., and D. Fink. 2006. *Sustainable Leadership.* **San Francisco: Jossey-Bass.**

In *Sustainable Leadership*, Andy Hargreaves and Dean Fink identify a framework for sustainable leadership. The framework consists of seven principles—depth, length, breadth, justice, diversity, resourcefulness, and conservation—that characterize leadership that is effective in the long term. Leaders whose leadership is sustainable have energy to continue to lead and are able to build on the history of their leadership to be even more effective.

Hess, F. M. 2008. *Common Sense School Reform*. New York: Palgrave Macmillan.

In *Common Sense School Reform*, Frederick Hess proposes a new agenda for school reform, one based on accountability and flexibility. Rather than promote any specific reform agenda, Hess argues that there are many ways to reform education, but that any successful reform effort must begin with creating a culture of competence, where excellence is rewarded and failure is not tolerated. He also promotes the notion that schools and school systems must be flexible enough to allow teachers and administrators to be innovative and creative in doing their jobs. Hess provides a number of recommendations for accountability, competition, creating an educated workforce, and effective leadership.

Izumi, L. T., and W. M. Evers. 2002. *Teacher Quality*. Stanford, CA: Hoover Press.

Lance Izumi and Williamson Evers identify characteristics of good teachers and good teaching, dispel some common myths about teaching and teacher credentialing, and assert that the quality of a student's teacher is the most important influence on that student's learning.

Kaplan, L. S., and W. A. Owings. 2002. *Teacher Quality, Teaching Quality, and School Improvement*. Bloomington, IN: Phi Delta Kappa Educational Foundation.

This book reviews and presents research on teacher and teaching quality and the necessity of both for school improvement that results in high academic achievement for all children.

Kimmelman, P. L. 2006. *Implementing NCLB—Creating a Knowledge Framework to Support School Improvement*. Thousand Oaks, CA: Corwin.

Paul Kimmelman provides a framework for leading schools to meet the requirements of No Child Left Behind through school improvement. The book includes examples of how other schools have been successful using a knowledge framework for continuous school improvement, processes and activities for putting a knowledge framework in place, and recommended resources and products that can support such an implementation.

Lambert, L. 2003. *Leadership Capacity for Lasting School Improvement*. Alexandria, VA: Association for Supervision and Curriculum Development.

In *Leadership Capacity for Lasting School Improvement*, Linda Lambert provides a process for schools to follow in building high leadership capacity among principals and teachers. She begins with five important strategies that leaders with high capacity for leading use: (1) skillful participation in the work of leadership; (2) inquiry-based use of data to inform decision and practice; (3) broad involvement in and collective responsibility for student learning; (4) reflective practice that leads to innovation; and (5) high or steadily improving student achievement. The book includes exercises to develop high-capacity leadership and real-life examples of high-capacity leadership in action.

Lipman, P. 2004. *High Stakes Education: Inequality, Globalization, and Urban School Reform*. New York: RoutledgeFalmer.

Pauline Lipman's book takes a critical look at how globalization and gentrification are serving to preserve the inequities of both the resources for and the learning outcomes of urban schooling. She uses the Chicago Public Schools policies and practices as examples of how those inequities are perpetuated by economic and social policies. According to Lipman, education will not be truly reformed until we have addressed the inequities of economics and social policies and have schools that "create new people for a new way of life."

Littky, D. 2004. *The Big Picture: Education is Everyone's Business*. Alexandria, VA: Association for Supervision and Curriculum Development.

In his book, Dennis Littky describes his work supporting education reform at a number of schools, among them an urban high school in Providence, Rhode Island. He also writes about the lessons he has learned from that work, and how other educators can learn from those lessons. Littky's book points out that standardized education measured by standardized tests—a one-size-fits-all approach—in reality fits no one, and that schools and teachers should be looking for what works for each child.

Marzano, R. J., T. Waters, and B. A. McNulty. 2005. *School Leadership that Works: From Research to Results.* **Aurora, CO: Mid-Continent Research for Education and Learning.**

In this book, Robert Marzano, Timothy Waters, and Brian McNulty review research about school-level, teacher-level, and student-level factors that characterize effective schools. The authors translate the factors into specific actions that schools can take to improve their practice and raise student achievement. The book includes a "Snapshot Survey" of the factors that research shows characterize effective schools. The survey can be used by school improvement teams, teachers, and school leaders to assess their own practice as a basis for planning for taking action to improve their schools.

Meier, D., and G. Wood, eds. 2004. *Many Children Left Behind: How the No Child Left Behind Act Is Damaging Our Children and Our Schools.* **Boston: Beacon Press.**

The authors of this book contend that No Child Left Behind can never fulfill its promise to ensure that all children will learn well for many reasons, not the least of which that it is underfunded, that the standards for students with disabilities and who are English language learners set them up for failure, and that the requirements for highly qualified teachers are not practical in many areas.

Nichols, S. L., and D. C. Berliner. 2007. *Collateral Damage: How High Stakes Testing Corrupts America's Schools.* **Cambridge, MA: Harvard University Press.**

In this book, Sharon Nichols and David Berliner discuss how standardized testing is being used and misused under No Child Left Behind. According to the authors, the use of standardized testing as the only measure of accountability not only uses the tests for a purpose for which they were never intended; that use also narrows the curriculum as schools and teachers focus instruction on the content of the test and creates pressures that undermine the validity of the test data. Nichols and Berliner provide accounts of adults who cheat to raise test scores of children, schools that push children out of school so that their potential low test scores are not included in the school's data, and schools and classrooms where inordinate amounts of time, some as many as several months of the school year, are spent on test preparation rather than on engaging children in a rich curriculum.

Noddings, N. 2007. *When School Reform Goes Wrong*. New York: Teachers College Press.

Nel Noddings critiques nearly every aspect of No Child Left Behind, based on the assertion that much of school reform fails to begin with asking the right questions. Indeed, she describes how schools, as well as the NCLB legislation, impose and adopt reforms without considering what even needs reforming. In the book, she argues that a moral and ethical approach to school reform requires addressing the inherent inequities in our educational system, and she proposes a set of strategies that she believes can lead to equity and improved academic achievement.

Noguera, P. A. 2007. *City Schools and the American Dream: Reclaiming the Promise of Public Education*. New York: Teachers College Press.

In this book, Pedro Noguera explains why urban schools and school districts are not successful in their reform efforts. He believes that policy makers and school administrators do not understand the conditions of urban schooling and urban life that prevent academic success for urban students. He proposes strategies for confronting those social and economic conditions to resolve the inequities and design schools that address the issues these children face. Unless the social and economic supports are provided, argues Noguera, urban children will not be able to attain higher standards, and schools will not be able to close the achievement gap.

O'Shea, M. R. 2005. *From Standards to Success: A Guide for School Leaders*. Alexandria, VA: Association for Supervision and Curriculum Development.

Mark O'Shea's book describes a process, the Standards Achievement Planning Cycle, that school leaders can use to help their schools meet educational standards. The book describes the process step-by-step, with examples of how the steps look when they are in place in a school. This book is an excellent resource for teachers and schools in the process of aligning their practice with standards.

Popham, W. J. 2008. *Transformative Assessment.* **Alexandria, VA: Association for Supervision and Curriculum Development.**

Formative assessment is an assessment process that both students and teachers can engage in during the instructional process to understand how the students' learning is forming, with the purpose of informing instruction. Formative assessment can also be used at the school level to determine how a school-wide initiative is forming. In this book W. James Popham explains why formative assessment is critical to the improvement of teaching and learning, as well as school improvement processes. He also shows how to analyze data from formative assessment and how to feed it back into the system for continuous improvement.

Popham, W. J. 2001. *The Truth about Testing: An Educator's Call to Action.* **Alexandria, VA: Association for Supervision and Curriculum Development.**

W. James Popham explains how the misuse of standardized tests to determine whether schools are succeeding is damaging to schools and to teachers. More importantly, Popham explains what the tests really measure and why they shouldn't be used to determine school success or failure. He proposes alternative measures teachers and administrators can use to be accountable, and he suggests ways that teachers and school leaders can take action against the misuse of standardized testing.

Pressley, M. 2006. *Reading Instruction That Works: The Case for Balanced Teaching,* **3rd ed. New York: Guilford Press.**

Michael Pressley's book presents research-based best practices for teaching literacy in a balanced approach that combines a skills-based approach with whole-language strategies that together help children to become good readers. Pressley presents strategies and techniques for teaching reading, explains the theory and research that support each of them, and shows how good teachers actually use the strategies and techniques in their classrooms.

Price, H. B. 2008. *Mobilizing the Community to Help Students Succeed.* Alexandria, VA: Association for Supervision and Curriculum Development.

In this book, Hugh Price builds a case for using the entire community to improve education. He argues that the community has many resources that are valuable to the reform process, and that the commitment of the community to education reform is critical to the process.

Rathvon, N. 2008. *Effective School Interventions: Evidence-Based Strategies for Improving Student Outcomes,* 2nd ed. New York: Guilford Press.

In this book, Natalie Rathvon provides 70 interventions that can be used to improve the classroom learning environment, student achievement, and student behavior. The research-based interventions can be used in pre-K through grade 12 classrooms on an individual, class, or school-wide level. The array of interventions include teaching strategies for specific curriculum areas, strategies for classroom management, and strategies for dealing with individual children. The interventions are explained in detail and include step-by-step procedures for using them with children, as well as combining them into a comprehensive program.

Reeves, D. B. 2004. *Accountability for Learning: How Teachers and School Leaders Can Take Charge.* Alexandria, VA: Association for Supervision and Curriculum Development.

In this book, Douglas Reeves calls for teachers to take the leadership in accountability and to transform accountability into a constructive decision-making process that leads to improvement of teaching, leadership, and student achievement. It is possible, according to Reeves, to develop accountability systems that are learner centered, that increase teacher motivation, and that lead to improved student learning, and the book outlines a process for doing so.

Rice, J. K. 2003. *Teacher Quality: Understanding the Effectiveness of Teacher Attributes.* Washington, DC: Economic Policy Institute.

Jennifer King Rice's book analyzes research on teacher quality and calls for using multiple measures that consider a number of dimensions when determining policies and procedures for determining credentialing and hiring teachers to build the kind of teacher workforce needed to improve teaching and learning.

Rothstein-Fisch, C., and E. Trumbull. 2008. *Managing Diverse Classrooms: How to Build on Students' Cultural Strengths.* Alexandria, VA: Association for Supervision and Curriculum Development.

Carrie Rothstein-Fisch and Elise Trumbull draw on teachers' experiences in classrooms with high numbers of immigrant children as they create a framework for understanding the cultural strengths children bring to their classrooms. The book describes that framework, and it also describes teaching strategies for enacting that framework in classrooms as part of school reform.

Salomone, R. C. 2003. *Same, Different, Equal: Rethinking Single-Sex Schooling.* New Haven, CT: Yale University Press.

Rosemary Salomone argues in this book that single-sex schooling has the potential for both academic and social benefits to children, particularly disadvantaged and minority children, when the programs are thoughtfully planned and implemented.

Saltman, K. J. 2007. *Capitalizing on Disaster: Taking and Breaking Public Schools.* Boulder, CO: Paradigm.

In this book, Kenneth Saltman argues that the goals of much of the current school reform relate not to improved educational outcomes for children, but to dismantling public education and creating opportunities for privatization and profit for businesses. He also argues that public education should be a democratic enterprise, with public oversight, and that current reform efforts undermine the involvement of the public in education.

Schlechty, P. C. 2001. *Inventing Better Schools: An Action Plan for Educational Reform.* San Francisco: Jossey-Bass.

Phillip Schlechty argues that schools will never be truly reformed until our focus changes from teacher and student test scores and mandated policy. Real improvement, according to Schlechty, will come only when the focus is on what he terms "knowledge work," work in schools that provides intellectual challenge and daily creative engagement for both teachers and students.

Schmoker, M. 2006. *Results Now: How We Can Achieve Unprecedented Improvements in Teaching and Learning.* **Alexandria, VA: Association for Supervision and Curriculum Development.**

In this book, Michael Schmoker asserts that teaching must change and improve if student achievement is to improve, and he argues that the development of professional learning communities in schools has the potential to improve instruction. Schmoker writes for school leaders, and he provides a set of leadership practices, grounded in the research on professional learning communities, for teachers and leaders to use as they work collaboratively to improve teaching. He also makes recommendations for the involvement in professional learning communities of school district administrators, state departments of education, and policy makers.

Taylor, B. M., and P. D. Pearson. 2002. *Teaching Reading: Effective Schools, Accomplished Teachers.* **Mahwah, NJ: Lawrence Erlbaum Associates.**

Barbara Taylor and P. David Pearson explore how reading is taught in schools and classrooms where at-risk students are learning to read well. The authors compare practices across schools and classrooms, and they also provide in-depth descriptions of teaching strategies in context in individual classrooms. Taylor and Pearson show in this book that effective teaching of reading is not just classroom practice; indeed, there are organizational factors that contribute to teachers' success in classrooms.

Tucker, P. D., and J. H. Stronge. 2005. *Linking Teacher Evaluation and Student Learning.* **Alexandria, VA: Association for Supervision and Curriculum Development.**

Pamela Tucker and James Stronge assert that including measures of student learning in evaluations of teachers can help schools improve student achievement. The authors describe how four school districts are doing just that. In their analysis of the four districts' teacher evaluation systems, the authors found four strategies for linking student learning with teacher evaluations. These include documenting how desired outcomes lead to student learning, tracking learners' progress on standards, setting annual goals for student achievement, and analyzing student test scores to look for significant changes. The book includes samples of teacher evaluation tools that include student learning as a factor of the quality of teaching.

Wehling, R. L., ed. 2008. *Building a 21st Century U.S. Education System*. Washington, DC: National Commission on Teaching and America's Future. http://www.nctaf.org/resources/research_ and_reports/nctaf_research_reports/documents/Bldg21stCen turyUSEducationSystem_final.pdf

This book brings together a wide range of authors, among them practitioners, researchers, policy makers, and business leaders, who think outside the box about the issues and problems faced by the U.S. education system. Each of the authors has been involved in the reform of education, and each chapter proposes ideas and solutions from that author's particular perspective.

Whitman, D. 2008. *Sweating the Small Stuff: Inner-City Schools and the New Paternalism*. Washington, DC: Thomas B. Fordham Institute.

In this book, David Whitman provides descriptions of six highly effective inner-city secondary schools where disadvantaged youth make gains in academic achievement that are much larger than what would be expected. Whitman attributes much of this success to the paternalistic practices of the schools. They are warm and caring, and adults in these schools form strong paternalistic bonds with students as they communicate high expectations for learning and behavior.

Zmuda, A., R. Kuklis, and E. Kline. 2004. *Transforming Schools: Creating a Culture of Continuous Improvement*. Alexandria, VA: Association for Supervision and Curriculum Development.

This book describes a set of "operating principles" for transforming a school district or school that use systems thinking as a means to school reform. The chapters explain the principles and proven examples of how those principles serve to create the culture of continuous analysis of the school district or school and how to use the data generated for improvement. The authors contend that the book can help school leaders "chart the course" for improving their school districts or schools.

Journal Articles
Bailey, J. 2000. "The Case for Small Schools." *Center for Rural Affairs Newsletter*. January. http://www.cfra.org/files/casefor smallschools.pdf

The Center for Rural Affairs in Walthill, Nebraska, publishes a newsletter that provides its constituents with information that will help them to be agents on behalf of issues that face rural communities. This article, however, provides statistics and other information about the value of small schools for children's learning that can be used in any community. The article summarizes a number of other papers and studies that build a case for the development of small, personalized education programs as a way to engage children effectively.

Darling-Hammond, L. 2005. "Teaching as a Profession: Lessons in Teacher Preparation and Professional Development." *Phi Delta Kappan* **87 (3): 237–240.**

In this article, Darling-Hammond proposes that the United States has much to learn about teacher preparation and professional development from what other countries do to prepare teachers and to provide support to them during their careers. As other countries have reformed their education systems, they have taken more systematic approaches to improving teacher preparation, beginning teacher induction, and teacher professional development, all of which have the potential to increase student learning and achievement. Darling-Hammond argues that such improvement can come only when there is a policy infrastructure that supports it, and when schools and school districts reallocate their resources to provide for it.

Hadderman, M. 2000. "Educational Vouchers." *ERIC Digest,* **Number 137. Eugene, OR: ERIC Clearinghouse on Educational Management.**

This ERIC digest provides information about educational vouchers, how they are being used in the United States, and where they are being used. It also discusses the political issues surrounding them.

Kunkel, C. 2007. "The Power of Key: Celebrating 20 Years of Innovation at the Key Learning Community." *Phi Delta Kappan* **89 (3): 204–209. http://www.616.ips.k12.in.us**

The Key Learning Community is a school that is organized around Howard Gardner's theory of multiple intelligences. Believing that all children have the potential to develop intelligences, the school's curriculum and learning experiences are designed to provide experiences that lead to the development and refinement of the intelligences identified by Gardner. The Web site of the school provides a wealth of information about how that is done.

Sadker, D., and K. Zittleman. 2004. "Single-sex Schools: A Good Idea Gone Wrong?" *Christian Science Monitor*, April 8, 9.

In their response to the Bush administration's proposed changes to Title IX to allow for the development of single-sex schools, David Sadker and Karen Zittleman argue that these changes do not represent sound education policy, nor are they based in research. There is very little research on the benefits of single-sex public schools, and the authors assert that the conditions they found in their studies of private girls' schools that were critical to the students' success there—smaller class size, supportive parents, teachers trained to work in single-sex classrooms, and strong academic focus—are often missing in public schools.

Voices in Urban Education. *http://www.annenberginstitute. org/VUE/*

Voices in Urban Education is a journal published monthly by the Annenberg Institute for School Reform. The articles in the journal address issues related to school reform in general, and more specifically, urban school reform. A recent issue, for example, had as its theme school environments, and the articles, authored by teachers, school administrators, and researchers, addressed such issues as democratic school architecture and peaceful schools. Information about ordering paper copies of the journal, as well as online access to it, can be found at the Web site above.

Reports

American Association of University Women. 2008. "Separated by Sex: Title IX and Single-Sex Education." Position paper. Washington, DC. http://www.aauw.org/advocacy/issue_ advocacy/actionpages/upload/SingleSexEducation.pdf

In this position paper, the American Association of University Women (AAUW) expresses its concern that new regulations that change Title IX to allow for single-sex education under No Child Left Behind have the potential to "strip girls of civil rights protections," since the words used in the new regulations are "substantially equal." AAUW believes that the purpose of Title IX is to ensure that the educational opportunities for girls and boys are equal, not substantially equal.

Berry, B., D. Montgomery, R. Curtis, M. Hernandez, J. Wurtzel, and J. Snyder. 2008. *Creating and Sustaining Urban Teacher Residencies: A New Way to Recruit, Prepare, and Retain Effective Teachers in High-Needs Districts.* Hillsborough, NC: Center for Teaching Quality. http://www.teachingquality.org/pdfs/AspenUTR.pdf

One of the challenges that many urban school districts face is recruiting and retaining effective teachers. This study, conducted jointly by the Aspen Institute and the Center for Teaching Quality, found Urban Teacher Residencies to be effective. The researchers describe the conditions that make Urban Teacher Residencies attractive both to prospective teachers and to school districts, as well as the costs involved in operating Urban Teacher Residency programs.

Corbett, C., C. Hill, and A. St. Rose. 2008. *Where the Girls Are: The Facts About Gender Equity in Education.* Washington, DC: AAUW Educational Foundation. http://www.aauw.org/research/upload/whereGirlsAre.pdf

In their analysis of 35 years of student achievement data by gender, race, and ethnicity, the authors of this report found girls to have made significant gains. Interestingly, though, the authors conclude that girls' gains have not been at the expense of boys' gains—both girls and boys have made substantial gains in academic achievement. The analysis does show that there are gender differences that may be accounted for by race and ethnicity, and that these differences must be addressed if there is to be real gender equity in our nation's schools.

Darling-Hammond, L., et al. 2008. *Democracy at Risk: The Need for a New Federal Policy in Education.* Athens, OH: Forum for Democracy and Education. http://www.forumforeducation.org/node/378

This report describes the state of public education in the United States and makes recommendations for reforming public education both to improve the quality of teaching and learning and to ensure that quality teaching and learning are available to all children. The report underscores the importance of free and public education to a strong democracy.

Education Trust. 2005. *Gaining Traction: How Some High Schools Accelerate Learning for Struggling Students.* Washington, DC. http://www2.edtrust.org/NR/rdonlyres/6226B581–83C3–4447–9CE7–31C5694B9EF6/0/GainingTractionGainingGround.pdf

This report is the result of a study that compared a group of "high-impact" high schools—schools that produced unusually large growth among students who began significantly behind academically—with "medium-impact" high schools to determine the factors that contributed to their success. The study identified the culture of the school, the academic core, the supports for students, the teachers and their assignment to classes, and time and other resources in the students' growth. The report identifies and describes the practices of the "high-impact" schools in each of those areas.

Forum on Educational Accountability. 2007. *Assessment and Accountability for Improving Schools and Learning: Principles and Recommendations for Federal Law and State and Local Systems.* Cambridge, MA. http://www.edaccountability.org/AssessmentFullReportJUNE07.pdf

The report *Assessment and Accountability for Improving Schools and Learning: Principles and Recommendations for Federal Law and State and Local Systems,* written by a panel of education and assessment experts, makes a set of recommendations for changes to the Elementary and Secondary Education Act. When No Child Left Behind, the current version of the law is reauthorized, the report calls for the law to "ensure that all children have a fair, equal, and significant opportunity to obtain a high-quality education" (Section 1001 of the Elementary and Secondary Education Act, No Child Left Behind). The changes the panel recommends are based on a set of six principles that, according to the panel, provide a vision for an assessment and accountability system that is fair and equitable.

Hoxby, C. 2004. *A Straightforward Comparison of Charter Schools and Regular Public Schools in the US.* Cambridge, MA: National Bureau of Economic Research.

Hoxby, C. 2004. *Achievement in Charter Schools and Regular Public Schools in the US: Understanding the Differences.* Cambridge, MA: Taubman Center for State and Local Government, Kennedy School of Government.

In these two reports, Caroline Hoxby provides an evaluation of charter schools in the United States. The reports give an accounting of the number of charter schools in the United States and how student achievement in charter schools compares with student achievement in regular public schools. According to Hoxby's analysis, children in charter schools in nearly every state outperform their peers in regular public schools.

James, D. W., S. Jurich, and S. Estes. 2001. *Raising Minority Academic Achievement: A Compendium of Education Programs and Practices.* **Washington, DC: American Youth Policy Forum. http://www.aypf.org/publications/rmaa/pdfs/Book.pdf**

This report describes programs that have been shown to be successful in raising minority student academic achievement. The researchers analyzed published evaluations of the programs to determine a set of factors common to the programs, and they recommend that new programs designed for minority students include the factors.

Mead, J. F. 2008. *Charter Schools Designed for Children with Disabilities: An Initial Examination of Issues and Questions Raised.* **Madison: University of Wisconsin. http://www.uschar terschools.org/cs/spedp/print/uscs_docs/spedp/reports.htm**

This report, funded by the U.S. Department of Education, provides a wealth of information about charter schools designed specifically for children with disabilities. The report is in the form of questions and answers about the nature of such charter schools and how they implement the regulations of IDEA and provide services to children with disabilities.

Moats, L. C. 1999. *Teaching Reading Is Rocket Science: What Expert Teachers of Reading Should Know and Be Able to Do.* **New York: American Federation of Teachers.**

Moats's report examines research on teaching reading and proposes changes to teacher preparation programs and teacher professional development to ensure that teachers are prepared to implement teaching practices that will help all children learn to read well. Moats calls for action for developing high-quality teaching of reading, writing, and spelling rather than criticism of teachers; she argues for teacher preparation programs, and for professional development to be revised in light of the research in reading.

New Commission on the Skills of the American Workforce. 2007. *Tough Choices or Tough Times: The Report of the New Commission on the Skills of the American Workforce.* San Francisco: Wiley.

This report updates the earlier report of the Commission on the Skills of the American Workforce. It analyzes the needs of the workforce that will be required for the United States to be competitive in the global economy and translates those needs into expectations for the nation's schools.

"Quality Counts: Tapping into Teaching." *Education Week* 27, no. 18 (January 10, 2008). http://www.edweek.org/ew/toc/2008/01/10/index.html

Quality Counts, published annually by *Education Week*, provides statistics about education in the United States by state. The publication "grades" education in several areas; in 2008, those areas included students' chances for success; student achievement; state standards, assessment, and accountability, transitions and alignment between levels of schooling; the quality of teachers; and school finance. The publication also includes a series of articles about each of the factors analyzed. In 2008, many of the articles focused on teaching quality.

Reeves, T. C. 2006. "Single-Sex Schools." *WPRI Commentary.* Thiensville, WI: Wisconsin Policy Research Institute.

While Thomas Reeves seems not to support a position relative to single-sex schools, his commentary does provide information about a number of issues, including the American Civil Liberties Union's litigation against single-sex schooling. He also discusses Leonard Sax's argument that the differences between boys' and girls' brains and brain function warrant single-sex classrooms.

Roy, J., and L. Mishel. 2005. *Advantage None: Reexamining Hoxby's Findings of Charter School Benefits.* Washington, DC: Economic Policy Institute.

In this report, Joydeep Roy and Lawrence Mishel reanalyze the data presented in Caroline Hoxby's evaluations of charter schools, and they use Hoxby's data to refute her findings. It is interesting to look at the reports side-by-side to compare them.

Stiggins, R. 2008. *Assessment Manifesto: A Call for the Development of Balanced Assessment Systems.* **Portland, OR: ETS Assessment Training Institute.** http://www.ets.org/Media/Conferences_and_Events/pdf/Stiggins/pdf

Rick Stiggins, an expert in designing assessments and assessment systems, calls for rethinking the purpose of assessment in schools. He argues that schools can no longer just use assessment to determine which students have learned; instead, they must use assessment to understand how students are learning so that they can intervene to ensure that all students learn well and meet standards. The manifesto calls for revision of criteria used to determine the quality of assessments to include the evaluation of the impact of assessment and assessment scores on student learning. Stiggins proposes a process, outlined in the manifesto, for selecting and designing assessments that are balanced, that lead to continued learning, and that provide information that helps educators plan for appropriate instruction for each student.

International Perspectives on Education Reform
Books
Apple, M. W., J. Kenway, and M. Singh, eds. 2005. *Globalizing Education: Policies, Pedagogies, & Politics.* **New York: Peter Lang.**

The authors of the essays in this book explore issues related to educational change and reform from the perspective of a global society. What will education mean when there is truly a global society? How can democracy be preserved? How can the voices of all be heard? How can public schools be globalized? In discussing these issues, the authors propose innovative and transformative educational policies, pedagogies, and politics.

Grindle, M. S. 2004. *Despite the Odds: The Contentious Politics of Education Reform.* **Princeton, NJ: Princeton University Press.**

Merilee Grindle analyzes education reform in Latin American countries through the lens of the political movements and perspectives that they represent. She shows how reformers have been strategic in choosing reforms so that they can be sustained, and staying the course, even against the odds. Education reformers can learn from the examples set by these reformers.

Klooster, D. J., J. Steele, and P. L. Bloem, eds. *Ideas Without Boundaries: International Education Reform Through Reading and Writing for Critical Thinking.* Newark, DE: International Reading Association.

This book presents the stories of teaching and changing, written by educators from central and eastern Europe and central Asia who have participated in the Reading and Writing for Critical Thinking school improvement project. The stories they tell show how these teachers have worked together to change their classroom practice and how they have been changed in the process.

Levin, B. 2001. *Reforming Education: From Origins to Outcomes.* London: RoutledgeFalmer.

In this book, Benjamin Levin describes large-scale education reform efforts in England, New Zealand, the Canada provinces of Alberta and Manitoba, and the state of Minnesota. Levin reviews the reforms and their results through the perspectives of their political origins, the laws that mandate or support them, and the processes that have led to the results. Through his analysis, Levin shows that there are many lessons to be learned from the experiences of others involved in education reform.

Rotberg, I. C., ed. 2004. *Balancing Change and Tradition in Global Education Reform.* New York: Rowman and Littlefield Education.

This book presents a series of case studies of education reform from countries that are involved in the process of reform. Iris Rotberg selected the countries because of what can be learned from each of the education reform processes of these countries, as well as their perspectives. She describes the reform process as one that involves a delicate balance between tradition, what has always been done, and change.

Spring, J. 2004. *How Educational Ideologies Are Shaping Global Society: Intergovernmental Organizations, NGOs, and the Decline of the Nation-State.* Mahwah, NJ: Lawrence Erlbaum Associates.

Joel Spring argues that there are conflicting ideologies at play in global education and education reform. He identifies the ideologies and analyzes their effects on the future of education as an institution of a global society. He concludes by exploring the future of global education policy and global school organizations.

Spring, J. 2007. *A New Paradigm for Global School Systems: Education for a Long and Happy Life.* **Mahwah, NJ: Lawrence Erlbaum Associates.**

In his book *A New Paradigm for Global School Systems: Education for a Long and Happy Life,* Joel Spring proposes to reform education by changing its very purpose. Instead of expecting education to lead to jobs that support the global economy, Spring suggests that the purpose of education should be to prepare people to lead long, happy lives. In addition to a strong argument for his proposition, Spring shows how education with such a purpose could be organized, how the curriculum could be designed, and how teaching and learning could look.

Sugrue, C., ed. 2008. *The Future of Educational Change: International Perspectives.* **London: Routledge.**

This book takes a look at educational change in several countries and a wide range of contexts to show, despite claims to the contrary, that much has changed and is changing in schools and educational systems worldwide. Ciaran Sugrue says her intent is that each effort at change "contributes toward the identification of some signposts and compass readings that become the rudder of educational change, a tiller that gives direction to the future" (p. 3). In other words, even if a change effort doesn't result in the change hoped for, at least something can be learned that can help with the next effort.

Journals and Journal Articles
Baines, L. 2007. "Learning from the World: Achieving More by Doing Less." *Phi Delta Kappan* **89 (2): 98–100.**

In this article, Lawrence Baines compares practices of U.S. schools with the practices of schools in other countries. He suggests that there are many practices U.S. educators can borrow from our international colleagues that might help U.S. schools improve students' learning, including shortening the school day and requiring less homework.

Darling-Hammond, L. 2008. How They Do It Abroad. *Time,* **February 14. http://www.time.com/time/magazine/article/0,9171, 1713557,00.html**

This article compares teaching conditions in the United States with those of teachers in Finland, Singapore, Sweden, Ireland, the Netherlands, Hong Kong, South Korea, Japan, Australia, New Zealand, and Canada—the highest achieving countries on international comparisons of student learning. Darling-Hammond argues that these countries all "prepare their teachers more extensively, pay them well in relation to competing occupations, and give them lots of time for professional learning." The result of providing such resources for teachers is that all children in these countries have well-trained teachers.

Grubb, W. N. 2007. "Dynamic Inequality and Intervention: Lessons from a Small Country." *Phi Delta Kappan* **89 (2): 105–114.**

Finland's student achievement ranks at the top of international comparisons. W. Norton Grubb takes a look at how schools in Finland foster equity and argues that U.S. schools have much to learn from Finnish schools.

International Journal of Educational Reform. **http://www.row maneducation.com/Journals/IJER/Index.shtml**

The *International Journal of Educational Reform*, published quarterly, provides information about political and educational issues related to education reform. The international perspective allows for insight into how education reform is taking place in countries around the world.

Levin, B., and M. Fullan. 2008. Learning about System Renewal. *Educational Management Administration & Leadership* **36 (2): 289–303.**

In this article, Benjamin Levin and Michael Fullan draw on the lessons they have learned about change from their experiences with education reform throughout the world. Based on that experience, they believe that the most important lesson they have learned is that improvement in student learning is the result of sustained effort to change teaching practices on a large scale. They list a number of factors involved in supporting change on the scale that is required, and they caution that the work of doing so is difficult.

Rethinking Schools, **1001 E. Keefe Avenue, Milwaukee, WI 53212; 414-964-9646. http://www.rethinkingschools.org**

Rethinking Schools is a quarterly journal that was begun in 1986 to promote education reform in general, and more specifically, equity in schools, and to critique educational policy, theory, and classroom practice in urban education through the lens of equity. All of the articles in *Rethinking Schools* are edited by classroom teachers. The journal is available online.

Rotberg, I. C. 2005. "Tradeoffs, Societal Values, and School Reform." *Phi Delta Kappan* **86 (8): 611–618.**

In this article, Iris Rotberg describes school reforms from several countries from the perspective of what the countries had to give up in order to adopt the reforms. She describes the processes these countries used to make the choices they did about reform.

Stewart, V. 2005. "A World Transformed: How Other Countries Are Preparing Students for the Interconnected World Of the 21st Century." *Phi Delta Kappan* **87 (3): 229–232.**

Vivien Stewart describes how other countries are preparing their children for life in the global era, and she compares what they are doing with what is happening in the United States. According to Stewart, efforts in the United States are local and small in scale; to be effective, funding must be allocated for teaching foreign languages and the international education that is needed to prepare students for the global era.

Zhao, Y. 2005. "Increasing Math and Science Achievement: The Best and Worst of the East and West." *Phi Delta Kappan* **87 (3): 219–222.**

Yong Zhao analyzes the mathematics and science teaching practices of the United States and compares them with teaching practices in China, Chinese Taipei, Hong Kong, Japan, Korea, and Singapore. He concludes that although students from these countries score higher than U.S. students on international standardized tests, there are strengths of U.S. teaching practices that should not be exchanged for Asian teaching practices.

Reports

Cuadra, E., J. M. Moreno, L. Crouch, Y. Nagashima, Y. Koda, D. Bundy, G. J. Kim, T. Welsh, I. Psifidou, Y. Wang, S. Sosale, and D. Abu-Ghaida. 2005. *Expanding Opportunities and*

Building Competencies for Young People: A New Agenda for Secondary Education. Washington, DC: The World Bank. http://siteresources.worldbank.org/EDUCATION/Resources/278200-1099079877269/547664-1099079967208/Expanding_Opportunities_Secondary.pdf

This paper, published by the World Bank, argues that secondary education plays a critical role in global development, and it proposes policy alternatives and options for reforming and transforming secondary education. While the paper is aimed at educators and policy makers in developing countries where secondary education is not universal, the reforms suggested can also inform educators and policy makers in the United States.

Levin, B., and J. Young. 1998. International Education Reform: A Canadian Perspective. Paper presented at the annual meeting of the American Educational Research Association, San Diego, California. ERIC Document No. ED424642.

Benjamin Levin and Jonathan Young compare education reform in Canada with mandated reforms in several other countries. The authors analyze the reforms in terms of the legislation that mandates them, the process of implementing the reforms, and the evidence of student outcomes related to the reforms. The article identifies commonalities and differences among the reforms and with reform in Canada.

Nonprint Resources

AAUW Title IX 35th Anniversary Resource Kit. http://www.aauw.org/advocacy/issue_advocacy/actionpages/upload/titleixResourceKit.pdf

The AAUW Title IX 35th Anniversary Resource Kit provides background information on Title IX, as well as resources to support advocacy for continued enforcement of Title IX. In particular, the kit includes a rationale for Title IX implementation in schools as well as a list of ways to ensure gender equity.

ASCD SmartBrief. http://www.smartbrief.com/ascd/

The *ASCD SmartBrief* is a daily electronic newsletter for educators. The *SmartBrief* contains reports and articles about a wide variety of topics, many related to education reform and improvement. Recent issues have included a report of research on the achievement of students who used vouchers to attend schools of choice, a report on the effectiveness of tutoring provided through No Child Left Behind, and a number of resources available on education reform.

Annenberg Institute for School Reform. 2006. *Tools for School-Improvement Planning.* **Providence, RI. http://www.annenberg institute.org/tools/index.php**

This Web site provides a database of tools for school improvement gleaned from successful school improvement projects throughout the country. Besides the tools themselves, the Web site includes descriptions of successful schools and promising practices of those schools, a guide for school improvement, and resources for using data to drive school improvement. There is also a list of resources to support school improvement efforts.

Asking the Right Questions: A School Change Toolkit. **http:// www.mcrel.org/toolkit/**

The toolkit includes information about a systems approach to schools as well as a process of needs assessment and reflective inquiry in designing reform plans. The toolkit addresses the factors shown by research to have the biggest impact on student achievement. It is intended to be used by school leaders and teams of teachers involved in school improvement and reform.

Center for Earth and Space Science Education. http://cesse.terc .edu/

This center, funded by the National Science Foundation and the National Aeronautics and Space Administration, has as its purpose "transforming science education from 'reading about science' to highly engaging and exploratory experiences in which students 'do science' by investigating and exploring the Earth around them and the universe beyond." The Web site has links to information, maps, books, posters, and listservs about Earth and Mars.

Center on Innovation and Improvement Information on the Need for and State of Education Reform. http://www.centerii. org/centerIIPublic/criteria.aspx

The Web site of the Center on Innovation and Improvement provides the opportunity to generate reports of data on education reform by state. Reports can be generated across states on supplemental educational services, on restructuring, and on school and school district improvement. Reports can also be generated by state; state reports may include information about standards and assessments, state regulations governing education reform, and education reform resources available in that state.

Education Reform Networks. http://www.edreform.net/

This is an electronic library of information about education reform organized and searchable by topic—instruction, classroom management, data-driven reform, digital equity, early literacy, equity, mathematics education, professional development school partnerships, pre-service technology infusion, professional development, teacher retention, and urban teacher education.

Edutopia. **George Lucas Educational Foundation. http://www. edutopia.org/**

The George Lucas Educational Foundation supports the development of interactive classroom environments, project-based learning, and the integration of technology as means to school reform. Three publications of the foundation—Edutopia.org, *Edutopia* magazine, and *Edutopia* video—provide information and support for developing schools and classrooms where learning is interactive and project based and where technology resources are used to support learning. Edutopia.org is an interactive site that includes an archive of examples of research and best practices; *Edutopia* magazine is a bimonthly publication available online; and *Edutopia* video offers video examples of the vision of the foundation in practice. These resources are all offered free of charge.

FairTest Examiner. **Newsletter published by FairTest, the National Center for Fair and Open Testing. http://www.fairtest.org/ resources/publications**

This quarterly newsletter published by FairTest provides information about testing reform and best practice in assessment and evaluation. It also reports on federal and state legislation on testing, and it critiques the misuse of tests and evaluation data. The newsletter is free, and the FairTest Web site provides access to the full archive of the *FairTest Examiner*.

Federal Resources for Educational Excellence. http://www.free.ed.gov

This Web site networks teaching and learning resources from federal government agencies. The resources are indexed by subject area (Arts & Music; Health and Phys Ed; History and Soc Studies; and so on), and they include links to information and primary sources in repositories like the Library of Congress, the Institute of Museum and Library Services, the National Science Foundation, the Endowment for the Humanities, and the National Institutes of Health. All of the materials available through the site may be accessed and used free of charge.

www.ed.gov/free/what.html

This Web site is a searchable database of teaching and learning resources from federal agencies. The database includes curriculum materials such as background information, facsimiles of primary documents, photos, and music, as well as lesson plans and teaching activities for every curriculum area.

Grants and Fellowships for Education Reform. http://www.edreform.com/index.cfm?fuseAction=document&documentID=2905

The Grants and Fellowships page of the Center for Education Reform Web site offers a list of grants and fellowships available for education reformers, teachers, and school programs. The list of grants and fellowships includes descriptions of each granting agency or foundation, the types of projects they support, the deadlines for applications, and the monetary amounts of grants or fellowships available from each agency. Each entry is linked directly to the granting agency for more information about that particular grant or fellowship.

IBM Reinventing Education Change Toolkit. 2007. http://www.reinventingeducation.org/RE3Web/

The Reinventing Education Change Toolkit, based on the work of Harvard professor and change expert Rosabeth Moss Kanter, was designed to help lead and implement change in schools and school districts. Part of IBM's Reinventing Education grant program, the toolkit was developed as a collaborative effort among IBM, the Council of Chief State School Officers, the National Association of Secondary School Principals, and the National Association of Elementary School Principals. The toolkit is free of charge from the Web site.

Just for Parents. http://www.uscharterschools.org/pub/uscs_docs/o/parents.htm

Just for Parents is a page on the Web site of U.S. Charter Schools. The Web page includes basic information about charter schools, information about finding and choosing appropriate charter schools, and information about how parents can support their children's learning.

LEA (Local Education Agency) and School Improvement Guidance. www.ed.gov/policy/elsec/guid/schoolimprovementguid.pdf

This 2006 document, published by the U.S. Department of Education, provides the latest guidance to schools and school districts in implementing the school restructuring provisions of No Child Left Behind. The information, in the form of questions and answers, is organized by areas of the law and the questions that have been asked frequently.

Math Forum@Drexel. http://mathforum.org/mathed/index.html

The Math Forum@Drexel is an Internet mathematics library. The library links to information resources for the reform of mathematics. In addition to links to information pages and sites, there are also links to research and to mathematics journals.

National Institute for Urban School Improvement Online Library. http://niusi.ed.greenriver.org/

This online library has links to annotated citations for journal articles and research about many aspects of school improvement and education reform.

No Child Left Behind. **http://www.ed.gov/nclb/landing.jhtml**

The U.S. Department of Education has a Web site that links to information about and resources for implementing No Child Left Behind. The site includes pages specifically for students, parents, teachers, and administrators. The pages link to research, descriptions of innovative programs, and a number of other Web sites that address the various aspects of No Child Left Behind, as well as education in general.

Pathways to School Improvement. http://www.ncrel.org/sdrs/

Pathways to School Improvement is a Web site that "synthesizes research, policy, and best practices" on a number of issues important to education reform. The specific issues addressed are assessment, at-risk students, family and community, instruction, leadership, literacy, mathematics and science, policy, professional development, and technology. The site provides links to a wealth of papers, essays, and audio files related to each topic. Visitors to the site can also request information about a specific topic. Pathways to School Improvement is a project of the North Central Regional Educational Laboratory.

Public School Insights: What is Working in Our Public Schools. *Learning First Alliance.* **http://www.publicschoolinsights.org**

The Web site of the Learning First Alliance, a partnership of education associations, includes descriptions of successful school programs, a "toolkit" of resources for teaching mathematics and reading, and a framework for recruiting and hiring good teachers for high-needs schools. The school district success stories include contact information for the school districts described.

SETDA Toolkit. **http://www.setda.org/toolkit/nlitoolkit2006/down loads.htm**

The SETDA (State Educational Technology Directors Association) Toolkit is a set of "tools," processes, and research associated with them for addressing several aspects of education reform. They include "Showing Evidence of Educational Technology Effectiveness," "Using Data for School Reform," "Technology's Role in Math Curriculum," and "Standards & Curriculum Alignment." Each of these sets of "tools" includes information for educators or policy makers and strategies for using that information.

Glossary

accountability   Accountability can be defined as the responsibility of states, school districts, schools, and teachers to report and justify their efforts to meet the requirements of state and federal government regulations regarding the quality of their education programs and their students' progress toward meeting curriculum standards. Accountability is a key component of the No Child Left Behind legislation; that legislation requires states to set standards for student progress toward becoming proficient in reading and mathematics. The legislation also enforces sanctions for schools that fail to meet the standards.

achievement gap   In the United States, students considered to be part of an ethnic or racial minority group have historically performed lower as a group on tests of student achievement than their white peers. This disparity in student test scores is called an achievement gap.

adequate yearly progress   The standard that schools are expected to meet annually in terms of student achievement is called adequate yearly progress. Each state must set standards for student achievement that increase annually so that all students reach proficiency in reading and mathematics by the school year 2013–2014. Adequate yearly progress is determined by students' scores on standardized tests. Schools with fewer than 95 percent of their students meeting state standards for adequate yearly progress are identified by their states as needing improvement.

bilingual education   Students experience bilingual education when teaching is done in more than one language, for example, classrooms where teachers use both English and Spanish as the languages for instruction. There are many models of bilingual education, two of which are transitional bilingual education, in which students are taught initially primarily in their first language with a gradual transition to English, and dual language programs, in which all children are taught in two languages with the goal of all of the children becoming bilingual.

charter school   A charter school is an elementary or secondary school that receives public funding but is generally governed outside the public school district in which it is located. Charter schools are chartered differently in different states. In some states the charters, or contracts to operate, are administered directly by the state, while in others the charters are administered by universities, and in a few, the charters are administered by the local school districts. Charter schools are usually not held to the same regulations as other public schools; their charters determine how and to whom the schools will be accountable.

compensatory education   Compensatory education is defined as educational services provided to children in addition to the services normally provided by public schools. Compensatory education is usually provided to children to compensate for the effects of poverty or disability. An example of compensatory education is the service provided to children under Title I of the Elementary and Secondary Education Act, No Child Left Behind. For schools where a significant proportion of students are considered living in poverty, Title I provides funding for educational services—additional instructional time, smaller class size, and so on—that is in addition to the basic educational services provided by the school district.

comprehensive school reform   Comprehensive school reform is an approach to improving schools that involves every aspect of schooling. It is based on the idea that a school is a system, and that changing one aspect of schooling will necessarily affect every other aspect of that school system. In comprehensive school reform, schools are explicit about examining every aspect of schooling to improve and revitalize the entire school. Schools involved in comprehensive school reform believe that strategies to improve the entire school result in more significant improvement than adopting new programs or improving one aspect of schooling at a time.

content standards   Content standards describe what children should learn and be able to do as a result of an educational program.

curriculum   Curriculum is what children learn in school. Curriculum theorists believe that there are several different curricula in every school—a stated curriculum, which is what the school claims to teach and includes in its written curriculum guides or textbooks; a hidden curriculum, things that students learn that are not included in curriculum guides; and a null curriculum, things that are intentionally not taught in that school.

differentiated instruction   Differentiated instruction is teaching that acknowledges that students learn in different ways and are ready to learn and demonstrate that they have learned in different ways. The promoters of differentiated instruction believe that teaching should be differentiated in terms of content—how students are taught; in terms of process—the activities that students do to learn the content; and in terms of product—how students demonstrate or are assessed on what they have learned.

dual school systems Before schools were racially integrated, several states in the United States required dual school systems. School districts in those states included one set of schools for white children and a second set of schools for black and other minority children. Until the U.S. Supreme Court ruled in *Brown v. Board of Education* that dual school systems were not legal, the doctrine of "separate but equal" set forth in *Plessy v. Ferguson* was used to justify the dual school systems.

effective schools Beginning in the 1970s, a number of researchers in the United States examined schools that were considered to be effective. Based on their research, a set of characteristics of effective schools was developed. Those characteristics, a list of which can be found in Chapter 6 of this book, have come to shape most of the education reform efforts in the United States.

free appropriate public education In the Rehabilitation Act of 1973, Congress determined that every child in the United States, regardless of disability, is entitled to a free appropriate public education (FAPE). What this means is that public school districts are required under the law to provide every child with an education, free of cost, that addresses that child's specific learning needs. A free appropriate public education also means that no child may be excluded from nonacademic or extracurricular activities by virtue of having a disability.

inclusion When there is inclusion for children with disabilities, those children are included in regular classrooms for most of their instruction; they may leave the regular classroom for special education services that specifically address their disabilities. Full inclusion extends the concept of inclusion in that children with disabilities in full inclusion programs remain in the regular classroom for all of their instruction; any special education services they require are provided in the regular classroom setting.

least restrictive environment PL 94–142 required that all children entitled to special education services be provided those services in the least restrictive environment. This meant that children with disabilities should be educated with and allowed to interact with their peers without disabilities to the fullest extent possible. In other words, children with disabilities should be educated in regular classrooms as much as their disabilities allow.

opportunity to learn standards Opportunity to learn standards are standards that describe the facilities, teachers, curriculum, learning experiences, instructional materials, and quality of education required to provide equity for all children in schools and classrooms. When standards were first proposed by the United States federal government, opportunity to learn standards were included; they were later omitted from the national discussion about standards. Proponents of opportunity to learn standards argue that unless students have equal opportunities to learn, they should not be held to the same standards of learning.

performance assessment Performance assessments are assessments that require students to apply their learning in the context of a task or activity. The student performances are rated or judged based on rubrics, or criteria that are agreed upon in advance, that represent the quality of learning expected. In a performance assessment, for example, students might be asked to solve a mathematics problem and explain both the solution and why they selected the particular solutions they used. Through such assessment, teachers can determine both whether students know how to apply mathematical concepts and algorithms and whether students use problem-solving strategies.

performance standards Performance standards are standards that accompany content standards. While content standards describe what students are expected to know and be able to do, performance standards describe what students must do to demonstrate what they know and can do. In other words, performance standards describe how well a student is expected to learn.

portfolio A portfolio is a collection of student work that can be used as an assessment tool. The portfolio includes samples of student work that show how that student's learning has developed over time. A number of school districts and states require student portfolios that show how students' writing skills progress, for example. When used as assessments, portfolios are typically judged or rated through the use of specific criteria called rubrics.

scripted direct instruction Scripted direct instruction is a method of teaching that involves teachers reading commercially produced scripts of lessons rather than developing lessons of their own. In such direct instruction lessons, children are the passive receivers of instruction, and their responses to such lessons are also often scripted, with teachers prompting the children's responses as part of their scripts. Critics of scripted direct instruction argue that children must be actively engaged in learning experiences to learn, that appropriate instruction must acknowledge children's differing learning styles and needs, and that teachers are in the best position to design lessons to meet the needs of the children in their classes.

standardized test A standardized test is a test that can be used to compare student performance across classrooms, schools, school districts, states, and so on. To be considered standardized, a test must be administered under standard conditions—for example, the same test items or questions, at the same time of year, with the same amount of time and the same level of support—so that the scores have the same meaning and can be compared.

standards The U.S. government has promoted standards as the basis for education reform in U.S. schools. States are required to set content and performance standards for the schools in their state, and they are required to design assessments that measure students' progress toward meeting the standards.

supplemental educational services Supplemental educational services are educational services provided to students in addition to the services normally provided to all students by a school or school district. Examples of supplemental educational services include English as a Second Language classes, additional instruction or tutoring in reading or mathematics, and special education services.

universal education Universal education is based on the concept that education is a basic human right and that all children are entitled to a good-quality education. Universal education is promoted by such organizations as the United Nations and the World Bank as part of national and international development.

vouchers An educational voucher is a public payment for education that can be used to pay tuition at non-public schools as a way of offering choice in children's education. Proponents of vouchers believe that offering such choice promotes competition among schools, which can improve schools and their offerings. A number of states in the United States offer vouchers to parents, and the entire public education system in Chile is based on vouchers. (See Chapter 3 for more information about Chile's voucher system.) Critics of vouchers argue that vouchers are rarely large enough to allow students to attend high-quality private schools, and that vouchers take financial resources away from underfunded public schools.

Index